From Heaven to Hell

A Diary of Zimbabwe

Maria Treacy

Pen Press

First published in Great Britain by Pen Press

All paper used in the printing of this book has been made from wood grown in managed, sustainable forests.

ISBN: 978-1-78003-344-0

Printed and bound in the UK
Pen Press is an imprint of
Indepenpress Publishing Limited
25 Eastern Place
Brighton
BN2 1GJ

A catalogue record of this book is available from the British Library

Cover design by Jacqueline Abromeit

Dedication

From Heaven to Hell: A Diary of Zimbabwe
is for Miriam, my dearest friend in
Orchard Terrace, Orchard Lane, Hampshire
and also
my sister, Lucy Ann of Enfield Green, Surrey,
who I cannot imagine living without.

Rhodesia to Zimbabwe

1924   Robert Mugabe was born.

1953   The Federation of Rhodesia and Nyasaland inaugurated.

1957   The African National Congress launched, with Nkomo as leader.

1959   The African National Congress banned (ANC).

1960   The African Democratic Party (NDP) formed.

1961   Agreement reached on a new constitution at a conference in Salisbury attended by Britain, the Rhodesian Government, Nkomo and Sithole (Ndabaningi Sithole, Encyclopaedia Britannica). Nkomo later repudiates the agreements. After sporadic violence, the NDP is banned. The Zimbabwe African People's Union (ZAPU) takes its place (Winston Field).

1962   ZAPU is banned. The Rhodesian Front, led by Winston Field, wins the general election.

1963   The nationalist movement splits Sithole and Mugabe. They break away to form the Zimbabwean African National Union (ZANU). Nkomo supporters form the People's Caretakers Council (PCC). Months of faction fighting followed the split, federation dissolved.

1964   Ian Smith became prime minister. Nkomo was then detained. ZANU and PCC banned. Sithole and Mugabe arrested.

1965   Unilateral Declaration of Independence on 11th November. The British government applies selective sanctions.

1966   Harold Wilson meets Ian Smith on HMS Tiger. The United Nations imposes selective sanctions.

1970   Rhodesia adopts new constitution then becomes a republic. Conservatives win British election.

1971   Ian Smith accepts terms for a settlement presented by Lord Douglas Home in Salisbury. The ANC is formed with Muzorewa as leader.

1972   The Pearce Commission finds settlement terms unacceptable to Africans. Guerrilla war began with attacks on white farms in North East Rhodesia.

1973   Border between Zambia and Rhodesia closed. Smith negotiates with Muzorewa.

1974   Revolution in Portugal to black rule in Mozambique, also Ian Smith's negotiations with Muzorewa were rejected by ANC. Vorster and Kaunda embark on a détente exercise. African leaders were released from detention. Nkomo, Sithole, Muzorewa and James Chickermara? signed unity agreement in Lusaka. Ceasefire in guerrilla war, but this fails to take hold.

1975   Herbert Chitepo was assassinated regarding talks between Smith and Nationalists on Victoria Bridge. Ian Smith negotiates with Nkomo.

1976   Major guerrilla incursions from Mozambique.

I took an enforced break from writing my book at this point, as in 2002 a friend and I were the victims of a nasty mugging outside my Zimbabwe home.

Saying goodbye to her one day outside our decorative wrought iron fences (which had replaced all the beautiful flowered hedges for security reasons), we were set upon by two smartly dressed African gentlemen, who proceeded to kick us and drag us up the road and driveway until I called out to one of my servants, which scared them off.

We were both black and blue, my friend's finger was hanging off where they'd bit it to get her car keys and my left shoulder was badly dislocated and the bones and ligaments severly damaged. This resulted in many operations, for me and my friend, and I now have plates in my arm and even with a splint, my left hand is completely useless. My right hand was also damaged, resulting in the reduced function of several fingers.

Zimbabwe is a dangerous place. The police worked on the matter for months and people were also helped by an excellent charity, ZANE (Zimbabwe: A National Emergency), based in Oxfordshire, who offer support and do so much for people in the country.

1979	Then hell let loose! We had the famous conference which gave the Jewel in the Crown to Mr Robert Mugabe. It was from 10th September to 21st December.
1980	Then we had the independence election run-up. After the election, the aftermath of war. Election aftermath – Zimbabwe National Army – a terrible integration process. Surrender and non-surrender of weapons. Activities of ZIPRA dissidents.
1981	Robert Mugabe and his ZANU-PF come to political power in Zimbabwe after British and Commonwealth supervised elections in 1980. Acclaimed by the British government and others. The elections were free and fair. In reality, the process was a complete sham. It has been seriously flawed by a murderous campaign of intimidation conducted against the black community by the political commissions of ZANLA – ZANU-PF military wing. Having got away with it in 1980, Mugabe repeated these brutal tactics in the 1985, 1990 and 1995 election campaigns. The result, of course, was no political opposition. The constitution was changed to suit his ruling elite. In the 1980s the ex-Rhodesians were trained by SADE to gather intelligence and destabilise Zimbabwe. Most of the jet planes, armour and major armoury at Thornhill were destroyed, also at Inkomo Barracks. Mugabe suppressed the report of the Commission of Enquiry into it.

In the early 1980s the North Koreans trained ex-ZANLA guerrillas into a new Fifth Brigade. It was trained to murder like a machine. It was launched into Matabeleland in 1983. It was just too dreadful for words and ended with the murder of some 15,000 people; they truly beat, raped, starved, maimed and tortured countless thousands more.

Times had changed so much. Twenty years later, Zimbabweans were dissatisfied with the ruling party's waste and rampant corruption. The trouble in the Congo did not help. The diamond and other mining concessions. The economy was nearly finished. The dollar had dropped unbelievably to an all-time low! Little did the Zimbabwean world know how much more it was going to drop. Quite honestly, Zimbabwe would agree with my title of this book, *From Heaven to Hell*.

Mugabe does not seem to care about the continual murders, food shortages and so much sickness, which is killing his nation – mainly AIDS. Then Mugabe tried to introduce a new constitution, which meant allowing him to continue in office as president for the rest of his life – this would have been the end! The opposite side, MDC, was run by Morgan Tsvangirai. The electorate rejected the draft constitution in a referendum. Mugabe blamed his defeat on the country's 60,000 whites out of a population of 13 million, blaming it on the farmers who supported the MDC. After farmers were murdered, war veterans took over the farms.

There were murders daily with rapes, beatings, torture and intimidation; all these lives tainted with worry and more worry. The bread basket of Africa just burst and was taken over by the war veterans. Mugabe actually launched the invasions of squatters led by his orders. In defiance of his own High Court, the farm invasions had intensified.

Since Zimbabwe's independence in 1980 (after the 'Lancaster Talks'), which gave Mugabe the 'Jewel in the Crown' everything changed; materials were short, towns were dirty, there were more beggars then we used to see, more thieving and stealing, and of course murders. The happiest and most reasonable country in the world – we did not have oil, but our land could not have had richer soil – for hundreds of miles on our beautiful, wide, dark black dolerite stone, with white lines on each side of the roads, there was majestic countryside, growing the tobacco, maize (the traditional diet for the Africans known as 'meali meal'), coffee, cotton, sugar, teas and vegetables. Our mines were the most magnificent; Sandawana emeralds, gold, diamonds and copper.

I could go on and on – the mines are closed now; the farmlands brown and empty! The farms have been taken over by ministers and war veterans, the owners murdered or tortured, losing homesteads and all they had ever worked for. We used to say it was the bread basket of Africa, now we go from town to town looking for bread, milk, butter etc. The veg is stale, withered and old, even the bananas and tomatoes are withered and black, but we buy them for 'millions' not thousands – the bank notes are changed and reprinted regularly!

Our beautiful city with its lilac and purple jacaranda trees, red flamboyant trees touching each other across the wide roads. Now the pavements are all cracked and broken; paper, Coke bottles, rubbish over the streets, we can no longer call Harare, known as Salisbury, our 'sunshine city'. Bars on all the windows in the shops in fear of riots, which were many. During the Rhodesian War and after, we carried guns in our handbags, and shopping was searched by special guards at each shop entrance, no matter how large or small the shop was – safety was spelt everywhere.

1982   The kidnap or tourists, attempted coup d'état by ZIPRA elements (Zimbabwe People's Revolution Army).

Rhodesia and the Commonwealth

1979   South Africans had appreciated that when the Conservative government under Prime Minister Margaret Thatcher took power in Great Britain on 3rd May 1979, it would recognise the internal settlement and government of Bishop Muzorewa! Margaret Thatcher, unlike her Labour predecessors, made it quite clear that she supported the internal settlement and that when she became prime minister recognition of Zimbabwe/Rhodesia as an independent sovereign state would follow, but after two weeks of taking office, she described ZANILA (and ZIPRA) as 'terrorists' like the IRA.

Forty-two delegations attended the Commonwealth, held in Lusaka from 1st – 8th August 1979 and Margaret Thatcher had shown her hand in advance, which had given the frontline states time to lobby support for the rejection of her proposals. The Commonwealth was no longer the 'gentlemen's club' of white-ruled states as it had been in the old days. The Afro-Asians with the frontline states in the vanguard were making plans to have Great Britain's status reduced, where she was just another member of state, not the acknowledged leader.

The British delegation suffered a great shock before the meeting started; the newest member, Nigeria, moved to expel South Africa from the Commonwealth due to her apartheid policies and suddenly expropriated the assets of Shell BP in Nigeria. Mrs Thatcher chose to ignore Shell BP directors, who had warned the British government in advance that this would be likely to happen. Also, there was the added threat of a Nigerian rumour to cut off all trade with Britain, worth three times its trade with South Africa. The Commonwealth secretary, Raphael, moved the agenda so that the plenary discussions of Zimbabwe/Rhodesia would be expelled from the Commonwealth. She knew jolly well that she was under intense pressure and no further help was available on the Rhodesia question from President Carter. He had failed to bring about a settlement as he was engaged in more areas of conflict, like France. He had promised to lift sanctions against Zimbabwe/Rhodesia but that was all.

Mrs Thatcher had no intention of painting herself 'beaten'. She decided to address the conference extempore, telling of the British government's willingness to meet the Commonwealth's demands – she would leave room for manoeuvres later. Sir Anthony Duff and Lord Carrington spent the time canvassing Commonwealth views, himself stating that this would not do; there could be no avoidance of clarity.

Bowing to pressure, Mrs Thatcher retired to bed leaving Sir Anthony Duff (civil servant and senior deputy under-secretary of state and the Foreign Office) in consultation with Lord Carrington. After spending the night drafting notes for the conference, it was indeed approved by Carrington the next morning and Mrs Thatcher read it out very speedily at the conference, taking two and a half minutes, her cold voice indicated immediately hat she had suffered a major defeat. Sir Anthony Duff did very well; he had destroyed any chance of the internal settlement being accepted and after minor amendments the British government were wholly committed to genuine black majority rule.

It was terrible, as their pre-UDI briefing notes for the Foreign Office dismissed Ian Smith as a simple-minded and obstinate bigot with a schoolboy attitude. Therefore Zimbabwe/Rhodesia in 1979/1980 was, in my estimation, the beginning of the end! Most of the people at the conference stayed at the Hilton Hotel in London and those dates will always remain in my mind – from 10th September to 21st December 1979.

1983   In September 1983 defence minister, Sydney Sekeramayi announced that the setting up of Fifth Brigade had been completed. According to many sources, the training given to them by the North Korean system was of an abysmally low standard. It is doubtful after such an elapse of time that the North Koreans had completely abandoned the 'human wave' tactics, which they and the Red Chinese had used so ineffectively during the Korean War in the 1950s.

It's now 2008 and so much is happening in Zimbabwe at the moment that I am writing about Robert Mugabe in this day and age to keep up with the present times. Let me write a sort of chronology of events relating to Robert Mugabe:

1924   Robert Gabriel Mugabe was born in Kutama, Zimbabwe (then Southern Rhodesia).
1945   Leaves St Francis Farm College in Kutama having qualified as a teacher.
1949   Obtains scholarship to University College of Fort Hare, South Africa, achieving the first of seven degrees.
1957   Moves to Ghana and meets Sally Hayfron.
1960   Gives first political speech, while home on holiday and joins National Democratic Party (NDP) under Joshua Nkomo, becoming publicity secretary.
1961   Marries Sally Hayfron. Zimbabwe African People's Union (ZAPU) formed to replace the banned NDP.
1962   ZAPU was banned, all leaders restricted.
1963   Zimbabwe African National Union (ZANU) was formed as rival to ZAPU.
1964   Mugabe and others detained.
1966   Three years old, Nhamo Mugabe dies in Ghana. Imprisoned Mugabe is denied permission to attend his own son's funeral.
1974   Detainees released from prison for settlement talks.

1975   Herbert Chitepo, head of ZANU in exile, is assassinated in Zambia. Mugabe and Edgar Tekere leave Rhodesia to join guerrillas in Mozambique but are initially placed under restriction there.

1977   Mugabe gains control of ZANU and its army.

1978   ZANU military leader, Rex Nhongo, crushes internal revolt aimed at toppling Mugabe.

1979   Lancaster House conference takes place in London. ZANU's military leader, Josiah Tongogara dies.

1980   Mugabe becomes prime minister of independent Zimbabwe.

1981   Apartheid South Africa embarks on campaign to destabilise Mugabe.

1982   Nkomo sacked from government following discovery of arms caches in Matabeleland. Trial in Harare of white airmen tortured on suspicion of sabotaging air force planes. North Korean-trained Fifth Brigade is unleashed by Mugabe in brutal campaign against dissidents.

1987   Mugabe and Nkomo sign Unity Accord merging to form ZANU-PF (Zimbabwe African National Union – Patriotic Front). Mugabe changes constitution becoming executive president.

1988   War veterans launch campaign for recognition of rule in liberating Zimbabwe. Edgar Tekere expelled from ZANU-PF for campaigning against one party state. Willowgate corruption scandal exposed. Mugabe begins affair with his secretary, Grace Marufu.

1990   Mandela released from prison in Robin Island. World Bank's Economic Structure Adjustment Programme (ESAP) begins in Zimbabwe.

1992   Sally Mugabe dies of kidney failure.

1995   Street riots in Harare, Zimbabwe, against rising prices and unemployment.

1996   Mugabe married Grace Marufu in Carish ceremony in Kutana.

1997   New Labour government under Tony Blair wins UK elections.

1998   Mugabe sends troops to the Democratic Republic of the Congo to intervene in civil war and plunder riches!

1999   Repressive action against Zimbabwe's media and judiciary increases. Mugabe is accosted by gay rights activists in London. Movement for Democratic Change (MDC) is formed in Harare. Relations with Britain deteriorate.

2000   Constitutional reforms rejected by electorate. Squatters seize white-owned farms. ZANU-PF wins narrow victory against MDC in parliamentary elections.

2002   Parliament passes law limiting press freedom. European Union imposes limited sanctions. Mugabe re-elected in presidential polls condemned as flawed by MDC and foreign observers.

2004   Leader of the MDC, Morgan Tsvangirai, acquitted of treason charges.

2005   US labels Zimbabwe amongst world's six outposts of tyranny. ZANU wins two kinds of votes in parliamentary election. Shanty dwellers and illegal street stalls destroyed in urban clean-up programme that leaves thousands homeless.

2006/7 Badly beaten up MDC leaders hospitalised after rally arrests. Power cuts for up to 20 hours per day throughout. Zimbabwe inflation soars. Five men charged with coup plot. ZANU-PF and MDC hold talks in South Africa.

One

Having just finished reading an excellent book by Heidi Holland (2008) – the untold story of a freedom fighter who became a tyrant – it makes one realise (as the saying goes) 'never judge a book by its cover'. This book has made me realise that 'there are two sides to every story!'

I knew Ian Smith personally and admired his ambitions until reading how Heidi gives both Robert Mugabe and Smith two completely different characters! In point of fact, I even felt sorry at times for Robert Mugabe in spite of his shocking performance in ruining one of the most beautiful and wealthiest countries in the world.

It seems there was far more racial bitterness between both sides than the everyday man in the street realised!

It is all so very sad how Robert Mugabe changed. During the first decade of his premiership he was definitely regarded as one of Africa's most inspiring leaders. All he achieved, such as his education and social welfare programs, were very welcome and admired, but during the next ten years things started changing. He travelled far too much and met all the powers that be all over the world, including royalty. The wonderful 'Jewel in the Crown' that Mugabe had inherited from Ian Smith, which had been in very good shape economically I must admit, began to falter by the '90s. It was quite a joke and at one stage Mugabe was very seldom in the country.

Because of the low-downs with Mugabe, our lovely country was being tarnished in the news more and more. We often heard of our wonderful farms being 'taken over'. It started in the '90s and at one stage I remember reading in our newspaper in 1994 that most of our money was spent and squandered by Mugabe's cronies instead of Land Reform. It was revealed that in 1994, 98 previously white-owned farms had been leased to Mugabe's senior officials and at a very low cost. People all over the world started to notice!

This went from bad to worse as in 1997 Britain made it quite clear when the international development secretary, Clare Short, wrote that there had been a disagreement between Tony Blair and Mugabe over Zimbabwe land redistribution plans during a meeting at the Commonwealth Conference in Edinburgh. Clare Short actually dismissed Zimbabwe's contention that Britain had an obligation to fund land redistribution in what was Rhodesia and she also made it quite clear that 'we do not accept the fact that Britain has a special responsibility to meet the costs of land purchase in Zimbabwe.' Then came cencroship, and the opening of British mailbags at Harare Airport.

So many farmers were murdered; having taken a lifetime of worry and money, the farmsteads were burnt down and servants and animals just killed out right.

When Ian Smith was in power, we wanted for nothing. Although there was a very bad time with petrol and I used to leave my car in a queue overnight, then at 6.00 am stay in it for one gallon or two, depending on what we could get! The black market started in full force; buying petrol coupons, changing money deals. In 2007 the bank had no money while I was there. Everyone trying to farix at a ridiculous price. The price of food rose to an unreal price – $2,000 to £1.

One never hears in history how political characters are such good friends, for instance Lord Christopher Soames and Mary Soames admired Robert Mugabe very much indeed, even when Lord Soames was the last Governor of Rhodesia. It was through Soames's patience and understanding that the friendship remained through very delicate times!

Then we have the times with Dennis Norman who always brought the very best out of Mugabe. He was really very good looking – seemed to dislike publicity – from what I can gather he started off life in Africa as a white farmer. He was totally honest and an excellent, hardworking man. He eventually became Zimbabwe's first agriculture minister and Mugabe often turned to him for help. He refused to be contaminated by racism. He was not a politician at heart, in spite of the fact that he served in Mugabe's cabinet four times. He seemed to go to the rescue often when needed by Mugabe. The Foreign Office officials had meetings with Dennis Norman in the hope that they could mend relations between Britain and Zimbabwe. Norman became Mugabe's travel companion on state visits all over the world in the first two decades after Independence in 1980.

In the world of tobacco days, Norman was known as 'The Burly King' or 'The Best Tobacco' and headed the Commercial Farmers' Union (CFU).

After sending some of CFU's staff to the head office for a crash course in agriculture just before the election, Norman agreed to oblige to his next change in office. Soames then told Norman that he was the new agriculture minister, but Norman said definitely no, it was the last job he wanted. Soames said it wouldn't be for ever. Mugabe greeted Norman by saying how delighted he was that he would be joining ZANU's government but Norman still insisted he had not made his mind up.

'All I am asking you to do is join the government as Deputy Minister of Mines.'

'No, I can't. I don't know the first thing about mines so help me out.'

'No, I can't,' replied Mugabe.

Norman made his excuses and stormed back to Soames's office.

'Count me out,' he told him.

That evening Soames called Norman to listen to the 6.00 pm news.

'Why?' asked Norman.

'Because you are in. You are the Minister of Agriculture.'

And so life continues with crime, black market and first-class corruption. What makes our beautiful Zimbabwe tick God alone knows!

Two

Let's go back in time to 2005 and reminisce, which is not so very long ago. The media simply did not get happenings reported to the world, only to Zimbabwe. Only now in 2008 is the world finding out the truth about what Zimbabwe has gone through since 1980 when Robert Mugabe came to power. So sad and a great tragedy for such a magnificent country.

Every year I return to Zimbabwe to see my friend. During this time, from 1989 onwards, violence was still in full force, intimidation was unbelievable and we all kept hoping and waiting, trying to find bread, milk, coffee, tea from town to town, ringing our friends on our cell phones to tell them where the food was. There was no water or food for days and also electricity cuts. At night, some of us had gas lights and cookers which helped, no matter how small, just for a standby!

For the last seven years I return to my wonderful friend with all sorts of food and material things which they can't see or buy. How wrong I was! On 14th December 2008, I catch an Air Zimbabwe flight; the best trip I have been on for many years. The service was absolutely excellent and I even had Scotch on board. The food was very good and beautifully serviced and the air hostesses were young and a 'breath of fresh air'; all black of course. I was upgraded to first class – what a joy! Even the gin and tonic was extra special, not forgetting the lemon. We were five hours late and the worst time was waiting in the lounge for hour after hour.

My luggage was, of course, overweight and a lovely old boy with a grey moustache and grey beard winked at me and said 'Have a good Christmas, love,' I was through!

I had Christmas cake, two heavy Christmas puddings, two large smoked salmon, nuts, chocolates, tea, sugar, brandy butter, cheese board with six different cheeses – not to mention Christmas gifts!

My darling friend, Maria, was waiting for me on arrival in spite of being so late. She really spoilt me when I stayed with her.

The road lights, which were a pale blue and at least 20 feet tall, were all shapes and leaning left, right and centre; completely rusty. The pot holes in our beautiful roads are to say the least very dangerous! The 'green' lights are treated as 'stop' lights and the red lights don't mean a thing, they just drive through them! Our beautiful suburbs, with shopping centres, which were spotless, are now rubbish centres; meali cobs everywhere; Coca Cola tins and bottles everywhere; paper, cardboard boxes, it is just worse than the African townships one sees on TV.

The banks are empty and another note is created – $50million! There are no more bank statements and I could not understand why I had no money in my account; I should have millions in it – nothing!

'It is all right, Mrs Treacy. The government has taken all the zeros off the money.'

This meant that I had no pension for one year. It was not allowed out of the country so I used to return to Zimbabwe once or twice a year to help my friend with money and buy clothes, which I can't afford in the UK, not this year! I was told to bring US dollars. My fare had gone up to £1,226.40 from £800 and I drained my savings to take US dollars to Zimbabwe. This is how much one still loves the country and all my wonderful friends there. To think, one man can ruin so many lives and a magnificent country with all its wealth that was!

While I was in Zimbabwe so much happened. On landing, human rights lawyer, Justina Mukoko, plus nine opposition leaders of MDS were held in prison. They were plotting to overthrow Mugabe (must be very brave to even attempt this).

The plot had been wildly discussed; Mukoko had been missing for at least three weeks. The search was intensive and carried on for the whole time she was missing. Then she suddenly appeared in court on a Wednesday in January. The judge said that she should be sent to hospital immediately, without delay at all.

Instead she was sent to the famous Chickurubi Prison. Another lawyer confirmed she was definitely there, which incidentally had no running water.

New York called for a human rights group and Mugabe admitted in a speech that food, medicine and US dollars were very scarce in Zimbabwe.

Maria, my dearest friend who I have stayed with when I have been in Zimbabwe on my last five trips, had the most terrible fall. Her knee was the size of a football and she had bruises on her face and arm. She stuck it for three weeks and then went to her doctor, which can cost an arm and a leg. The doctor drained the fluid off her knee and gave her ointment. She was one of the lucky ones with a good doctor. Also, of course, regardless of pain, she carried on working and living normally, not feeling sorry for herself no matter what!

One day we had a shopping trip in our Land Rover with the dangerous, deep potholes filled with rain. It was so hard to see how deep they were and we stopped at the lights on a main crossing only to see in the middle of the road a beautiful lady's handbag with notes and a wallet on the ground. Obviously someone had snatched it out of someone's car at the lights. That handbag was still there two days later – no police around when one needed them and no-one dared take it.

Second week in December 2008 and again the law court has ordered the release of the 38 prisoners who should never have been in jail in the first place. The streets, in parts, had thousands of Zimbabwe dollars on the pavements, they are so useless. It makes me feel quite sick when I think of how hard my darling Brendan, my husband then, worked for this country as attorney general.

For the first time in 58 years of living in Rhodesia/ Zimbabwe I find shopping an absolute nightmare! We are living in a world of US dollars. To my astonishment the 'Spar' shops have everything one could wish for in the way of food BUT there is never any change for the US dollar. One shop gave me two lollipops, another four bread rolls and another an IOU. Zimbabwe dollars would lose millions. The supermarkets even take petrol coupons in lieu of money. If one started to say 'forget the change' we would lose out by thousands every day. Somehow everyone seems determined to get their money's worth – and why not?

It is now the beginning of January 2009 and the thunder is rumbling day after day but there is very little rain. 'Climate change' seems to have caught up with Africa after all. In spite of the political problems, we still manage to keep up the colonial way of living. There seems to be no class distinction, everyone knows their place and accept each other accordingly, with help, concern and friendliness.

In August 2008, I was still in the UK living in our 'sheltered home' private flat with the best security one could have. Every room has a card should one have a fall or is in trouble. We all have our own hallways and a box with certain buttons on it and should anyone outside press your flat number it beeps. We press our second button to speak to the caller, release it to listen to them and press the third button to open the door (only if you wish to). We also press the third button to stop unwanted calls for a few minutes. Also, we can see on TV who it is! We also have an automatic fire alarm for smoke and each flat is monitored at a box in reception with the number of the flat shown. We have a public lounge for residents, eg for coffee mornings, Irish coffee mornings, Halloween, St Patrick's Day, New Year, Christmas, bingo, private parties etc. You name it, we have it; raffles, tea parties—but back to August 2008!

On a more cheerful note, my darling Alistair was taking me to Willow Mead for coffee; thatched roofs and long buildings for lush vegetables and booze and a lovely café right out in the country. Yes, the very same Alistair in my autobiography. We were going to stay together after July and look after each other. It may have to be in the UK and not Zimbabwe as it is almost impossible to live there now. Yes, Alistair is the person I dedicated *Never a Dull Moment* to (this book, after many requests, is going to be re-edited). I can't wait to spoil him for ever.

In January 2009, the news from ZWN News by Blessing Lulu read as follows:

Washington – Zimbabwe's president, Mr Robert Mugabe, has told his ministers that he is dissolving the cabinet signalling his intention to make a new state of ministers in defiance of international pressure for him to share power with the opposition. As such, a government will not be joined by either formation of the Movement for Democratic Change, political sources said on Friday. Top officials in Mr Mugabe's government and the ZANU-PF party said most of his ministers have received letters that went out on 1st January but some who were away will receive them on Monday. They said that Mr Mugabe could form a new cabinet as early as the coming Tuesday.

A report in the state-controlled Herald newspaper on the one hand suggested the letters to the ministers terminating their executive appointments were effecting a mere cabinet shuffle and that many of those receiving termination letters lost their parliamentary seats in the March elections so could not continue as ministers beyond three months from their October appointments. But the Herald, at the same time, said the Mugabe spokesman, George Charamba, indicated that President Mugabe was going ahead with the formation of a new government. The Herald continued, 'This is pursuant to the invitation (Mugabe) extended to the two MDC formations to submit their preferred lists of ministers and for their leaders to come forward and be sworn into office in line with the 15th September agreement.'

Government sources say that Mugabe is moving ahead to form a government because MDC founder, Morgan Tsvangirai, prime minister designate under the power-sharing accord signed by the two parties on 15th September, spurned his invitation to join a national unity government. Tsvangirai received the letter on Christmas Day and sent his response two days later, saying all outstanding issues had to be first satisfactorily resolved. These included the composition of the cabinet and other top political appointments – governors and ambassadors. Tsvangirai also demanded a halt to the abduction of the MDC and civic activists by state agents and the release of about 40 individuals abducted since October, who had lately resurfaced in police hands, only to be charged with conspiring to overthrow the government.

Rival MDC formation leader, Mutambara, is said to have told Mugabe this week that it would not be possible for him to enter into a unity government that didn't include Tsvangirai. Justice minister, Patrick Chinamasa, told VOA (Voice of America) in a brief interview that he was in the dark and referred questions to chief cabinet secretary, Musheck Sibanda, who, however, could not be reached. Secretary general, Welshman Ncube of the Mutambara MDC formation, told VOA it would spell disaster if Mr Mugabe attempted to form a government without the MDC chief whip, Innocent Gonese of the Tsvangirai MDC grouping. He said that Mugabe has been making many illegal decisions, which threaten the future of the power-sharing process.

Offering a legal perspective, Chairman Lovemore Madhuku of the National Constitutional Assembly called Mr Mugabe's latest rule academic offering the opinion that the president and his ministers were in any case operating outside the boundary of the constitution.

While all this was happening in Zimbabwe, the High Court on 2nd January refused a request by a top human rights activist, detained on accusations of plotting to overthrow the government, to be taken to hospital for treatment after alleged torture. Contradicting an earlier order by the same court, the judge, Alphius Chitakunye, made the incredible order that if she should be taken to hospital it would be for the purpose of examination otherwise she would be treated in hospital. Beatrice Mtetwa, the lawyer for rights campaigner, Justina Mukoko, told reporters that Chitakunye's order was contrary to an earlier order by a fellow High Court judge on 24th December that Mukoko and eight rights and opposition activists be released to hospital.

'The law has completely broken down in Zimbabwe,' said Mtetwa said after the ruling. 'Even if we go to another court, we may well get a similar ruling. The court also dismissed contempt of court charges against the police for defying the High Court order to release Mukoko and the others to hospital,' she said.

Nelson Charnisa, national spokesman of the main opposition, Movement for Democratic Change (MDC), has played down the ability for his party to quickly stem the number of cholera deaths if it were to join the government immediately. Charnisa said if the party was to sign the power-sharing deal on the table, it still would not have any real power to help the humanitarian crisis, as the cholera death toll crept near the 1,600 mark, clocking more than 40 deaths in two days, according to the World Health Organisation.

Agencies also underlined the need to end the months of political uncertainly which has made raising funds to help the country to get back on its feet difficult. At least 5.5 million people – over half of the population – will need food aid in the first quarter of 2009, according to the World Food Programme.

The food security situation, cholera and political problems are exacerbated by hyper-inflation and widespread infrastructural collapse. A power-sharing deal brokered by the South African Development Community (SADC) said the MDC and the ruling ZANU-PF is deadlocked in September 2008.

'The humanitarian situation is seriously affected by the political situation,' said George Tadonki, head of the United Nations Office for the Co-ordination of Humanitarian Affairs (OCHA) in Zimbabwe. 'The UN is working hard at all levels to reach a political settlement, which has now become very urgent because of the cholera outbreak.'

'The MDC must sign the power-sharing pact and then they will be in a position to get the ball rolling to help the country out of the humanitarian crisis which now needs urgent attention,' said Thabo Masebe, spokesman for the South African president, Kgalema Motlanthe, who is also the SADC chairman.

Charnisa explained that an amendment to the constitution which being into the law the power-sharing deal being between Robert Mugabe, leader of the ZANU-PF party, Morgan Tsvangirai, the MDC leader, and Arthur Mutambana, an MDC breakaway party, in September 2008 will only become effective after it has been endorsed by parliament, which does not sit until 20th January.

'If we become part of the government now we will have no muscle! We are not yet empowered,' said Charnisa. 'We do not want to become an accessory to a government who has not shown any genuine willingness to power share. The recent abduction of MDC activists apparently by the state security apparatus has also fuelled tensions. Tsvangirai has said he will ask him national council to vote to walk away from the deal, if the abduction of MDC activists do not cease and if all those seized by the state agents have not be released by 1st January,' continued Charnisa.

Justina Mukoko, head of local rights group Zimbabwe Peace Project, who had been reported missing since the beginning of December along with eight other activists were charged last week with recruiting Zimbabweans to undergo military training to overthrow the Mugabe government. Despite a High Court ruling to release activists, they remained in custody.

Reacting to the failure to follow the ruling, Motlanthe's spokesman, Masebe, said, 'We are saying the MDC must become part of the inclusive government, but at the heart of the MDC's reluctance to sign the deal is also the allocation of governors' posts and key ministries.'

'All these issues can be resolved within minutes if there is political willingness,' said Charnisa. 'We want to be able to provide a real change in government and not become part of a symbolic act.'

Comment from The Star (South Africa) on 3rd January: 'If ever proof were needed that ZANU-PF should no longer control the police, then the last week's events around Harare courts should provide it. Peace worker, Justina Mukoko and about 24 others, after being abducted and held in secret locations for weeks, were supposed to be sent to hospital or even freed on Christmas Day in the evening, according to an order from the High Court judge, Yunus Omerjee. Instead they remained locked up. It is also no use presidential spokesman Thabo saying there are many issues that need to be addressed by a unity government, he (Mukoko and company) is one of them.

'In a unity government as it stands now, ZANU-PF would control justice and ZANU-PF and MDC would jointly run the home affairs ministry, which control the police. No country in the region has even tried to co-manage a ministry so imagine the first experiment within SADC, carried out with an incompetent ZANU appointee. If SADC believes that Robert Mugabe won't shift on allowing MDC sole control of the police and he already has the armed forces and intelligence, then South Africa will have to push him hard and they have plenty of non-military weapons.

'It is not that the police haven't defied the courts before. Human rights lawyer, David Coltart, spent years defending people loyal to the then opposition, ZAPU and other prisoners locked up without trial, or held after the courts ordered their freedom. Zimbabwe had a state of emergency then a handful of traitors in its ranks and hits from South African security forces, although its efforts were, in retrospect, muted. There is no record of our professional police force in Rhodesia or Zimbabwe, although there were spasms of impartiality in both eras. At least early Zimbabwe had a preponderance of professional judges. Without control of the police, forget any unity government if Thabo Mbeki believes that Morgan Tsvangirai only got his passport because South Africans leant on Robert Mugabe.'

'The charges of nine of those who appeared in court again on Monday add up to treason with the death penalty. They are charged with recruiting or trying to recruit people of military training in Botswana to topple Mugabe. It was obvious that Botswana would be accused of harbouring MDC insurgents as soon as President Ian Khama spoke out against Mugabe. His treason and similar charges are a favourite of ZANU-PF. They have done it to all their political opponents. Secretary general, Tendai Biti, is similarly charged. His treason charges arise from a document written by Military Intelligence. It is a document littered with clichés of what MI believes is 'Rhodesian speak'. Biti is an intellectual and a lawyer and could never, even if he tried, write the childish, semi-literate language of which he is accused.

The document, about the way forward under a MDC government and attributed to Biti, was first published in the wicked newspaper, The Herald, in April. Biti laughed it off and issued a denial and behold, it appeared a few weeks later on a charge sheet with treason attached!

A comment from The Guardian on 29th December: 'They did similar to Morgan Tsvangirai, then MDC secretary general, Welshman Ncube, and the party's then agriculture spokesman, Nelson Gasela, three weeks before the violent 2002 presidential election. Twenty-four hours' time, they had a Canadian crook, Ari Ben Menashe, and paid him more than one million US dollars (admitted in court) to produce a video proving Tsvangirai plotted to kill Mugabe. The CIO (Central Intelligence Organisation) which devised this plot did not care whether or not it got a conviction. The charges took two years of the accused's lives and drained the MDC of funds. Even if the MDC gets home affairs, Mugabe still has the right to appoint the commissioner and the police have many ways it can circumnavigate the law. Nevertheless, for the morale of the police, at least, ZANU-PF must be moved from day to day control.'

Morgan Tsvangirai is the people's choice, as he easily beat Mugabe in the first round. It is rough on ANC members to be snide about Morgan Tsvangirai; Zimbabweans want Tsvangirai and he is brave enough to try and fix his country. Without the MDC in control of home affairs, the region will have to find a solution other than a unity government, the catastrophe north of Musina.'

The UN is gridlocked over the question of its responsibility to protect. Can Barack Obama break the stalemate?

The United Nations Security Council is supposed to deal with matters of international peace and security, but it won't be able to fix the crisis in Zimbabwe. Why? Because the council is at an impasse which is worth more: human rights or sovereignty. The council has five permanent members who have the right to vote any resolution that comes to the council's table, and as soon as Russia, China and the three Western powers remain in the same dynamic the Bush years have brought to the UN, the stalemate remains. Will Barack Obama change things? If you ask Russia or China, the Western powers' continued appetite to intervene inside other nations' affairs, ostensibly to ensure human rights for us all, is just another way the West has tried to extend the sphere of influence. This is because when the US used the pretext of bringing democracy to the Iraqi people as a reason to invade Iraq, it made the rest of the world fuse the idea of humanitarian interventions with Western abuses of power. So the Iraq war caused a rift that is still being felt by the UN on a daily basis. However, it's going deeper than that and secretariat employees who were at the UN when Colin Powell dangled his vial of anthrax and tried to scare the council into authorising Bush's war, are still traumatised by what they witnessed, which was basically the moment when Bush came to shove over something called R2P.

The case against Saddam Hussein was always a dubious application of the theory but the core issue remains the same today. Does a nation's right to decide its own affairs include the right to abuse the human rights of its citizens? The US and EU fall on the side that says protecting human rights troops borders, but most of the other major powers think they have the right to exert total control over their territory. The Guardian knot of a question – a nation's right to non-meddling in its internal affairs by other countries, its sovereignty, versus the international community's responsibility to ensure human rights for all, is the number one burning question at the UN right now.

Of course, this being not just UNHA but also acronym HQ, the whole discussion has been boiled down to R2P (responsibility to protect). The former name of the doctrine that says borders are nothing and human rights are everything.

Little verbal battles inside the council tend to harp on the divisions: 'I must say I liked the statement of the US reminding the members of the Security Council that states that their activity must refrain from the use of the threat or the use of force.' (Comment from The Guardian, 29th December 2009.)

This sparked the Russian permanent representative of the US, Vitaly Churkin, in a Security Council meeting in Georgia to say, 'And I would like to ask the distinguished representative of the United States – weapons of mass destruction, have you found them yet in Iraq or are you still looking for them?'

The problem is that this dynamic of reflexive disagreement on R2P has become a well worn track. If the Western powers today take an initiative on a conflict, Russia and China will block it with a precisely calibrated anti-initiative. When cyclone Nangis struck Burma, France the UK and the US all wanted to intervene somehow but Burmese military junta wanted to retain total control over their country. China, which sees Burma as within its sphere of influence, blocked the Security Council from doing anything about the situation. They even managed to stop the Council from mentioning the name of Aung San Suu Kyi, the main political opposition candidate. In as much as the Security Council is a microcosm of international politics, this has bad implications and ending up in a precise give-and-take like this between the West and the rest is destructive too because it means that the world is destabilised by something as confusing as the Mumbai terrorist attacks. The powerful nations are locked in to reacting against events in the set pattern they've become accustomed to, not acting on the merits of the case itself.

So something must be done, but will Obama change the dynamic? Unlocking the impasse could only be done by coming to an agreement over R2P. The new ambassador of the UN, Susan Rice, is on record saying that she'd rather 'go down in flames' than fail to do something about Dafus. So it seems clear that the Americans are still interventionists and so in the end, the question turns out to be whether Rice can convince the rest of the world that after Iraq, there is a difference between a neocon interventionist and a humanitarian one. How exactly that could be done is a question above my pay grade, but it will be interesting to see Rice and Obama finesse it because if anyone can do it, it has got to be them.

There are also indications that Russia and China are willing to hear them out. Earlier in December, both the current and former presidents, Medvedev and Putin, made positive comments about Obama that seemed to say that Russia is willing to work with the US come January. As far as China is concerned, whatever they are thinking the country does have a pragmatic side that Obama might be able to appeal to. Rarely did it seem so appropriate to recall Deng Xiaoping's explanation of what pragmatism is: the idea is that a cat is a cat if it catches the mice, regardless of whether the cat is black or white.

Three

Tuesday 24th February 2009 – Reporter Grant Ferrett, Editor David Ross – File on Four, Radio Zimbabwe. Actuality of swearing in ceremony:

Mugabe: I, Robert Gabriel Mugabe, do hereby call upon you, Morgan Richard Tsvangirai to take the oath as Prime Minister.

Ferrett: As Robert Mugabe embarks on a power-sharing deal with the opposition, the biggest challenge facing the uneasy alliance is to reverse the country's calamitous economic decline.

Actuality of Tsvangirai: I, Morgan Richard Tsvangirai, do swear that I will be faithful and bear true allegiance to Zimbabwe.

Ferrett: But foreign donors and investors remain deeply sceptical there can be any real change until the 85-year-old president leaves power. As they watch and wait, Robert Mugabe and his allies retain control of many of the levers of power and patronage which have helped them become rich.

Makumba: They have government-issued Mercedes Benz; most of them stay in government houses. They also have four-by-four vehicles. The state funds all of that. It is like they are not in Zimbabwe.

Ferrett: File on Four has uncovered some of the ways in which the select group has enriched itself while impoverishing an entire country. We investigate the vice president's sale, in a multi-million pound gold deal in Europe and ask if sanctions are anything more than a political gesture that's backfired.

Lamb: We stand charged of complicity and failing to take an effective action to bring to an end a despicable regime, which is causing such horror for its population. These sanctions are just not worth the paper they are written on.

Signature tale actually at Victoria Falls:

Ferrett: This is one of the world's great tourist attractions. The falls mark the border between Zimbabwe and Zambia. As Zimbabwe descends ever further into economic ruin and chaos, business on the Zambian side of the bridge booms. New hotels are being built to accommodate the surge in visitors. Many of the new arrivals in the Zambian resort town of Livingstone are not wealthy Western tourists, but impoverished Zimbabweans, desperate to escape their country's economic meltdown.

Actuality at bus station:

There are thousands of Zimbabweans in Livingstone; many of them are street vendors touting for trade around the bus station, selling bootleg CDs and tourist souvenirs. Among the usual array of carvings and beads on offer, there seems to be a new addition, a symbol of Zimbabwe's disintegration – Zimbabwean dollars.

Actuality of vendors describing ten trillion dollar bank notes:

Vendor: This is ten trillion.

Ferrett: So that's a ten?

Vendor: Trillion.

Ferrett: A trillian-dollar note?

Vendor: Yes.

Ferrett: So that's ten with one, two, three, four, with twelve zeros?

Vendor: Yes, twelve zeros.

Ferrett: Ten with twelve zeros. And how much is ten trillion dollars worth at the current exchange rate?

Vendor: Two US dollars.

Ferrett: So, ten trillion Zimbabwe dollars is worth two US dollars?

Vendor: Two dollars, yes. This money will go to Zimbabwe.

Ferrett: Can you use this ten trillion-dollar note in the shops?

Vendor: No, you can't buy anything. They don't want it. Only US dollars and Rand.

Ferrett: All the Zimbabweans told me their main aim was to send money to support their families. I visited a group of street vendors who for the past two years have lived in a township in Livingstone. Each night three of them cram into a single room to cut costs. The less they pay out the more they can send home.

In the room:

Vendor: You can see three metres and a half metres by two and a half metres.

Ferrett: About three metres by two and there are three of you in one room.

Vendor: We also cook outside. We can't cook inside, there is no room inside.

Ferrett: And it is quite noisy here.

Vendor: And it is quite noisy. There is a bar, that's why there is music. If it is raining, there will be water in here, running water.

Ferrett: Going past the front door?

Vendor: Yes.

Ferrett: You don't have any mattress here?

Vendor: No, we don't have any. We are just sleeping on these.

Ferrett: On these reed mats?

Vendor: Yes.

Ferrett: An estimated four million people have fled Zimbabwe, or about a third of the population. The majority of those who remain need food aid. Unemployment is estimated at 94% but amid the economic chaos, a few hundred well-connected members of President Mugabe's ZANU-PF have become very wealthy. While many Zimbabweans overseas are scraping together money to send home to keep their families alive, some of these elite are looking in the opposite direction, trying to pursue valuable business deals outside Zimbabwe.

This will give you a slight idea of what goes on in our wonderful Zimbabwe. Felix Eimes was working with a company? in the commodity broker business. Commodities like gold and steel, to make deals as a broker for them.

In November last year, Felix Eimes, who's based in Frankfurt, made contact with a young Zimbabwean commodities trader living in Madrid, Nyasha del Campo, she offered to sell him more than three and a half tonnes of gold. It was a genuine offer and was in her legal possession or 'they' had the information that the gold was already physically at the airport in Nairobi and ready to be transported and was quite sure that she is in possession of the gold. Oh yes, and she is acting on behalf of two companies. Ferrett asked how much it would cost – the first transaction is equivalent to US$20 million.

Ferrett: You said the first transaction. There would be subsequent transactions if that was successful?

Eimes: Yes, it was planned to do it on a monthly basis, to make one transaction each month of about US$20 million which was planned from Nyasha del Campo's side.

Ferrett: When I looked into the plan more closely, he began to have misgivings. First, the gold appeared to originate from the Democratic Republic of the Congo. While there is no international embargo against gold exports from the DRC, there are long-standing sensitivities. The United Nation and human rights groups have called for stricter regulations to ensure the proceeds don't end up fuelling the conflicts, which have raged in the Congo for more than a decade. I am looking at a copy that you have made available. It says in French, Democratic Republic of the Congo, certificate of origin. There are lots of official stamps on it. What's the significance of that document?

Eimes: This is the certificate, a statement where the gold comes from.

Ferrett: So the gold comes from the Congo, but a lot of refineries do not work with gold from the Congo, like our refinery would not accept this gold. This is not because of an international ban, but this is the decision from refinery to refinery.

Firstar had another concern. It discovered that Nyasha del Campo was the daughter of one of Zimbabwe's most powerful families, the Mujurus. Her mother, Joyce, is vice president and her father,

Solomon, is a former head of the National Army, which deployed troops in the Congo from the late 1990s in return for mining and logging concessions.

John Makumbe, Associate Professor of Politics at the University of Zimbabwe, has been following the Mujurus' fortunes for many years.

Solomon Mujuru has since retired from the army and he is a businessman! He is into farms and it is known that he has six farms and is into mining. He is also into manufacturing. He is literally in every sector. Joyce Mujuru is the wife. She is vice president of Zimbabwe, appointed by Robert Mugabe himself. She is very much into business and she has shares in many companies in Zimbabwe, including in companies that are involved in diamonds here in Zimbabwe, but also in many other ventures throughout the country.

Within the DRC there are huge exploits being made by both Soloman Mujuru and Joyce Mujuru and sometimes with Robert Mugabe himself.

Ferrett: Those business dealings may well be legitimate, but both Joyce Mujuru and her husband, Solomon, are on a list subject to sanctions in the EU and United States. They're accused of undermining democracy, human rights and respect for the rule of law and Felix Eimes says Joyce Mujuru was central to the gold deal being offered by her daughter, Nyasha, from her base in Spain. She promised (according to Eimes) us in order to complete this transaction her mother will pay the total amount that is necessary to transport the gold from Nairobi to Zurich. This is equivalent to about 150,000 to 200,000 euros in transport costs and at the end of the day, the money transaction was completed and the gold was also ready to be shipped by a security firm.

Reporter Ferrett of File on Four, BBC, has also seen copies of emails from Nyasha del Campo in which she refers to her mother's role in the proposed deal. In one to her husband, later copies to Finstar, she writes about her mother sending money to pay lawyers in Kenya.

Reader in the studio: I have informed that my mother still needs to make payments to our lawyers in Nairobi in order to start the process.

The vice president's involvement comes up in another email, this time to Firstar itself:

Reader in the studio: Right, Eimes said it is too sensitive on documentation for her mother and that is not possible to make us bank documents available because her mother's name is on them.

Ferrett: The vice president's involvement comes up in another email to Firstar itself. There's a copy of an email from Nyasha del Campo which says: 'As far as the transaction receipt is concerned, we can forget that as my mother has forbidden me to disclose it.' So she is saying her mother can't give documentation.

Former guerrilla fighter for Robert Mugabe's ZANLA army, ? Mutasa, describes himself as a staunch supporter of President Mugabe. He sees nothing untoward in Zimbabwe's vice president funding deals to sell large quantities of gold in Europe.

Mutasa: This is Congolese gold acquired quite legitimately so no problem with that. That is business.

Ferrett: You say you would not have a problem if that gold was sources from the Congo and this was a legal deal, but should the vice president of Zimbabwe be involved in gold deals in Zimbabwe or even Europe? Surely she has a job to do in Zimbabwe rather than getting involved in mineral exports to the rest of the world?

Mutasa: All I am saying is what she does exactly outside her role as vice president business-wise is not a problem as long as she is able to discharge her role as vice president.

Ferrett: So a deal in which the vice president is involved in selling three and a half tonnes of gold, you say you really don't see any difficulty with that?

Mutasa: It is possible for somebody to engage in a legitimate business enterprise, but I think you have to look at it in context of the fantastic smear campaign that has been going on. Joyce Mufuru has been a target of that kind of thing, just like Mugabe himself.

Ferrett: You mean there is a propaganda campaign internationally against Robert Mugabe?

Mutasa: Oh yes! A very globally orchestrated programme.

Ferrett: But it's a fact, not propaganda, that as Zimbabwe as a whole sinks ever deeper into poverty, those closest to Robert Mugabe have become conspicuously wealthy.

If you were to visit some of the upmarket residential areas, you would think that you had landed in Beverley Hills. There are some magnificent properties and I believe that many of the people who built those houses could be picked up by an honest tax collector who could say, in order to build this house, you must have misrepresented your earnings, otherwise you wouldn't have been able to built a house that clearly cost about five lifetimes' salary at the declared rate. There really are some magnificent properties.

John Robuso Robertson, an economics analyst in Harare, says many of these fortunes have been amassed not in spite of the economic meltdown, but because of it. Access to foreign exchange is the key. Most shops no longer accept the local currency; instead foreign exchange that holds its value has become highly sought after. Most Zimbabweans have to pay exorbitant rates on the black market but the reserve bank governor, Gideon Gono, has granted a select few the privilege of buying foreign exchange from the Central Bank at extraordinarily favourable rates. For this small elite, the exchange rate is just a thousandth of the black market rate!

If you can buy your foreign currency at a thousandth of the price that other people are paying, you can very clearly import things and then sell those goods as if you had paid the market price for the foreign currency and you can also claim that you paid import duties. This is something else the government gave themselves, the privilege of duty-free imports. If you are high up enough in the political hierarchy, they would give themselves sort of money to pay for fuel or to pay for luxury motorcars, so it was empowering themselves to make money without having to have any special knowledge. It was just the use of such privileges that permitted these huge fortunes to be made.

Gideon Gono recently published a book about his exploits as reserve bank governor, entitled *Zimbabwe's Casino Economy*. Zimbabweans have lost out on a grand scale, thanks to his disastrous gamble with inflation, but so far the governor himself has emerged a winner. He's become fabulously wealthy serving Robert Mugabe. His new mansion in Harare's northern suburbs is reported to have 47 bedrooms. Last year he defended his decision to keep printing Zimbabwe dollars, regardless of the effect on inflation.

Gono said that extraordinary circumstances call for extraordinary interventions. The days are gone when we should be worried about whether this is fiscal policy, whether this is monetary policy; we're talking about lives here, saving lives.

In other words, Mr Gono's answer to Zimbabwe's problems was to keep the printing presses churning out ever more worthless Zimbabwe dollars. As the local currency devalued, the governors and the ZANU-PF elite became still richer because of their access to hard currency at favourable rates. John Makumbe again, who stated that Gideon Gono is Father Christmas. Basically he collects all the revenue that comes into the Zimbabwean government. It is kept at the Reserve Bank of Zimbabwe and Central Bank and he dishes it out willy-nilly basically, without necessarily following any budget, to the party and to individuals within the party, to Mugabe and his family, without any accountability whatsoever.

The constant problem for Mr Gono and his senior ZANU-PF colleagues has been how to get more foreign exchange. Zimbabwe's exports have collapsed and tax revenues have dwindled. One scheme approved by the Reserve Bank governor involved selling shares in London in what are known as dual-listed companies; those listed at more than one stock exchange, as John Robertson in Harare explains:

'There are only a few dual-listed companies, but the principle one among them was 'The Old Mutual'. The Old Mutual is a very large insurance authorised pension fund company set up in Africa. The Reserve Bank in Zimbabwe would have to authorise people to buy shares in Zimbabwe and sell them abroad and that authority was very seldom given to anyone but themselves. That was another of the privileges they could offer and say, well, when we buy shares or when people we know (part of the inner circle) buy shares, we can authorise them to sell those shares in another country market and earn the foreign currency. So it was a means of converting Zimbabwe dollars into foreign currency.'

One of the few people allowed by Gideon Gono to sell shares outside Zimbabwe was a businessman by the name of Mohammed I. Mohammed was granted the privilege of becoming the sole private importer of desperately needed fuel into Zimbabwe.

Patrick Smith, the editor of Africa Confidential, explains how the arrangement worked.

Smith: What he is doing through his London operations is to use the money from The Old Mutual shares bought in Zimbabwe, which he trades on the London market and uses the profit from those dealings to then buy oil and bring that back into Zimbabwe and sell it to the distribution companies at a time when he has literally no other competition, except the state-owned oil company. So it is an extremely lucrative business and it is made more lucrative by the fact that he doesn't have any more competitors. It's whatever price he and his pals in the government choose to fix.

Ferrett: What evidence have you uncovered that this is actually taking place in London?'

Smith: We have an invoice from Mr Mohammed's company, which is called Revenscourt Corporation Ltd and it's talking about a consignment of diesel to Zimbabwe and it states quite clearly on the invoice, which refers to Mr Mohammed's bank in London EC2 and then names the consignee in Southern Harare.

Ferrett: And that's an invoice dated 20th November?

Smith: Yes. The 20th November 2008 and that's when this deal went through.

Ferrett: Mr Mohammed is not on the list of those subject to a travel ban as sanctions in Britain and the European Union. Is he doing anything contrary to the regulations?

Smith: He certainly doesn't appear to be breaking any EU sanctions or any British laws by this but it does raise the question of the nature of the sanctions' regime on Zimbabwe. Any sort of deal where the government is able to exercise its patronage by giving procurement contracts to its business pals, which enables them to bring in essential commodities into Zimbabwe and sell them for huge profits is outrageous. That they should use the British or European Union financial systems to do that seems to be absolutely contrary to the spirit of the sanctions they're meant to be imposing on Zimbabwe.

Ferrett: Mr Mohammed has not responded to our request to tell us his side of the story, but what of Gideon Gono's lavish lifestyle? What does the ZANU-PF loyalist and former guerrilla fighter, Alfred Mutasa make of his ostentatious display of wealth? He reportedly has a 47-room house and a fleet of luxury cars. How is that possible?

Mutasa: I can't comment on the veracity of those statements as such. Let's assume that is the case and in Zimbabwe it is possible. If you are good enough at farming and so on, and from what I hear Gono has a very big farm where he has been farming very successfully, so he is a good farmer as well as being a good banker. It is possible. It is quite possible. There are people, like some Zimbabwean generals I know, they are very good farmers!

Sanctions were imposed on Zimbabwe in 2002 by the European Union and the United States and others. They were intended to send a signal of disapproval and to isolate the president. Mr Mugabe and his senior colleagues were also designed to promise human rights and the rule of law. There are now more than 200 individuals and 40 companies whose assets in Europe are liable to be frozen and are subject to a travel ban, but the fact they have been so narrowly targeted has severely limited the effectiveness of British banks in Zimbabwe for several years.

He believes they are, in effect, helping to keep Robert Mugabe in power.

Lamb: For example, banks including Standard Chartered are required to participate in an agricultural loan scheme. This is providing loans to people who've benefited from the land grab and bear in mind it wasn't the people from Zimbabwe who benefited from the land grab, it's the ruling elite, those close to Zimbabwe. It's also the case that any commercial bank operating in Zimbabwe is required by the government to reinvest 40% of its profits in government bonds. So in these sorts of ways these banks are providing financial support and sustenance to the

Mugabe regime and it seems to me ultimately to be counterproductive to sustain the regime in that way.

Ferrett: Do you think the banks should be taking action themselves then? Should they be saying to themselves we are not prepared to work in Zimbabwe under these circumstances?

Lamb: I recognise there is a dilemma. The banks argument is that if they were to comply with the spirit of the sanctions and stop the report, the loans for those on the EU list would have to cease business in Zimbabwe and that would result in hundreds, possibly thousands, of people losing their jobs and I don't take that concern lightly. Even a country as dysfunctional as Zimbabwe needs a banking sector to function and Mugabe has been sustained because of the operation of British banks and I think ultimately that has prolonged the agony for this country and for its people.

Ferrett: We asked Standard Chartered, which operates through a wholly owned subsidiary in Zimbabwe, for an interview. We particularly wanted to ask about their role in providing loans to those who illegally acquired land following the invasion of white-owned farms. They declined, but issued a statement saying they had taken a long-term decision to continue working in Zimbabwe to look after the interests of their 860 staff there.

Lamb: Standard Chartered Bank, Zimbabwe, is required to hold government securities, just as the bank is required to invest in approved assets to meet statutory reserve requirements in every other country in which it operates. Likewise all banks in Zimbabwe are obliged to administer applications for working capital loans for the local agricultural sectors, which are funded entirely by the Reserve Bank of Zimbabwe.

Ferrett: Within the last two weeks, Norman Lamb has used the Freedom of Information Act to gain access to correspond between Whitehall departments in the Foreign Office and Treasury civil servants are considering whether Standard Chartered has breached sanctions. They concluded that because it's operating through a subsidiary incorporated in Zimbabwe, there's been no violation. What Norman Lamb says suggests that the sanctions regime is virtually meaningless.

Lamb: I have here an internal FCO briefing document from August last year and it says that Standard Chartered risk real reputational damage if seen to be passing funds to the government of Zimbabwe. Understand that Standard Chartered has been diverting money to the government of Zimbabwe due to legal obligation to do so, but must realise the repercussions of giving money to those responsible for this crisis and so the Foreign Office is clearly fully aware of the extend of which British-based banks are sustaining the Mugabe regime. Until now this has remained secret. What we've exposed is that these sanctions are just not worth the paper they are written on.

Ferrett: Would you like to see sanctions looked at again?

Lamb: It is no more than rhetoric and tokenism if we are talking touch but actually doing nothing effective. I think it just brings the whole process of sanctions into disrepute and we stand charged of complicity and of failing to take an effective action to bring to an end a despicable regime which is causing such horror for its population.

Ferrett puts those arguments to the Foreign Office minister with responsibility for Africa, Mark Malloch-Brown. A Freedom of Information request, which has just been answered reveals emails between government officials apparently scrambling to find reasons not to stop banks operating in Zimbabwe. It seems that we have sanctions so long as they don't inconvenience anybody.

Malloch-Brown: No, I think that is just a misunderstanding of it. We have sanctions intended to inconvenience and make it as uncomfortable as possible for the elite around Mugabe. We're absolutely determined that we should not make life harder for ordinary Zimbabweans and we think the closing of these banks would do just that and frankly, they would also make our own humanitarian aid operations impossible because we use these banks to put money in the country, which we can spend locally. You know we cannot turn a blind eye to big British business interests. It is about being very steady and clear-eyed in what we are trying to do here, which is squeeze the elite and protect ordinary Zimbabweans.

Ferrett: Those banks, one of which, Standard Chartered Subsidiary, is wholly owned by a British company. They're handing over loans, millions of dollars sometimes (loans, of course) as part of this land redistribution programme. That makes a mockery of sanctions if banks can do that, doesn't it?

Malloch-Brown: Well, look, I'm not going to get into, you know, who's lending what to whom because frankly, you know it's commercially confidential information which I'm not privy to and you know I'm not necessarily sure the sources who have given you that are privy to it either. You know, what I know is the leadership of Standard Chartered, as well as British headquartered mining companies involved in the country as well, you know, have continuously assured us that they minimise their relations with the regime.

Ferrett: But it's not only the activities of multinationals which have attracted criticism. Concerns have also been raised over small companies and some individuals who've been operating in Britain.

Sunningdale, Berkshire

Ferrett: Last month, the European Union added another batch of names of individuals and companies to the list of those subject to sanctions for their role in propping up Robert Mugabe's government. No fewer than ten companies were listed at a single address here on London Road in Sunningdale, a wealthy commuter town in Berkshire. The man behind those businesses, whose assets in Europe have now been frozen, is John Bredenkamp, a former captain of Rhodesian rugby and sanctions buster for Ian Smith's Rhodesian government during the days of white minority rule in the 1960s and 1970s.

It's John Bredenkamp's more recent activities which have caught the attention of campaigners.

Patricia Feeney of the pressure group, Rights and Accountability in Development, has followed his dealings for the best part of a decade, largely as a result of Zimbabwe involvement in the war in the Democratic Republic of the Congo. She believes he should have been subject to sanctions far earlier.

Feeney: It was about 2002 when there was a series of UN expert panel reports into the causes of the conflict in the Democratic Republic of the Congo. It looked at the illegal exploitation of the national resources of the Congo and listed among those who were profiting from this John Bredenkamp, among others. They suggested and recommended to the UN Security Council in 2002 that Bredenkamp, among others, should have a travel ban imposed on them and that there should be financial restrictions placed on their companies.

Ferrett: Mr Bredenkamp denied any wrongdoing and was allowed to carry on working out of Britain. Patricia Feeney says there was no desire on the part of the British ministers to take action, in spite of the UN findings.

Feeney: We raised this with Patricia Hewitt, who was then the head of DTI. We met with Chris Mullin at the Foreign and Commonwealth Office when he was the foreign Africa minister and we then met with Hilary Ben throughout 2002/2003, trying to push the British government to take whatever action it could. We found it a very uphill task. There seemed to be very little appetite. We wrote to Jack Straw in March 2006 and we were really just fobbed off.

Ferrett: In November the United States announced that it would freeze John Bredenkamp's assets, describing him as a 'Mugabe regime crony'. Mr Bredenkamp rejects the allegations and says he has known Robert Mugabe for more than 20 years. But the US government, or rather Treasury, said he'd a sophisticated web of companies to financially prop up the regime. It was only in January, after Washington had taken action, some seven years after the international concerns were first raised, that Britain and the EU followed suit.

For Patrick Smith, it suggests a broader reluctance on this side of the Atlantic to tackle businessmen.

Smith: They want sanctions to make a rhetorical point against political appointees but they don't want to go for the financial infrastructure and I would say it is not just Bredenkamp. I mean, it's a raft of people that if they had gone for, if the Europeans had gone for those characters, those business people, much earlier, I think they would have had a lot more leverage in Zimbabwe and perhaps persuaded South Africa to do the same. Instead of which you've seen a messy process of the Europeans gradually coming round to imposing sanctions almost when it is too late.

Ferrett: But of all the criticisms of sanctions, perhaps the most powerful focuses not on the many loopholes and limitations, instead it is a political point which Robert Mugabe spares no opportunity to emphasise.

Mugabe: The problem we have had is a problem that has been created by a former colonial power wanting to continue to interfere in our domestic affairs. Why, why, why the hand of the British? Let us ask that.

Ferrett: For Mr Mugabe and his supporters, Zimbabwe's problems can be explained by sanctions. They deny they're targeted only at the elite. The economics analyst in Harare, John Robertson, says sanctions have had no effect economically and have been counterproductive politically and should therefore be dropped altogether.

Robertson: The sanctions have not been real in the sense that they made any difference whatsoever to the economic activity. ZANU-PF has made political capital out of sanctions to a far, far greater extent than I think was ever anticipated by the people who imposed them. In other words, ZANU-PF has been able to claim that the entire reason for the decline of Zimbabwe's economy has been the sanctions. So they have made political capital out of this in a way that has been thoroughly dishonest and unfortunately too readily believed by a large proportion of Zimbabwe's population. This is because the media is under the control of the government and radio, television and the daily newspapers can pour onto the total population every single day the claims that the country is suffering from sanctions and the only reason this is a food shortage or a jobs shortage, and any other problem, is because of sanctions. I do believe if the world would announce the removal of sanctions so that the people here would see how little difference it makes.

Ferrett: That is not an idea that wins favour in the Foreign Office. The minister, Lord Malloch-Brown, hopes real change has now begun in Zimbabwe and this is not the time to change course. Malloch-Brown made it quite clear what he thought.

Malloch-Brown: The sanctions have contributed, but you know, these were sanctions where we kept the gloves on because we didn't want to harm ordinary Zimbabweans so they've only been targeted at individuals and lately at companies which are directly kind of involved in the regime.

Ferrett: What you have ended up with is a sanctions policy which has no discernible effect other than to entrench President Mugabe's position because he's repeatedly misrepresented the sanctions as general economic sanctions and in that way rallied support among same other African leaders.

Malloch-Brown: He's concealed it, you're right, because when he talks about sanctions what he's really complaining about is that the World Bank and the IMF won't give him big cheques to keep going and you know, even if we didn't have any sanctions, he would find some way to blame the Brits!

Ferrett: But the policy has given President Mugabe a PR opportunity and in fact, far from stopping him from establishing his grip on power even further, it's actually helped him – it has been counterproductive.

Malloch-Brown: Yes, it's been a PR prop to him, but everything the UK does is a prop to him.

Ferrett: But does that mean that you will put aside sanctions?

Malloch-Brown: I don't think so, because you know, actually they have been pinching a nerve. They are never the answer, but they do help. I think they have contributed very significantly to him feeling he had to do a deal with Morgan Tsvangirai.

Ferrett: Perhaps now is the time to abandon sanctions altogether?

Malloch-Brown: Because, you know, he has got to show evidence that he and the people around him are genuinely committed to this deal. If political prisoners are released and if the violence stops and if there's a clear roadmap to elections, we'll start to lower the stick. But you know, given that we think it was pressure on Mugabe to get him where he is now, the last thing we are going to do is, you know, put the stick down.

Four

A bit of good news today.

20th March 2009 – 'Farmers promised protection in new economic plan' – The Times

Zimbabwe's five-week-old Unity Plan Government promised yesterday to protect the few white farmers that remain from intimidation that has forced thousands to fleet their land in the last few years.

Announcing a plan to rescue the country's shattered economy that calls for $5 billion (£3.4 million) of aid, Tendai Biti, the new Minister of Finance, promised that no more white-owned farms would be seized.

The government's so-called 'land reform programme' authorised by President Mugabe, has forced 4,000 white farmers from their land prompting famine in what used to be considered a bread basket for Africa. President Mugabe, seated next to Mr Biti on the podium as the economic plan was announced, restricted himself mostly to appeals for Western governments to lift what he called 'the inhuman, cruel and unwarranted sanctions' that he claims are the cause of the country's economic failure.

Under his rule, the country has suffered economic disaster; hyper-inflation has rendered the currency all but worthless. There are severe shortages of the most basic goods and a failure of healthcare and sanitation has sparked a cholera outbreak.

The nine-month programme would depend on assistance from the Monetary Fund and World Bank and Western governments. Mr Biti also said that the distribution of funds would be transparent, making the finance ministry under him 'the primary channel' of this programme. Critics of Mr Mugabe said that under stewardship, funds flowing into the country were often diverted from their destination.

Mr Biti, whom Mr Mugabe had arrested under fake treason charges ten months ago, said the rescue package should allow the people of Zimbabwe to have decent jobs and incomes and ensure that hospitals and schools are once again functioning.

The prospect of securing foreign loans seemed remote in September when Mr Mugabe and the opposition leader, Mr Morgan Tsvangirai, signed a power-sharing agreement. British and American officials promised that 'not a cent would be forthcoming in aid if Mr Mugabe was still in charge'.

However, Mr Tsvangirai's increasing influence in the government has encouraged donors who now say they want to see key reforms before parting with funds. Mr Tsvangirai, who is now prime minister, was not at the launch but with his children in South Africa mourning his wife, Susan, who died in a car crash two weeks ago.

A team from the IMF, which is visiting Zimbabwe, said the country was still some way from meeting the conditions from receiving fresh funds. It wants to see the country in a position to repay arrears on existing loans.

'Zimbabwe needs to pay the outstanding amounts. We can't just step in and share out the budget,' a senior visiting IMF official told a group of civil organisations this week. 'We want to assess the situation over the next few months to see sound policy changes. In the meantime,' she said, 'the IMF are recommending humanitarian aid rather than funds to finance the running of the government.'

On 18ᵗʰ March, The Zimbabwean newspaper brings us shocking news that Susan, Morgan Tsvangirai's wonderful wife and so-called 'mother of the nation', was killed in a car accident. The driver of the car, or rather truck, that killed Susan appeared in a chivhu court this Monday, 16ᵗʰ March 2009, and charged with culpable homicide. He was released on bail for US$100 and will appear in court on Monday 23ʳᵈ March and was asked to surrender his passport, not to interfere with state witnesses and stay at his given address.

However, it is said 'The Dictator' is mesmerised as Morgan Tsvangirai takes the lead after years of decline at the hands of ZANU-PF. It takes only three weeks in the hands of the unity government for Zimbabwe to begin its turnaround.

Prime Minister Morgan Tsvangirai is absolutely forging ahead in looking for solutions to the country's problems, leaving all adversaries – former ones, of course – behind in standing.

Only three weeks of being in office as the head of government and he had already made the nation feel his presence through price reductions for basic commodities such as food, transport, accommodation and healthcare. Civil servants are now getting their salaries in US dollars, while private companies are also charging prices in stable international currency in a move aimed at bringing down hyper-inflation.

Tsvangirai is travelling throughout the African continent and the world sourcing funds for food, education and healthcare and agriculture.

People are already witnessing some significant changes. They are beginning to see who the real leader is between Robert Mugabe and Prime Minister Morgan Tsvangirai.

Ceriphas Michimbirike of Kuwadzana in Harare said that nearly all supermarkets, or rather major supermarkets, in the country were selling all kinds of foodstuffs and basic commodities had dropped in price sharply and it was easier to travel to different places with a few of the problems the long-suffering people were used to.

Most of us thought this change would take so long to take place and bear fruit, but Morgan Tsvangirai's work rate has taken the nation by surprise.

Teachers who left the country for neighbouring states such as South Africa, Botswana, Zambia and elsewhere overseas, are coming back home under Morgan Tsvangirai and now the US dollar has been introduced.

The professionals who left their beloved country (now see) that home under this new 'Prime Minister Morgan' never looked so homely.

'Tsvangirai is creating a conducive and enabling environment for everyone to come back to Zimbabwe,' said Michimbirike.

Thabani Sibanda of Waterfalls, Harare, said the only cause for concern was the ZANU-PF regime, which instead of joining hands to improve people's lives, was now into witch hunting and arresting all opposition activists; a move he claimed was scaring away those outside the country.

'The hindering obstacle is the partisan state security, including the police, who have scores to settle with opposition activists,' said Sibanda.

'A drive across the countryside revealed that the United Nations food agencies were now reaching starving villages. Food is now reaching everybody though it is not enough, but we can see the positive changes. Food is reaching everybody and agencies that were being denied access to provide relief aid to the majority are being allowed to travel freely,' said Chingeto Muzavazi of Murewa.

'We believe Tsvangirai should visit us throughout the country to make an assessment of the people's suffering to speed up food distribution, healthcare and collapsed education as a result of teachers who left the country for greener pastures.

'I am quite convinced that under Morgan Tsvangirai, the green pastures would not be in Botswana or South African, England or America, but once again back home,' CAJ News wrote.

A tribute to Susan Tsvangirai by Debbie Jeans, of The Zimbabwean newspaper on 12th – 18th March 2009, read:

'In one brief moment in time – Susan Tsvangirai out of this world and into the next, leaving behind her a nation in mourning and a formidable legacy.

'For millions of us wherever we are in the world and into the next, she was, and always will be, the mother who gave birth not only to six children but also to a new Zimbabwe.

'She stood by her man and family through what we can only say was at the most terrifying, treacherous, dangerous and life-threatening years; committed in mind, body and spirit to the cause, getting out there and doing whatever it took to fight the good fight to bring hope, love, guidance and leadership to her countrymen and women. That Saturday morning in Zimbabwe was sombre. An underlying feeling of sadness mixed with anger at the injustice of it all.'

Debbie Jeans spoke to some people who were deeply upset and clearly the impact of this tragedy will be felt far and wide for a long time.

45

'As we go about our own days, I am certain that the Tsvangirai family will be in our thoughts and as such, we would do well to honour Susan's sacrifice that she died a true heroine of Henry Olongo's "Our Zimbabwe" of our hearts and souls. She joins the sacrosanct list of those who will never be forgotten in the struggle for the Promised Land. With Susan's legacy behind us, embedded within her birthright, her qualities of love, patriotism, courage, humility and grace shall surely shore up our own strength and commitment to continue this long walk to freedom.

'Let her ultimate sacrifice remind us to look deeply and honestly into our own souls to ask the same question Susan's life answered with our resounding "YES".

'"In the evening of my life I will look to the sunset and the question I will ask only God can answer. Was I brave and strong and true? Did I fill my world with love my whole life through?"

'We will not forget. We will not falter when called to make the sacrifices needed to make the difference so that at the end of our own lives we may look back and know that we did all we could and ultimately helped to spread the life which enveloped the darkness hanging over our beloved land.

'God bless you, our prime minister and the Tsvangirai children. Your loss is our loss. Your pain is felt throughout the world. You are not alone. You have never and will never walk alone. We pay tribute to our great lady in our prayers, thoughts and actions. We are so, so sorry.'

The healing of evil can be accomplished only by the love of individuals, a willing sacrifice is required. I do not know how this occurs but I know that it does. I know that good people can deliberately allow themselves to be pierced by the evil of others, to be broken by others, yet somehow not broken, to even be killed in some sense and yet still survive and not succumb. Whenever this happens there is a slight shift in the balance of power in the world.

Dr Scott Peck

Five

'Mutambana blasts government for crash tragedy' and 'Zimbabwe to arrest land thieves'

Good for Morgan! At long last the poor worried farmers will feel safe. Mr Tsvangirai said the recent land invasions 'are actually acts of theft'.

President Mugabe has said the government will continue to seize white-owned farms as part of his Land Reform Policy, yet President Robert Mugabe and leader Morgan Tsvangirai joined each other in a power-sharing government last month. The seizure of white-owned land is one of Mr Mugabe's defining policies but critics say it has destroyed the economy.

The occupation of farms resumed shortly after the power-sharing government was sworn in, with some accusing hard-lined allies of Mr Mugabe of trying to scupper the deal.

Prime Minister Morgan Tsvangirai, announced 'I have asked the Minister of Home Affairs to ensure that all crimes are acted upon and the perpetrators arrested and charged. This government is aware that most of the ongoing disruptions of agricultural production, which is being done in the name of the land reform process, are actually acts of theft.' Mr Tsvangirai was addressing civic society diplomats and business leaders in one of his first public appearances since the death of his wife in a car crash earlier this month (March 2009).

'Those continuing to undertake these activities will be arrested and will face justice in the courts. I have asked the Minister of Home Affairs to ensure that *all* crimes are acted upon and the perpetrators are arrested and charged.

However, there are two home affairs ministers in the unity administration, as neither side would concede control of the ministry, which is responsible for the police.

Last month, Mr Mugabe said, 'There is no going back' on land reform, despite a ruling from the South African Development Community (SADC) Tribunal last year that the seizures were illegal.

The government's seizure of white-owned farms and land since 2000 was often accompanied by violent invasions by supporters of Robert Mugabe.

Mr Morgan Tsvangirai has long criticised the way land reform was carried out. But a commitment to continue the policy was a key part of the power-sharing agreement.

I picked up the following news from Peter Biles, BBC News, South Africa:

'Politically though, it leaves the MDC in considerable disarray just when the party is trying to consolidate its position in Zimbabwe's new inclusive government, which was formed on 13th February 2009. Regarding the death of Susan Tsvangirai, it is, without doubt, a personal blow to Zimbabwe's new prime minister, Morgan Tsvangirai, as well as the couple's family and their close friends in the Movement for Democratic Chance (MDC).

'Only a few days ago the MDC proudly announced it had launched a new website for Mr Tsvangirai. The front page this week carries the tragic news of Susan Tsvangirai's death in a car crash. It could not have happened at a worse time.'

'Given the long history of car crashes involving prominent Zimbabwean political figures, there will inevitably be speculation in some quarters that this was more than a road accident.

'He will immerse himself in his work and that is the one thing that will get him through this,' wrote Sarah Huddleston, Tsvangirai friend and biographer.

Those with long memories in Zimbabwe, as I have since the 1950s when roads were trips of tarmac on each side. When we had to give by law our servants a weekly ration of meat, jam, sugar, meali meal etc and see they had a little hut with a garden at the back of the house. All homes had large gardens then. My first husband had two acres of land and built two houses in Highlands.

I put every blade of grass, every fruit tree and hedge in from scratch.

One of the main car crash deaths was the ZANU guerrilla leader who was killed in a crash in neighbouring Mozambique in December 1979, just after the signing of the Lancaster House agreements that led to Zimbabwe's independence and when Robert Mugabe was given 'the jewel in the crown' – wonderful Rhodesia, now Zimbabwe.

At that very time, Tongogara had been seen as a political rival to Robert Mugabe. Mugabe mistrusted Tsvangirai deeply.

Morgan Tsvangirai said the crash which killed his wife was an accident and he does not suspect foul play, BUT the MDC has become understandably cautious in its public statements following the death of Susan.

'We have to wait for the police report. This is something we take as an accident until proven otherwise,' said Nelson Chamisa, the party's spokesman to SABC Radio in Johannesburg.

'As a party, we are going to proceed with thorough investigations that are independent. This is necessitated by rift speculation and suspicion in the country,' he added.

President Mugabe was among the first to console Mr Tsvangirai on hearing the news of his wife's death. Mr Mugabe went to the Avenue Clinic in Harare, accompanied by his wife, Grace, and a delegation of senior ZANU-PF ministers.

BBC News reported: 'Even if he was Superman, this tragedy would negatively affect Morgan Tsvangirai to do his job.' (Welshman Ncube, MDC faction.)

However, the mistrust and animosity between ZANU-PF and the MDC still runs deep as the country tries so hard to move forward, under a power-sharing government.

When Central Bank governor, Gideon Gono turned up at the Tsvangirai family home in Harare the weekend after the tragic accident to pay his respects, he had to face a crowd of MDC supporters gathered outside. They threw trillions of worthless Zimbabwean dollars. Mr Gono has managed to retain his position at the bank (I wonder why) in spite of his spectacular mismanagement of the country's economy.

Mr Tsvangirai is no stranger to adversity. At the hand of President Robert Mugabe's administration, he faced vilification, arrest, beatings and was accused of treason.

But the personal tragedy of losing his wife will perhaps raise questions about his future as Zimbabwe's newly appointed prime minister.

Personally, I would feel more than ever determined, for the sake of his beloved Susan, who stood by the MDC cause and Morgan's dreadful life putting up with so much through standing by the MDC!

Family friend and biographer, Sarah Huddleston, believes Mr Tsvangirai *will* be able to carry on the fight for Zimbabwe. The children (nine) will be the source of a great comfort to him. He's also dedicated.

Welshman Ncube, the secretary general of the smaller MDC faction, MDC M, says 'The prime minister, Mr Morgan Tsvangirai, remains the key person in the inclusive attention despite the troubled times. He had a daunting task of trying to run a government in a country where just about everything has collapsed. You need him at his best, with his undivided attention.

'Even if he was Superman, this tragedy would negatively affect his ability. It is a severe blow to the capacity of the government to address the myriad challenges we face as a country.'

From BBC News – Brian Hungwie visits the scene of the car crash near Harare in which Zimbabwe's prime minister, Morgan Tsvangirai, was injured and his wife, Susan, killed.

'A Land Cruiser lies on its back 24 hours after the car crash, drawing the attention of motorists. Inside the mangled remains of the vehicle, a continuous warning sound has been ringing all day. The doors are open yet the keys are still in the ignition. A shattered windscreen and broken car windows tell an ugly story as the Toyota Land Cruiser rests on its roof beside the road. Two policemen are on constant guard but strangers are not allowed up close. Vehicles are slowing down around the fatal scene. Curious onlookers disembark, say little and some weep as they catch a glimpse of the lonely, miserable vehicle.

'It is difficult to imagine how Mr Tsvangirai escaped relatively unscratched as the heavy vehicle rolled three times after the collision with an oncoming lorry. One immediately feels pity for his wife Susan, his pillar of strength and mother of the couple's six children.

'Questions are asked. The Masvingo to Harare road is a two-lane route. The place where the crash occurred is on a kilometre-long (0.6 miles) stretch of clean road, sandwiched between two commercial farmlands.

'"People don't want to believe it was an ordinary accident. They wanted to kill Morgan Tsvangirai," one taxi driver says.

'The road, however, evidently requires rehabilitation but calls for such repairs have fallen on deaf ears over the past years, despite horrifying fatalities involving haulage lorries, buses and ordinary cars.

'As the nation ponders on the latest tragedy, many questions are being asked and concerns are being raised over the security of many government officials' vehicles. How a convoy of three vehicles, with one in the middle carrying the second most important person in the land, got involved in a car crash is what has perplexed many people. The oncoming lorry, which apparently belonged to a partner of the US government aid agency, USAD, is supposed to have crossed into the prime minister's path, sideswiping the right bumper of his Land Cruiser, which then rolled off the highway.

'Rumours in Harare include: "If you look at the circumstances surrounding the accident, they show that there was not as much security as one would have wanted. Not that one can prevent an accident, but I am sure it must give a lot of lessons about the security framework," says Dr Lovemore Maduku, chairman of a constitutional reform pressure group.

'"It is very depressing, I think, happening too within the first three weeks of the new inclusive government. It is indeed unfortunate that the public will find it unbelievable that it could happen and threaten the whole framework of the government," Mr Maduku continued.

'Already Harare is awash with rumour and speculation. People don't want to believe it was an ordinary accident, even if you tell them Mr Mugabe visited Tsvangirai in hospital hours.

'After the crash a taxi driver said, "Why did the oncoming vehicle target his vehicle when there are hundreds of other vehicles that use the same road every hour, it's a busy road?" he asked. "They wanted to kill him."

'At the scene of the crash, deputy mines minister and MDC legislator, Murisi Zwizwai, is refusing the buy into the story that the encroaching vehicle hit a pothole or bump before crossing the road or lane.

'"Where are the potholes or even bumps here? Do you see one? It is just a clear road," he said, almost throwing up his hands in exasperation.

'"There was a lot of talk around a pothole that is alleged to have caused the accident. It was only proper that we visit the scene. From my assessment, there is no pothole to talk about as far as this accident is concerned," Mr Zwizwai said.

'Huge embarrassment. At the clinic where Mr Tsvangirai was treated, there was very heavy security, state agents and police. It appeared like a state expression of loyalty to give any credence to conspiracy theories.

'"From now on security around the prime minister will be tighter. I think they will test whatever he drinks and eats first, to make sure he doesn't die. It is in their interest to keep him alive," said a senior MDC official barred from entering the clinic after the accident.

'The treatment centre was besieged by hosts of politicians from across the political divide. Inside were Central Bank governor, Mr Gideon Gono, defence minister, Emmenson Mnangagwa, head of Central Intelligence, Happyton Bonyongwe and other party deputy ministers.

'"Rarely do prime ministers get involved in car accidents. Plane crashes are more understandable," said a retired army official. "It shows lack of planning, co-ordination of close security transporting those VIPs in the country." He says that when such a situation arises, countless reports are filed, many questions asked and people tend to lose their jobs. "This incident," he added, "is no exception."

"What makes this incident more serious is that it is such a huge political embarrassment to the state, particularly President Mugabe that he is failing to provide adequate protection to his prime minister in government. Logic would have demanded that a police escort be provided to warn other traffic so that this tragedy could have been avoided," finance minister, Tendai Biti, said before breaking down at a party news conference.

'"The authorities must understand that omission," Mr Biti added.

'His tears hint at the growing level of anger and emotion within his party. At his home in Harare, there was weeping and wailing all night as relatives and friends tried to come to grips with the tragedy.'

Six

'Can Tsvangirai fix Zimbabwe's basket case?' – John Madslien, BBC News

Zimbabwe's prime minister, Morgan Tsvangirai, has declared that his first priority will be to fix the country's 'basket case' economy.

It is a challenge of biblical proportions – even when leaving aside the problems of sharing power with President Robert Mugabe.

The expenditure needs of government stretch from the North Pole to the South Pole, while its revenue options are as terse as the shortage verse in the Bible, observes the All Africa News Service.

With most of Zimbabwe's schools and hospitals closed, its roads and sewers in tatters and with at least eight in ten people out of work, there is no shortage of areas where expenditure can be clocked up, but raising the cash is a trickier task.

Take Mr Tsvangirai's first promise to his people: 'Every health worker, teacher, soldier and policemen will receive their pay in foreign currency until we are able to stabilise the economy.'

Doing so would make sense, given that the UK dollar and the South African rand have become de facto currencies in Zimbabwe, with most shops refusing to accept the Zimbabwean currency as payment. This has also rendered the salaries currently paid to civil servants pretty much worthless.

In turn, many have been forced to seek an alternative income, whether from other jobs or turning to corruption, while others have simply left the country.

No assistance

The question is whether civil servants should be paid in a currency that will pay for their food or rather where the government will get the money from.

The impact on Zimbabwe has been particularly severe (Economist Intelligence Unit)

Unlike many African nations which receive aid from wealthy nations, Zimbabwe saw the International Monetary Fund turn off the taps a decade ago. Donors from the US and European Union (EU) have said they will neither ease economic sanctions or provide development assistance until it is clear that Mr Tsvangirai has truly managed to wrestle power from Mr Robert Mugabe.

First, the EU would want to see 'tangible signs of respect from human rights, the rule of law and macro-economic stabilisation', it said in a statement.

'We'll just wait and see,' agreed US State Department spokesman, Robert Wood, calling for evidence of 'good governance' and particularly real, true power-sharing on the part of Robert Mugabe.

Direct investment into Zimbabwe from abroad has also all but collapsed, which leaves the government with just one way to get hold of foreign currency, namely exporting.

Severe impact

In the recent past, more than half its export earnings have plummeted from gold, platinum, ferrochrome and nickel mines.

'It would not work unless Zimbabwe accepted that South Africa would control its economy, which would make it virtually a province of South Africa,' said Azar Jammine, senior economist at Econometrix.

In recent months, these earnings have plummeted as global prices for precious metals have slumped with some mining companies mothballing operations until demand picks up again.

'The impact on Zimbabwe has been particularly severe,' according to the Economist Intelligence Unit.

'All four sectors are in serious trouble, partly because of the global downturn, but also the collapse of basic infrastructure, especially electricity and water supplies.'

Zimbabwe's other foreign currency earner, agriculture, is a shadow of its former self after the wholesale looting of farms by Mr Mugabe's cronies during the early 2000s when productive and profitable farms were either wrecked or left to rot.

These days they do not even produce enough to feed the country's starving population.

'Seven million people are in need of food said,' says Mr Tsvangirai, so it's clear that significant export earnings from agriculture are out of the question!

The country no longer has a tourism industry to speak of and it could take years before visitor numbers pick up.

I personally remember during the Rhodesian war days when terrorists were everywhere. We went to places in convoys with police. It did not stop our living! I remember the wonderful times when Ian Smith was in power – we had everything and coped with the war as well. The wonderful holidays at Kariba and Victoria Falls on the 'booze trips' up the Zambezi across the river. We carried guns to go shopping, seeing all the security guards in every shop entrance, searching our shopping bags and handbags. There were bars on all the windows.

We had bombs going off in restaurants; the Bamboo Inn and the Pink Panther Steakhouse. People were shot at the tills for money. We kept on living. One of my hairdressing salons in Montigua Avenue, Chez Marie, had a bomb in the letterbox! I finished a perm in a police car. We all stuck together with no violence.

It's all in my autobiography, which I had published in 2007 called *Never a Dull Moment*.

Indeed, to make Zimbabwe attractive to tourists, the country's reputation for deadly HIV/AIDS and cholera epidemics will need to be tackled and the rule of law must be re-established.

Unhelpful and unacceptable

With little scope for raising sufficient foreign current for export, another solution has been put forward. Zimbabwe should adopt the South African rand as its currency. South African president, Kgalema Motlanthe, has suggested this, but there are plenty of sceptics.

'It would mean that Zimbabwe would have to follow very different policies to what they have followed up to now,' says Rudolph Gouws, chief economist at Rand Merchant Bank.

'This would ensure that Zimbabwe give up its monetary fund and exchange rate policy sovereignty,' observes Alide Basnois, economist with the Governance of Africa's Resources Programme of South Africa Institute of International Affairs.

'Such a move would also leave Zimbabwe with a very tight fiscal space in which to manoeuvre and pull itself out of its misery,' he reasons in an article in The Cape Times. 'And as the rand would be overvalued relative to Zimbabwe's situation, it would destroy the competitiveness of its exports and hence remove any chance of export in recovery,' he continued.

As such, adopting the rand would only 'paint Zimbabwe into a corner in its bid to survive its economy' which is not the main reason why is an unlikely scenario.

'It would not work unless Zimbabwe accepted that South Africa would control its economy, which would make it virtually a province of South Africa,' adds Azan Jammine, senior economist at Econometrix.

Mr Mugabe in particular would resist any dilution of Zimbabwe's eco sovereignty, while Mr Tsvangirai would see it as an attempt by South Africa to be party to the agreement via the back door, some reasoned, insisting that adopting the rand would be unhelpful and politically unacceptable to Zimbabwe.

2nd December 2009 – 'Political battle' – BBC News

An economic solution to Zimbabwe's woes is clearly not forthcoming at this stage, so expect Mr Tsvangirai to focus on his political battles.

He will have to fight on two fronts: at home he will need the power-sharing agreement with Mr Mugabe to work. While on the international arena, he will need to convince both government leaders and investors that he has truly established himself as the nation's genuine leader. Only then will sanctions be lifted and both aid money and inward investment begin to flow.

Without such input from the international community, there is little hope that Zimbabwe's economy can begin to recover and the country's humanitarian crisis be brought to an end.

'You will not eat' – The Zimbabwean

A headman tells MDC villages, 'You will not eat.' Poor Morgan, he is trying so hard to try to save Zimbabwe but world leaders are demanding real change before and aid can flow.

With a general election looming, the South African government attention has been diverted from the Zimbabwean crisis, they are also on record as having said that (RB2) Gideon Gono must be removed from his post before aid can be released. Western governments have taken a similar line on Gono, who they accuse of fuelling hyper-inflation and corruption. They are also demanding a definite move to real democracy.

The IMF, who has been on a fact-finding mission in Zimbabwe, said there would be no money forthcoming from Brittoon Woods Institutions until the country paid back its outstanding loan and took steps towards implementing sound economic policies.

It is reported that President Robert Mugabe has been sending messages to his regional counterparts as the country falls into a major financial crisis, which could affect its security situation.

Zimbabwe's $5 billion (about R50 billion) short-term economic recovery plan unveiled last week appears certain to fail unless the rule of law is urgently restarted as demanded by international donors.

Finance minister, Tendai Biti's plan includes an end to price control and the easing of foreign exchange controls as well as focus on spending on agriculture and infrastructure. But he has hinted at drawing Zimbabwe into the rand monetary fund or area and insisted that the rule of law would have to be restored before recovery was possible.

A minister in the new government who did not wish to be named said, 'Nothing has been agreed with the South Africans yet. It is a bit disappointing because after the role they played in

58

pushing for this unity government, we would have expected them to come in with quick aid to help stabilise their own creation.' (Staff reporter, Zimbabwe Mail, 14th March – 1st April 2009.)

Going back to the headman saying, 'You will not eat', there certainly is reason for this to be the truth. The ZANU-PF village administration is using food aid donated by South Africa and farm implements from the reserve bank as a weapon, denying them to political opponents as nearly three quarters of the people here face starvation.

Village heads and the district ZANU-PF administration, who control the food distribution, are also staunchly refusing to embrace the new inclusive government.

An investigation by The Zimbabwean has revealed that the headman, Gora, whose real name is Benjamin Dzama, together with the ZANU-PF district leadership, are punishing opponents, mainly members of the MDC, by manipulating the supply and distribution of food aid from South Africa, farming implements from the RB2, as well as food aid from humanitarian agencies, the Catholic Relief Service and Help the Aged.

Gora is also manipulating the registration of people eligible for international relief in all areas that fall under the administration of Chief Mashayamombe. This practice is rife in Kwaramba, Zvavarfarja, Gora and Ghonhiwa villages.

The Zimbabwean can then reveal that corruption and profiteering is rampant and the majority of recipients for the aid are either relatives of the chief or headman or girlfriends of those in positions of authority. All MDC supporters have been told that 'hamulunu' which is slang meaning 'you will not eat'.

At the centre of this scandal is ZANU-PF district chairman, Vimbai Mapininga, who is also the nephew of the chief ZANU-PF women's league district commission, Anna Dzama and district men's political commissioner, Luke Chadehumba.

This team has told the villages to disregard the Global Political Agreement, saying that ZANU-PF had cheated Prime Minister Morgan Tsvangirai into being his public relations manager to get international funding for the country.

They told supporters at Marigumura Business Centre that the modus operandi would not change and it was business as usual, 'MDC supporters are the enemy.'

Our investigation has shown that these officials have diverted large quantities of grain at tremendous profit to the black market. They have abused the maize seed, groundnuts, beans, Compound D and ammonium nitrate fertiliser donated by the South African government under a R300 million Christmas present to Zimbabwe.

They have also denied MDC supporters in this area ploughs, scratch carts, barrows, knapsacks, fertiliser and seed that came from RB2. The first instance came in December and the second in February. In all instances, MDC supporters were told 'hamulunu' (you will not eat).

24th February 2009 – 'Zimbabwe elite seek to evade sanctions' – BBC

One of the richest and most powerful people in Zimbabwe has been trying to sell gold in Europe in a deal stretching from Nairobi to Zurich, the BBC has learnt, in defiance of international sanctions.

The vice president of Zimbabwe, Joyce Mufuru, with her husband Solomon, are among a small elite who have prospered in Zimbabwe as the rest of the country falls into ever deeper economic chaos.

As most of the country suffers, UN estimates suggest 75% need food while unemployment is at 90%, they and theirs have become wealthy.

Despite EU sanctions against Zimbabwe being in place since 2002 and extended this year, Mujuru has allegedly been trying to fund a multi-million gold deal in Europe, which the BBC has uncovered.

She was involved in a planned deal to sell almost four tonnes of Congolese gold to a company called Firstar.

Mrs Mujuru is one of more than 200 senior officials linked to President Robert Mugabe, who remains subject to a travel ban and an asset freeze in the European Union in spite of the creation of a power-sharing government with the opposition earlier this month. They are accused of undermining democracy, human rights and the rule of law.

The proposed gold deal focused on Mrs Mujuru's daughter, Nyasha del Campo, a commodities trader based in Spain.

Firstar firstly says that although the offer, made in November 2008, to sell 3.7 tonnes of gold came from Nyasha del Campo, it was the Zimbabwean vice president who was central to the deal.

Felix Eimes, who works for Firstar and is based in Frankfurt, told the BBC, 'She promised us that in order to complete this transaction, her mother would pay the total amount necessary to transport gold from Nairobi to Zurich.

'This is equivalent to 150,000 – 200,000 euros (£130,000 – £175,000). The person behind the deal and the person that organises the funding for the deal with her mother.

The BBC has seen copies of emails indicating that Mrs Mujuru was also paying the legal costs.

Firstar says it pulled out when it released who Mrs Mujuru was, it also placed the mother and daughter on the blacklist, deciding it did not want to do business with them.

The certificate of origin for the gold stocks confirms that it comes from the Democratic Republic of the Congo (DRC).

The Zimbabwean vice president has been unavailable for comment. Her daughter in Madrid says she is consulting her lawyers.

Father Christmas

While the sanctions were not breached in this instance, it does suggest that those at the top of the ZANU-PF are trying to use others, including relatives, to get around them.

Mrs Mujuru's husband, Solomon, was head of the army after independence in 1980 and is believed to retain some influence within the military.

The couple have extensive business interests in Zimbabwe and beyond.

'Within the DRC, there are huge mining exploits which are being made by Solomon Mujuru and Joyce, his wife,' said Jake Makumbe, Associate Professor of Politics at the University of Zimbabwe.

'For a select few, the economic decline in Zimbabwe has helped them to become very wealthy. If you were to visit some of Zimbabwe's upmarket residential areas, you would think you had landed in Beverley Hills. There are some magnificent properties,' says John Robertson, an economic analyst in Harare.

Privileged access to hard currency from Zimbabwe's central bank and unusually favourable rates is the key much of this conspicuous consumption.

'Gideon Gono, Reserve Bank governor, is Father Christmas,' says Mr Makumbe.

The revenue that comes into the Zimbabwe government is kept at the Central Bank and he dishes it out willy-nilly to individuals within the party, to Mugabe and his family, without any accountability whatsoever. Gono is referred to as 'Mr Inflation'!

He has presided over a policy of printing evermore worthless Zimbabwe dollars in order to keep pace with rising prices.

The new finance minister, Tendai Biti, of the long-time opposition Movement for Democratic Change (MDC), has described the Central Bank as 'totally diseased and at the core of economic decay'.

Sanctions first imposed by the EU, the United States and others in 2002 have been condemned by President Robert Mugabe and his supporters as being at the root of the country's problems.

There are now 203 individuals and 40 companies banned from travelling to the EU's 27 member states and doing business there.

'The problem we have had is a problem created by a former colonial power wanting to interfere in our domestic affairs,' said Mr Mugabe in September 2008 when signing the power-sharing accord with the MDC.

But critics of the sanctions say they have been too narrow and poorly enforced.

'These sanctions are just not worth the money and the paper they are written on,' according to Norman Lamb, an opposition Liberal Democrat member of parliament in Britain. 'We (in Britain) stand charged of complicity and of failure to take any effective action to bring to an end a despicable regime which has caused such horror for its population.'

The Foreign Office minister, Mark Malloch-Brown, rejects the criticism saying they contributed to forging a hard-fought power-sharing deal. He says of the sanctions, 'They have been pinching a nerve. I think they have contributed very significantly to him (President Mugabe) and felt he had to do a deal with MDC leader Morgan Tsvangirai.'

Despite calls from several African countries for the measures to be removed. He says they will remain in place until Mr Mugabe and those around him show they are truly committed to implementing the deal with the opposition.

April 2009

We are still learning of day-to-day unnecessary greed and illegal happenings in spite of the power sharing! Who in God's name can we trust or believe in?

'Now the Zimbabwe dollar is officially dead. The embattled country's national currency is no longer in use,' Economic planning minister, Elton Mangoma, said at the weekend. 'It will remain out of circulation for at least a year while the country moves to boost its industrial production and three-fold. There is nothing to support the value of the Zimbabwean dollar,' Mangoma said.

The government approved the use of foreign currency in January, to curb runaway inflation that had decimated the value of the Zimbabwean dollar to junk status.

Dollarisation has reversed hyper-inflation with the consumer price index of inflation falling at least 3% for two months in a row, according to the Central Statistical Office.

Mangoma made the declaration hardly a month after finance minister, Tendai Biti, projected the imminent death of the Zimbabwean dollar.

'The death of the Zimbabwean dollar is a reality we have to live with. Since October 2008 our national currency has become moribund,' Biti said while presenting a revised 2009 budget in parliament.

Professor Steve Hanke, a senior fellow of the Casto Institute in Washington, said in a commentary, 'Ashes are all that is left of the Zimbabwean dollar, a remnant of paper money. Until last weekend, Zimbabwean paper money dollar notes circulated alongside foreign money and currencies, but its real value was tiny, its use had become limited and its value against the US dollar had been eroded dramatically.'

Finally, the government has bowed to economic reality and scrapped the Zimbabwe dollar altogether. Economists say legalising the process of dollarisation, the replacement of the local money with the US dollar, was the masterstroke of the new administration.

The switchover to foreign currency helped the country considerably, allowing stores to reopen and restock their shelves. However, the country will need to get a lot of support to recover from the crisis brought on by the decades of misgovernance by a corrupt elite.

The government is seeking US$8 billion but a sceptical international community that has the capacity to bankrupt Zimbabwe's reconstruction is insisting it will not provide support until there is evidence that Mugabe and ZANU-PF are committed to genuinely sharing power with the new prime minister, Morgan Tsvangirai, leader of the MDC.

At Zimbabwe's peak hyper-inflation in December, it failed to beat Hungary's world record of hyper-inflation which is set at 195 million%, per day, in 1946. However, Zimbabwe easily beat Yugoslavia's 1994 hyper-inflation mark of 313 million%, per month, to secure second place in the record books!

The power-sharing government led by Prime Minister Morgan Tsvangirai has prioritised rebuilding the devastated Zimbabwean economy since taking office in February 2009.

Magoma said the government decided the Zimbabwe dollar should only be brought back when industrial output returns to about 60% capacity from the current average of 20%.

Seven

The NCA threatens protests if government adopts Kariba draft

The announcement of the Special Committee came three days after a pressure group agitating for constitutional reform. The National Constitutional Assembly (NCA) voiced its objections to parliamentarians at a heated meeting in Harare last Thursday, 9th April 2009, rejecting attempts by politicians to spearhead the constitution-making process.

The pressure group, which in 2000 successfully campaigned against a government-driven constitution, had demanded a new and democratic constitution written through a people-driven process, not a parliamentary-driven process.

The NCA threatened to confront Zimbabwe's new transitional government over its plans to foist on the people a constitution written by six ZANU and MDC politicians on a houseboat on Kariba last year (2008).

The NCA, a broad coalition of churches, students, political parties and civic groups, said it would roll out street protests if the so-called 'Kariba Draft' is used as a working draft during the constitution-making process.

But constitutional and parliamentary affairs minister, Eric Matinanga, said last Thursday that article 6.1 of the GPA (Global Political Agreement) states that committee may set up sub-committees that will include representatives of civil society as well as members of parliament. Each sub-committee will be chaired by a member of parliament, something which has also created friction with the NCA.

The select committee is mandated to hold public hearings and engage in consultation it considers necessary for the constitution-making process. But the NCA says it is opposed to the dominance of politicians in the process.

'It (the agreement) argues that the process should be driven by ordinary Zimbabweans led by civic society organisations. It claims that the people have the right to author their own constitution, yet prescribes for them a process where politicians, through parliament, have the final say as to the content of the constitution,' said the NCA chairman, Dr Lovemore Madhuku, who is also a 'constitution at law' expert.

Madhuku said in the agreement the parties boast about having already authored a constitution which they adopted in Kariba on 30th September 2007.

The draft constitution, written by Patrick Chinamasa and Nicholas Goche of ZANU-PF, Tendai Biti and Elton Mangoma of the mainstream MDC, Priscilla Misihairabwi-Mushonga and Professor Welshman Ncube is referred to in the draft as the 'Kariba Draft'.

'It is this Kariba Draft which ZANU-PF and the two formations of the MDC seek to sneak through as a new constitution for Zimbabwe,' Madhuku said.

'This is unacceptable. The NCA totally rejects it. The NCA therefore calls upon the people of Zimbabwe to unite and continue to push for genuine democratic, people-driven constitution led by an all-stakeholders constitution commission.

'As NCA, we do not believe or accept that ZANU-PF and MDC as political parties or as government have the right to unilaterally determine the process by which and through which a new constitution for Zimbabwe should be written,' Madhuku said.

'We believe that a constitution can only be as good as the process through which it is created and thus the process for creating the constitution is as important as the constitution to which it gives birth. Furthermore, the process itself must be legitimate, transparent and accepted by all the stakeholders! This is not the case with the current constitution-making process.'

Madhuku said ZANU-PF and the MDC were using? constitution-making process in which the ? political parties by and large were keen on imposing a constitution on the people of Zimbabwe.

'This is unacceptable as the constitution has to be written for the people, by the people,' Madhuku said. 'By spearheading the constitution-making process through parliament, ZANU-PF and MDC are attempting to usurp the power of the people. The ZANU-PF and MDC process essentially leaves out of the constitution-making process important stakeholders and currently do not have representatives in parliament.'

It is still April 2009 and a government of national unity has been formed in Zimbabwe. Commentators are looking back at the unity agreement of 1987, which was between Robert Mugabe, the Zimbabwe African Union Patriotic Front and Joshua Nkomo's Zimbabwe African People's Union. Actually, Unity Day has been celebrated every year to commemorate it. Survivors and revivers of ZAPU are now warning Mr Mugabe's new partners of the dangers of a unity agreement.

Their own experience was that ZAPU was swallowed up in the belly of the ZANU-PF python and many people are saying that the same thing will happen to Morgan Tsvangirai's Movement for Democratic Change.

But while it is certainly true that the MDC cannot yet protect its own supporters against the Central Intelligence Organisation, the police and the army, there are important differences between the two unity agreements.

Put simply, the 1987 event was a fusion of two parties. Some of the same dramatic transformations have happened on both occasions.

After 1987, for instance, Dumiso Diabengwa, ZAPU's intelligence chief, went from being imprisoned on a charge of treason to appointment as Minister of Home Affairs.

After the agreement in 2009, Tendai Biti has gone from facing a charge of treason in court to becoming Minister of Finance. So far, so similar.

But the recent agreement is nothing like as much of a triumph for Mugabe as 1987 when, after years of military and police pressure on his supporters in which 20,000 people died, Nkomo had no alternative but concede dominance to Mugabe.

A supposedly new party emerged from the unity agreement but it was still called ZANU-PF and it still used the same symbols of the clenched fists and the cockerel. Nomo was allowed ceremonial status and ex-ZAPO men were allowed to dominate local government in Western Zimbabwe, but the government controlled the central state.

An amnesty was declared for all those who had committed political violence.

The emergence of the single party was supposed to portend the creation of a one-party state and ZANU-PF ? up the percentages of its combined voter support.

'We worship the majority as Christians worship Christ,' said Eddison Zvogobo. 'This time round it is very different. This is a coalition government. There is an agreed statement of principals in which ZANU-PF tries to bind the MDC to its doctrines of sovereignty and the MDC seeks to restrain ZANU-PF by commitments to human rights.'

Nevertheless, the two parties remain quite distinct and both have made it quite clear that they look forward to competing against each other in an election as soon as possible.

In September 2008, when the agreement was first signed, Mugabe called his party to revive itself so that it could achieve a smashing electoral victory and he would never again have to suffer the 'humiliation' of working with Morgan Tsvangirai. During the long delay between the agreement and its implementation, Tsvangirai called for internationally supervised elections as an alternative to coalition.

Those who worship the majority won by the MDC in March 2008 or the claimed presidential majority won by Mugabe in the uncontested election in June. Armed police were present, and I was one out of God knows how many to be refused a vote. A crowd of us got together again in the afternoon insisting on a vote.

There is no amnesty this time round, which is why police are still able to arrest a nominated MDC deputy minister, Roy Bennett, and why many ZANU-PF fear prosecution for crimes against humanity.

When there is another election, the old XAPU will contest it. If the 1987 agreement was designed to usher in intense competitive multi-party 'democracy', the MDC will not be covered up or swallowed up and digested by the python. But it may emerge covered in slime. It is part of one of the most expensive cabinets in Zimbabwe's history. Now in charge of the economic ministries, it may be blamed for failure to bring about recovery.

So everything will be done with an eye to electoral advantage and the most important thing of all is to seek to create conditions in which a fair election can be held.

Terence Ranger, a veteran historian and commentator on Zimbabwe is an emeritus fellow of St Anthony's College, Oxford. Email: terence.ranger@saint.ox.ac.uk.

As I write all the daily, weekly, or even monthly ups and downs, so much is happening. This is still April 2009, 17th April and I read that 'Mugabe torturers confess their sins as church starts quest for reconciliation'. I was always taught one should never combine politics, but it seems to be the only hope we have to ask Almighty God to help us.

Here is an instance in The Times on Friday 17th April 2009:

Harry is a former torturer. He is also at the heart of an experiment to bring peace and reconciliation to Zimbabwe. Ten months ago in the bloody run-off to the Zimbabwean presidential elections, he was a commander of a torture group/base for Robert Mugabe's ZANU-PF party in the sprawling township of Chitungwiza, 20 miles (30km) south of Harare.

He was one of thousands of previously untouchable ZANU-PF who murdered as many as 180 people and tortured thousands to make sure that the election went Mr Mugabe's way. He controlled mobs of rampaging youths who sought our supporters of the Movement for Democratic Change (MDC) and subjected them to unspeakable torture.

Now, seven weeks after the establishment of the coalition government between ZANU-PF and the MDC, he cannot sleep at night for fear that his house will be burnt down in retribution. He says that he is so racked with guilt he contemplates suicide.

He is frightened to go to the grocery store and he will not accept a meal from anyone in case it is poisoned. After sending a night in the bush, Harry talks only when we drive to a secluded spot far from the crowded, garbage-strewn street that he lives on.

'Maybe one morning I will wake up murdered,' he says. 'I know other people won't forget what happened.'

They may never forget but there is some hope that they may 'forgive' thanks to a new reconciliation effort. Last October three researchers from the Catholic Commission for Justice and Peace (CCJP) in Zimbabwe began interviewing hundreds of torture victims.

'It is just too horrible,' said Joel Nkunsane, a co-ordinator. 'We were reopening the wound. We were listening and then we would leave them in pain without giving them any help.'

The church-funded organisation set up a reconciliation process in Chitungwiza, starting with a three-day group therapy workshop involving 17 victims. Getting ZANU-PF perpetrators to attend was far more difficult but they managed to attract seven, one of whom was Harry.

'He was sweating and shaking when he started,' said Mr Nkunsane. 'The guilt with him is still there. He said what he did was evil, that he caused death and suffering. He and the others said they wanted to look into the eyes of his neighbours and stay in harmony, they want to go back and talk it out.'

George Simango, 28, is the head of one of the wards and MDC in Chitungwiza. On the night before the election, he was dragged out of his home and beaten and had boiling water pour over him. Red hot embers were shovelled into the t-shirt that he was wearing and he was forced for lie on it. Mr Simango has kept the burnt t-shirt.

'For the time, I cannot forgive, but revenge is not the way. The only thing I want is a law that they should confess and giving details of what they did and who sent them.

Mr Nkunsane also believes that a public acknowledgement of the acts of violence that goes right to the top of the political parties responsible is critical for a process of reconciliation across the country, along the lines of a post-apartheid Truth and Reconciliation Commission in South Africa.

'I fear they may go for a process through a blanket of amnesty, call it a time of madness and say let bygones be bygones,' he said. 'If that happens there is never going to be a time that we can have another election without bloodshed.'

Now on 17th April 2009 it is still happening. Human rights activists are ordered back to jail. Who in God's name can we trust?

'The human rights in Zimbabwe had a 12-week-old unity government in Zimbabwe and suffered a grievous blow when 18 activists had their bail revoked and were returned to prison, on what are widely regarded as trumped-up charges of plotting to overthrow President Mugabe,' writes Martin Fletcher of The Times.

Morgan Tsvangirai's Movement for Democratic Change (MDC) said the ruling against Justina Mukoko and her colleagues seriously threatens not only the life and health of the inclusive government, but its longevity and durability.

Ms Mukoko, 41, has spent eight years documenting state violence as the head of the Zimbabwe Peach Project. She and the other activists were imprisoned last year and held without charge for many weeks. Their lawyers say they were tortured to try to make them confess to recruiting people for terrorist training.

Mr Tsvangirai, the prime minister, demanded their release before entering a unity government with Mr Mugabe's ZANU-PF party in mid February but they were not freed on bail until 2nd March.

Mrs Mukoko looked stunned at the decision to return her to prison. Supporters wept. Three activists were not in court, they were still being treated for injuries they received during their imprisonment.

Farmers, what a heartache we have. We were the bread basket for the nation, our tobacco, cotton, coffee, maize, citrus fruit. The poor farmers that worked so hard were murdered, evicted and tortured. The government has admitted they owe the farmers millions and are paying it back with fertiliser. Their accounts were siphoned without any authority whatsoever. The country's beleaguered Central Bank governor, Gideon Gono, revealed in a huge advert that he had spent US$18 million destined for accounts belonging to tobacco growers. Wheat farmers are owed about US$2 million. The Central Bank has already admitted spending more than US$30 million belonging to gold mines.

Gono, who is under pressure to step down, said through an advert that the Zimbabwe government is paying back the farms with fertiliser. 'Those wheat and tobacco farmers with bags of fertiliser and those who are owed money by the government through the Reserve Bank are being repaid in the most direct way of supporting their current season's production activities,' said Gono.

Last week in April 2009 he came under fire from finance minister, Tendai Biti, for borrowing US dollars from the international banks without authority. Biti wants Gono's conduct investigated but President Robert Mugabe has blocked the move. Since then, Gono has placed huge adverts in state-owned newspapers explaining what he has done with the money; from buying cars for ministers and MPs to funding dubious farming schemes. Gono has laid it bare for the public to see.

The unusual stance by insular government comes amid rising tension between Gono and his boss, Biti. Influential members of Mugabe's ZANU-PF party have hailed Gono as a 'sanctions buster'. Speculation is rife that Gono will be relieved of his position.

Then in September: 'Members were threatened with expulsion and the loss of their parliamentary seats,' wrote Violet Gonda.

A member of the Mutambana MDC formation, Senator David Coltart, has charged that the recent election of Lovemore Moyo as the new Speaker of parliament was illegal. However, the Tsvangirai spokesman, Nelson Chamisa, described Coltart's statement as 'hogwash' and 'total rubbish'.

The Tsvangirai MDC beat ZANU-PF for the first time in Zimbabwe history for the position of Speaker in parliament last month. Moyo, who is the party's National Chairperson, beat Paul Temba Nyathi from the Mutambana MDC by 110 seats to 98. Coltart claimed that the vote was illegal on the basis that some Tsvangirai MDC MPs showed their ballots to their vice president, Thokozani Khupe, and this, according to him, broke Section B of the standing leaders of the parliament of Zimbabwe that says the vote should be secret.

Coltart said, 'This is a Commonwealth-wide provision that safeguards the central principles of a democratic government and ensures that a neutral Speaker is elected.' The senator alleged, 'On the evening of Sunday 24th August 2009, a meeting of the MDC parliamentary caucus was held and its members were threatened with expulsion and the loss of their parliamentary seats if they voted for Paul (Temba Nyathi).'

Coltart believes if the Tsvangirai MDC hadn't broken the rules some of the MPs would have voted for Nyathi. This is an allegation that has been roundly denied by the Tsvangirai MDC. The party said they had agreed that Moyo was their candidate and it is not feasible to say that some of their MPs would have voted for another candidate.

Chamisa said Coltart was not in parliament when the election was held. He accused the senator of 'working with ZANU-PF to reverse their victory'.

Chamisa said, 'I can tell you that all the MPs, including Mr Mnangagwa, who is usually very difficult to accept and understand processes, was congratulated by our speaker.'

The spokesman said Mutambana formation has not been able to live with the reality that they have been defeated in a fair political process and are now abusing and misinterpreting the law. The Tsvangirai MDC won 100 seats in parliamentary elections in March, ZANU-PF received 99, Mutambana 10 and the remaining seat is held by an independent.

Political commentator, professor John Makumbe, said that if the rules were violated then the matter can always be taken to court but pointed out that it's a process that is easily manipulated by ZANU-PF, which controls the courts. He also said that because of the composition of the parliament, it is a fact that MPs from the other parties voted.

Eight

It is now May 2009. Living in the UK makes it very difficult to keep up with the times and happenings in Zimbabwe. Having lived there for 58 years, I have many friends there and so with letters, phone calls, newsletters and radio, also of course TV and the newspapers, I can give my readers a fair amount of weekly and monthly knowledge about how our wonderful Zimbabwe is surviving with its battle for peace and a democratic way of living!

11th May 2009 – 'Now we can sit down and laugh' – Wilson Johwa

Zimbabwe prime minister, Morgan Tsvangirai, on Friday congratulated and credited former president, Thabo Mbeki, for the formation of the country's unity government and whose work he described as irreversible.

Tsvangirai said that although he had had 'personal fights' with Mbeki, he still respected him. Zimbabwe's Global Political Agreement, which formed the basis for a unity government, was due to Mbeki's efforts.

In a candid talk to a mainly business audience in Johannesburg, Tsvangirai took stock of his time in the inclusive government, now almost 100 days old.

Tsvangirai also mentioned that all parties owe Mbeki a debt for his efforts. 'I am pleased to report we have made progress in a range of 500 billion% to 3% at the end of March. Income values were being restored while previously empty supermarket shelves are now a thing of the past.'

Tsvangirai acknowledged the persistence of market distortions; however, he also said the restoration of the rule of law had been frustratingly slow. He blamed this on 'residual resistance' by a faction of the ruling ZANU-PF who were accustomed to a culture of 'entitlement and impunity'.

Tsvangirai said the inclusive government is here to stay and those who could not live with it were rendering themselves irrelevant. He found it very frustrating as the country could do lots more a lot faster if the spirit was that of partnership rather than opposition. Yet the small improvements made in people's lives proved the Movement for Democratic Change (MDC) was correct in joining the unity government.

'I am confident that we will pull through this process until the people of Zimbabwe can choose their government freely,' he said.

The MDC president said that the first time he went to dinner with Mr Mugabe was the most difficult one and a half hours of his life. 'I thought of running away.' However, he has since mustered the courage to face up to what had been required. 'Previously I could not countenance a situation where I could say "President Mugabe", but now we can sit down and laugh. It requires patience.

'Although the country needed huge injections of international aid, this would largely depend on what Zimbabweans themselves do, particularly with regard to the rule of law. There are still massive challenges, especially in the health and education sectors.'

He said he was not discouraged. 'The will of the people is stronger than the resistance of the few.'

While the first three months were about setting tangible targets for government departments, he said economic stabilisation and democracy were mutually dependent. Tsvangirai, who has executive authority over the security agencies, said he was not worked over their reluctance to accept him.

'I am not going to waste my time worrying about who salutes me when people have no food and the country is collapsing,' he said.

Various commissions were on the cards to implement the charges that were needed. For instance, next week the parliament was due to set up a media commission; another 'initiative' mechanism to engage Zimbabweans on what process they wanted to follow in bringing about national healing. Tsvangirai said failure to heal would trap Zimbabweans in a history of hatred and acrimony, but reconciliation could not be achieved without truth and justice.

8th May 2009 – 'The activists were in the custody of state spies' – Zimbabwe Independence

The attorney general's office has revealed the names of some of the members of the Central Intelligence Organisation (CIO) and the police who were involved in the abduction of human rights and MDC activists last November.

Eighteen human rights and MDC activists, among them Zimbabwe Peace Project director, Justina Mukoko, were allegedly abducted, kept incommunicado and tortured between November and December last year by state security agents.

Notices of indictment for trial in the High Court served on some of the activists this week revealed the role the CIO and the police played when the activists were reported missing last year. They also revealed that the activists were in the custody of state spies, though the police professed ignorance of their whereabouts until late December, when they issued a press statement saying the abductees were in their custody facing banditry charges.

A perusal of the notices revealed the assistant director external in the CIO, retired Brigadier Ashen Walter Tapfumanei, Police Superintendents Reggie Chitekwe and Joel Tenderege, Detective Inspectors Elliot Muchade and Joshua Muzanango, officer commanding CIO homicide Crispen Makendenge, Chief Superintendent Peter Magwenzi and Senior Assistant Commissioner Simon Nyathi, were involved in some of the abductees' cases.

In the notice of indictment served on Regis Mujeye, the attorney general's office said Tapfumanei would tell the High Court when the trial opens on 29th June that on 29th November last year 'caused' the accused 'to be collected from a secure place' where he was being held in connection with banditry allegations.

Mujeye, freelance journalist Shadreck Anderson Manyere, Prime Minister Morgan Tsvangirai's former aid Gandhi Mudzingwa, the DCT security director, Kisimusi Dhlamini and party members Zacharia Nkomo, Chinoto Zulu and Mapjumo Garutsa, are facing five country of twice bombing Harare Central

Police Station, Manyama River bridge, rail bridges and Harare CID headquarters at Morris Depot.

He (Tapfumanei) will state he captured the first accused's (Dhlamini's) statement on video in which he narrated his involvement, especially the bombings, and implicated the second accused person (Mudzingwa).

He reads the notice, "The first accused's statement, which was captured on video was given freely and voluntarily.'

Chitekwe will tell the court that he was requested by the CIO on 25th November 2008 to assist them in conducting a search at the residence of Dhlamini, where he allegedly recovered a cardtex and safety fuse in his toolbox in the bedroom underneath his bed. The police officer will also testify that he interrogated Dhlamini, who then implicated that Mudzingwa, Zulu, Manyere, Nkomo and Mujeye.

Chitekwe will also testify that he was requested by the CIO to assist them in searching Mudzingwa's home on 13th December last year. The security agents asked him to search Manyere's house. The police officer will claim that they recovered a tear-smoke grenade from Mudzingwa and 48 rounds of 9mm ammunition cartridges at Manyere's residence.

The notice revealed that the seven accused persons were officially handed over to the police on 22nd December last year, who had kept them in their custody since they were allegedly abducted in November the same year.

On 22nd December 2009, he (Makendenge) was handed over with the seven accused persons by state security agents, who were holding them in a safe place whilst conducting investigations into acts of insurgency, banditry, sabotage and terrorism, which the accused had committed.

The notice read 'On the same day, he was handed the following exhibits by state security agents, i) 48 x 9mm rounds of ammunition, ii) a cardtex and a safety fuse and iii) a tear-smoke grenade. The following day Muchade recorded the accused persons' warned and cautioned statements in the presence of Muzanango.

In another indictment notice served on MDC-T youth chairman for Zvimba District, Callen Mutemagau, Tapfumanei and Nyathi were involved in the case.

Mutemagau is jointly charged with MDC-T national executive member Concillia Chinanzvana and fellow party members Fidelas Chiramba and Violet Mupfuranhewe on allegations that between 19th July and 30th October last year, they recruited Tapena Niupfuranhewie and other party youths to undergo military training in Botswana for the purpose of committing acts of banditry.

The attorney general's office said that Tapfumanei would tell the High Court when the case opens on 8th June that he used Tapena as an informer in the alleged recruitment of the youths. Nyathi will testify that on 31st October, Chiramba and Violet were arrested by Magwenzi on the banditry allegations and their warned and cautioned statements recorded. They were released on 4th November from police custody.

The two accused persons, according to their lawyers, were then abducted. 'He (Nyathi) will state that on 22nd December 2008, the accused persons were handed over to Chief Superintendent Magwenzi by state security agents and on 23rd December he interviewed them and later recorded warned and cautioned statements,' the notice read.

In another notice of indictment served on the MDC-T activist Manuel Chinanzavana, who is jointly charged with Mukoko, Audrey Zimbudzana, Broderick Takawira and Pita Kaseke, Magwenzi will testify that the five accused persons that were handed over to him by the CIO on 23rd December while Tapfumanei will confirm that he interviewed the suspects and recorded a video in connection with their case. Chinanzavana, Mukoko, Zimbudzana, Takawira and Kazeke will face trial in the High Court on 20th July on allegations that between April 2008 and 31st October 2008 they recruited Richard Hwasheni to undergo military training in Botswana for purposes of banditry in Zimbabwe.

11th May – 'Stench of Mugabe's decaying rule'

Harare. If the state of the toilets in public and even private buildings in Harare were a measure of the inclusive government progress, then it has failed miserably. In the courts, in the ministries, in all public buildings and some privately owned office blocks, the putrid smell of human waste is perhaps President Robert Mugabe's most telling legacy.

Emaciated prisoners are held in fetid cells where water pipes have not been fixed since the days of Rhodesian rule, another legacy of ZANU-PF's staggering failure, which goes beyond ten years of political turmoil since the Movement for Democratic Change, to produce some of the best education results into shells. Some of the bricks and mortar are still there but the windows, desks, doors, blackboards and, of course, books, are missing.

Despite the aversion to maintenance, Mugabe's power is slowly ebbing, mostly because he can't get hold of the cash for his power base. The redetention on Tuesday of activists accused on a repetitive plot – trying to overthrow Mugabe – was the most serious ZANU-PF breach of the political agreement to date, even if 15 were freed on bail 24 hours later. There are so many breaches of the political agreement it is absolutely astonishing that it is still there at all. But neither side has any alternative. As one diplomat said after the arrests, 'Prime Minister (Morgan) Tsvangirai can't threaten to walk out more than once so he has a very difficult balancing act, but we do wish he would speak out more politically and critically. Mugabe never gives up, even as his control, now limited to a diminishing group of thugs in the riot police and their senior officers, the hardcore of the Central Intelligence Organisation (CIO) and military intelligence, is waning.'

The ordinary policeman is more interested in organising a roadblock to extract bribes from motorists than looking for the mythical weapons Mugabe claims photo journalist Shadreck Manyure, still in hospital, had stashed somewhere among his laptop and cameras. It has begun to dawn on ZANU-PF civil servants that the US Marines, the British Army, on Zimmer frames, have not been massing on the border as their CIO have been telling them.

Mugabe has been at this particular game – keeping them on a war footing – for a mythical invading force for decades. His methods are not working as well as they used to but he is not finished yet. Three times in one week he has put off a meeting to address his violations of the political agreement. Will he make concessions after he has attended President Jacob Zuma's inaugurations? Probably not. Then what? Then the MDC will have to recommend that the SADC tries to resolve outstanding issues, which even some of its apologists recognise are indeed outstanding.

Emerging from this mish-mash unity government, insights into ZANU-PF are mostly spectacularly incompetent and Mugabe knows it! He even makes jokes about some party officials behind their backs over lunch.

Mugabe at the ripe old age of 85 is in control of his petulant generals and not the other way around, as so many people think. He is not senile, nor is he in poor health. He is definitely the chief manipulator and is trying to work out how to get his hands on foreign funds to rescue ZANU-PF from obliteration. The party has run out of money and it has always needed huge resources to keep going. The CIO needs projects to keep money flowing to its coffers and there are fewer and fewer ways of creating new enemies to jump-start campaigns and deploy personnel.

The cancellation of the Zimbabwe dollar was the blow Mugabe hadn't counted on. As John Robertson said last week, 'Central Bank governor, Gideon Gono, can no longer manipulate the exchange rate allowing ZANU-PF cronies to exchange one US dollar for trillions of Zimbabwean dollars.'

Mugabe also uses his other weapon 'charm' to disarm his opponents. 'He is so charming sometimes we have to remind ourselves what he has done to us personally and to the country,' said a top businessman after meeting Mugabe.

If Mugabe were to die or retire, his departure, in practical terms, would not be noticed. He plays no role in government operations except the arrests and violence, disruption and theft of crops from white-owned farms.

Could he stop that? Well, YES he could, but he chooses not to. The white farmers were always going to be a safe target, according to one CIO official. ZANU-PF tried to manipulate a teacher's strike, but it was outmanoeuvred by the progressive teacher's union because teachers would rather earn $100 than nothing. Mugabe has had nothing to do with the reopening of hospitals, schools and a few gold mines or the token payment of civil servants in a currency they can use.

These are the fruits of a unity government so far, as well as much less political violence, fewer arrests and shops groaning with imported groceries. Meanwhile Mugabe has to constantly violate the political agreement of last September to push the MDC into the corner. He needs to find a way to protect himself from the taint of gross violence during last year. None of his agents who committed the violence on his orders have been prosecuted, even though their names are known and there are witnesses longing to testify. So that is another reason he fouls the political agreement. He is looking for a foul to get him off the hook.

Nine

Although so many times we get 'repeats' in the papers, on the radio and in general gossip, forgive me if I have also repeated myself in my daily research on what was once the most beautiful and wealthiest of countries in the world. Now we look in hope and pray that Morgan Tsvangirai will perform a miracle.

May 2009 – Johannesburg

In an impassioned appeal, Zimbabwe's long-suffering prime minister, Morgan Tsvangirai, has called for people to get over their obsession with his long-time enemy, President Robert Mugabe. He urged the millions who have abandoned the Southern African nation to return to rebuild its ruined economy.

Tsvangirai, who has been beaten up and tortured by Mugabe's thugs over the years, said victims of repression and the perpetrators of the crimes should reconcile. He addressed white and black exiled Zimbabweans in an audience at South Africa's University of the Witwaterstand, the first open forum Tsvangirai has addressed since forming a unity government with Mugabe in February 2009. But the message was also intended for sceptical Western nations.

'Don't be too paranoid about your obsession with Robert Mugabe because he isn't going away. He is there,' Tsvangirai said. 'Robert Mugabe is definitely part of the problem, but he is also part of the solution, whether you like it or not.'

He was responding to a man who declared, to applause, that Mugabe 'has almost single-handedly destroyed the country, the last two elections and yet is still there—why do you have to sleep with the enemy—and not the simple solution that Mugabe goes?'

The United States, former coloniser, Britain and others have called for Zimbabwe's leader of 28 years to retire and being suspicious of Mugabe's commitment have not offered development aid, despite desperate pleas that the unity government could collapse. Neighbouring countries and an African bank have pledged $650 million in credit lines; far from the $2 billion the government says it needs this year.

The power-sharing agreement was shaken badly this week (Tuesday 12th May) when a magistrate revoked bail for a human rights advocate and 14 others abducted illegally and sent them back to prison where they allege they were tortured. They are accused of terror charges, widely seen as trumped up. Their redetention was seen as a move by Mugabe to put pressure on outstanding issues that have dodged the unity government for months.

The magistrate ordered them freed the following day, acting on orders from Mugabe and Tsvangirai, and said, 'As far as I am concerned, the issue is resolved,' but he made no mention of a journalist and two of his aides, who remain under police guard in the hospital for treatment from alleged torture.

Tsvangirai said on Friday that his and Mugabe's parties had resolved nearly all the outstanding issues and that an announcement would be made on Tuesday. Zimbabweans and others will be looking to see if Mugabe has made major concessions and if Tsvangirai has again been forced to compromise.

The former trade union leader and long-time opposition veteran admitted on Friday that he had agreed to share power from a position of weakness as tens of thousands of homes burnt and Zimbabweans were infected with cholera.

'More than 4,000 died and school and hospitals shut down as public services collapsed. Hundreds of people have been killed and thousands of homes were ruined through state-sponsored violence,' he said, 'while thousands were starving as inflation topped 500 billion%. We could not be the authors of death,' Tsvangirai said, adding that he keeps at the front of his mind the greater good of the people of Zimbabwe.

While Tsvangirai declared his country was open for business and eager for investment, he said the need to share land and business with black Zimbabweans was not in dispute but that his government realises it needs to renegotiate how that will be accomplished. The often violent seizures of white-owned commercial farms was the start of Zimbabwe's plunge into an economic, political and lawless morass that today has most people in former food export dependent on foreign handouts!

Mugabe said the land would go to landless peasants, but instead gave them to generals and cronies who let fields fall fallow. Tsvangirai said an independent land commission must be set up to redistribute land.

When Zimbabwe became independent in 1980 after a guerrilla war to end white supremacist rule, some 4,500 farmers owned two thirds of the richest land.

'Land is an unfinished national agenda which means that until it is resolved, it will continue to be an emerging issue every time there is conflict,' Tsvangirai said. 'Don't continue to be stewing in your own hatred,' he urged people. 'Zimbabweans must never forget that if we do not reconcile and rebuild and look to the future, this country will be forever trapped in this history of tribal and political violence.'

Harare. President Robert Mugabe's controversial Land Reform Programme took on a new twist on Wednesday when a court ordered the eviction of a man who is not a farmer. Ian Campbell-Morrison lives in the Vumba Mountains in Eastern Zimbabwe, next to a hotel where he is a green keeper. He and his wife live in a cottage on a plot not much bigger than a suburban garden, where she tends flowers.

'The Campbell-Morrisons used to farm tobacco and coffee but the government seized their farm and land and their beautiful farmhouse and gave it to a government official, leaving them their cottage and the garden around it,' said Hendrick Oliver, director of the Farmers' Union, made up mostly of Zimbabwe's remaining 350 white farmers.

A magistrate in the nearby city of Mutare nevertheless sentenced Campbell-Morrison to a fine of $800 for 'illegally occupying state land' and ordered the couple to be off the property and banned by this following Saturday.

The Campbell-Morrisons are one of 140 white farming families facing eviction from their land in the latest tactic in Mugabe's violent, lawless campaign to fore white landowners –

numbers about 5,000 when it started in 2000 – off their farms. The action is in the name of redistribution of land to go back to the Zimbabweans, but which has instead made a million farm workers homeless and set off the collapse of the once-prosperous country' economy.

Mugabe has declared all white-owned land to be state property and banned formers from taking the government to court. The evictions and violence have continues despite the establishment in February of a power-sharing government between Mugabe and former opposition leader, Morgan Tsvangirai, with an agreement to restore the rule of law and to ensure security of tenure to all landowners.

Tsvangirai, now prime minister, began by promising to end lawlessness, promising that, 'No crime (by invaders) will go unpunished.' But the police, under the control of staunchly pro-Mugabe security chiefs, continued to refuse to act against the most well-heeled Mugabe loyalists, grabbing productive farms and selling their crops.

Western governments have refused to provide finance for the recovery of the country's economy from world record inflation and discrimination of production under Mugabe until there are clear signs of reform in the re-establishment of the rule of law. The restoration of peace and security on the farms is cited as a key condition.

But there was shock this week when Tsvangirai referred in an interview to 'isolated incidents of so-called farm invasions that had been blown out of proportion.'

'He's talking like Mugabe now,' said a Western diplomat.

Throughout Tuesday night on Mount Carmel Farm in the Chetgutu District, farmer Ben Freeth and his family were terrorised by a mob of invaders who rolled blazing tyres at their thatched-roof cottage and homestead.

At the weekend, an 80-year-old woman was assaulted by police who were removing her son from his farm and on Friday another farmer was beaten by a Mugabe supporter.

'There has been no resolution or even recognition that there is ever a problem,' said CFU President Gifford, who is trying to stop a government official cutting down what is left of his timber plantation and selling it to the government of neighbouring

Zambia for telephone poles. Gifford is due to appear in court in February for 'illegally occupying state land'.

'This is happening in a country that has become the world's most dependant on donors for food,' he said. 'Until this government respects the rights of its own citizens and investment agreements, no-one will even look at this country.'

Ten

That beautiful sunny sky was looking down on us. Oh, how we took so many daily things for granted. I for one did, in the 58 years I lived in Rhodesia, later called Zimbabwe. That wonderful cloudless sky, so blue and sunny. The old servants who used to kneel down and clap their hands, saying, 'Good night and thank, you madam,' and 'Good night, boss.' Wearing their dark uniforms in the morning and white uniforms in the afternoon and when evening meals were served.

One morning, Allan, our house boy, had just brought our daily tea tray in at 6.00 am, our normal time. I jumped out of bed and opened the window. The many colourful birds seemed to be singing extra loudly. I looked over the swimming pool towards the colourful rose garden, and there was the post boy, singing away with a load of mail for us. Amongst it, I noticed a letter with 'British Embassy' on it. This letter showed the time we were living in!

8th May 2009 – Zimbabwe Settlement Scheme

The government is offering assistance to British people who have been resident in Zimbabwe for at least the last five years, and wish to resettle in the UK. The help is available to British citizens aged 70 or over, and to others who are vulnerable for reasons other than their age. They will be interviewed by British officials in Zimbabwe to see if they meet eligibility requirements and immigration controls, and will be allowed to bring spouses, partners and dependents with them once they reach the UK. They will be offered social housing, state benefits and support, subject to a means test. Up to 1,500 elderly and disabled British citizens have received letters from the British government offering this help. The Department of Health has announced that British citizens arriving from Zimbabwe under the UK Border Agency Resettlement Scheme are exempt from chargers and should not be asked to pay for any hospital treatment they require.

The letter did not affect me in any way as I was on my yearly trip to see my friends again in Zimbabwe. It was the very last time I went there.

In Zimbabwe life still goes on the same. We shall see what they say at the conference in Australia, while the Queen is there. Zimbabwe is on the agenda...

29th May 2009

Up to 500 destitute Britons living in Zimbabwe are to be repatriated after their savings and pensions were wiped out by President Robert Mugabe's economic policies. The first five will return this weekend after the British Embassy in Harare arranged for them to be flown home.

The group, which includes former colonial administrators, wives and civil servants, have seen their assets destroyed by hyper-inflation. Before expats left the country, they were asked to report neighbours involved in fraud. Their airfares are being paid by the British taxpayer and officials said each person would be given permanent accommodation in Britain and the same entitlement to state benefits as any other pensioner.

Fred Noble, a 78-year-old Scot, will return to Fife this weekend, 51 years after he and his wife departed with £100 for what was then Britain's Crown colony of Southern Rhodesia. He worked for Rhodesian Railways, retiring on a pension with medical aid 13 years ago.

'I helped more people than helped me in Zimbabwe,' said Mr Noble, who lost his wife four years ago. 'I deserve a Christian burial. I don't want to get ill in Zimbabwe.'

He was the second pensioner to apply for repatriation at the British Embassy. Mr Mugabe's bankrupt regime stopped paying his pension five years ago, leaving Mr Noble dependent on his investments. When inflation (Zimbabwe's) reached more than 230 million%, the value of his portfolio plunged to less than one penny.

'We didn't do anything wrong, we paid our taxes and invested for our old age. My wife used to say, "All this place has now is sunshine, we are simply wasting our lives here." My sister in the UK sent me £1,600 and it has gone now,' said Mr Noble. 'I was the second to apply to go and we had two weeks to prepare to leave.'

To find his new life in Britain, he will sell his 1969 car and television for about £250, but some prized possessions will stay behind. 'I have an elephant-skin waistcoat – I was dandy you know – and two pairs of handmade shoes, the best that Rhodesia produced,' said Mr Noble. 'I'll give them away. I will take photos of the Bible my wife gave me and my Robbie Burns'

Anne Budden, 83, is leaving the land of her birth because she can no longer be a burden to her daughters in Zimbabwe. She said, 'They keep on saying I should change my mind, but I must. Their husbands are nearing retirement and my hip operation took my last money. We had lived well on our three pensions.'

Mrs Budden, who was widowed two years ago, lives in a rented flat in Harare paid for by her daughter in Harare. 'I have a lovely life, shielded from what is going on outside, with space, nice people and my own garden. I will miss that, especially my two daughters in Zimbabwe who protected me from hardships.'

Although she has spent a lifetime in Africa, Mrs Budden has always cherished her attachment to Britain. 'I am leaving the country of my birth but going to the land of my ancestors,' she said. 'I have the two weeks and I have a daughter in the UK.' She will move to Farnborough near another friend from Harare, who will also leave this weekend. 'We need to support each other as we start our new lives,' said Mrs Budden.

The British have quietly identified pensioners with British citizenship and no means of support but the embassy declined to comment on the official repatriation scheme. About 1,500 pensioners (Zimbabwean pensioners) have no foreign citizenship, no family and no means of escape. As each penniless Briton departs, a new charity will be able to give more help to those who are left behind. The charity, (ZANE) Zimbabwe: A National Emergency, will be their only lifeline.

29th May 2009

The people who were leading the victimisation of the Movement for Democratic Change (MDC) supporters towards last June's presidential run-off elections in Buhera are pleading with their respective traditional leaders to be given production, as MDC-T supporters are insisting that they want revenge.

Headman, Josiah Mabvuregudo, in Ward 17 of Buhera Central constituency under Chief Nyahanu, confirmed, 'These people come to my home wanting to know what I will do in case they are assaulted by the MDC-T, who are swearing that they will not rest unless they revenge. I used to tell these people to go back and wait, so that they could see if the MDC-T supporters mean what they said. One of the people who came was beaten seriously last week. Now I am referring all the issues to my boss, who is Chief Nyashanu.'

Mabvuregudo said he informed the police at Sanga Police Camp to assist in limiting cases of violence. 'We have informed the police to be alert. As a leader, I am worried as the tension between ZANU-PF and MDC-T supporters in my area is increasing instead of going down,' he said.

Radio VOP was informed that some people have already fled to towns to skip potential punishment by MDC-T supporters. The situation is not unique to Buhera as member of parliament for Gutu North, Edmore Maramwidze Hamandishe, said he was also facing similar circumstances in his area. 'I think something should be done to cool down the emotions of people who were victimized in last year's elections. Currently, no justice has been done and if the government fails to do justice on behalf of the people, then the people will take the law into their own hands,' said Hamandishe.

Thomas Matema, an MDC-T supporter, said the inclusive government was taking too long to take the victims of political violence. He also said people should be arrested for failing to pay back whatever they looted during or towards last year's election. However, MDC-T president and prime minister, Morgan Tsvangirai, recently told thousands of party supported that victims of political violence were going to be compensated.

President Robert Mugabe earlier this year swore in three ministers of National Healing Zimbabwe, which was urged to undergo a national healing process and drew three new ministers from both ZANU-PF and MDC-T. The organisation for National Healing, Reconciliation and Integration has reportedly begun work on the establishment of a mechanism for national healing and reconciliation to create a new environment to remove tensions in society.

The organisation, chaired by John Nkomo, includes ministers of state Mrs Sekai Holland and Mr Gibson Sinbanda and was established in the office of the president under the Global Political Agreement. Calls have been raised for the removed of John Nkomo as president, or rather chairman of the organisation following the looting of a man by his bodyguard in a farm invasion power struggle.

In an interview with ZBC in Harare recently, the under-fire ZANU-PF said the group is on a mission to meet and consult various sections of Zimbabwean society and come up with the best way of conducting the healing and reconciliation process. The member said the organisation had already held consultations with some groups such as traditional healers, spiritual mediums and other groups, making their contributions to enrich the process and give the mechanism a true Zimbabwean character.

29th May 2009 – Blessing Zulu, Search News

Zimbabwe prime minister, Morgan Tsvangirai's branch of the Movement for Democratic Change on Tuesday dismissed an assertion by President Robert Mugabe that Reserve Bank governor, Gideon Gono will not step down, calling it unacceptable.

The Tsvangirai MDC wing issued a statement saying Gono and attorney general, Johannes Tomara, must both step down, also demanding a forensic audit of the Central Bank.

A deadlock between Mr Mugabe and Mr Tsvangirai, the latter backed up by deputy prime minister, Arthur Mutambana of a rival MDC formation, has been referred to the South African Development Community and African Union. The two African unions ushered Zimbabwe's national unity government into existence and stands as it guarantors.

91

Political sources aid Gono, in desperation, has launched a media campaign to frame the calls for his resignation as a personal vendetta by MDC finance minister, Tendai Biti.

The state-controlled Herald newspaper reported on Tuesday that a prison guard at Harare's notorious Chickurubi Prison, was arrested on charged that he acted on orders from Biti to seek incriminating evidence against Gono concerning a farm mechanisation programme.

Biti dismissed the accusation, lodged through the state newspaper, calling it fictitious. Reports say Gono has threatened to resign, complaining that he had largely been abandoned by Mr Mugabe's ZANU-PF party, his only defender being information minister, Webster Shamu, Information Ministry permanent secretary, George Charamba and independent parliamentarian, Jonathan Moyo, a former information minister.

Meanwhile, Biti has drafted amendments to the RB2 Act, which provide for a non-executive director to take over as chairman of Central Bank. Gono has criticised the amendments, saying they would strip him of his powers.

Spokesman, Nelson Chamisa, of the Tsvangirai MDC formation, told VOA that the decision as to who will run the Central Bank is one that should be reached by all three governing parties, not just ZANU-PF.

Economist John Robertson said, 'Sweeping reform is needed at the RB2 if the needs to secure reconstruction financing are to be met.'

The International Monetary Fund and other multilateral financial institutions have refrained from demanding Gono's departure but have urged reform. A team from the IMF is currently in Harare to provide technical assistance including on Central Bank governance.

How wealthy can a country be and then have nothing in general?

The Kimberley Process, the global body created to curb trade in gems used to fund conflict, will visit Zimbabwe again next week to investigate claims of diamond smuggling and related violence, The Herald said, citing an unidentified government official.

A team will visit Zimbabwe's diamond-producing mines in Thurowa, River Ranch and the Chiadzwa diamond fields, also known as Marange. The Harare-based newspaper said on its website that there were 'suspicions and allegations' that Zimbabwe's security forces killed scores of illegal miners in Chiadzwa. 'The Chiadzwa fields contain the largest concentrated reserves in the world.' It added that Zimbabwe produced about 695,000 carats of diamonds worth $31 million in 2007, according to the most recent data from the Kimberley Process.

May 2009 – ZW News

A small piece of history was made in Harare yesterday when the Zimbabwe Law Society was able to stage a demonstration without getting beaten up. The last time they tried was two years ago when they were set upon by riot police and lashed until they had welts and bruises. Yesterday's protest was over the arrest of Alec Muchadehama, a senior human rights lawyer.

Lawyers marched to the Ministry of Justice carrying placards. As they arrived, they were met by four riot policemen with batons and a senior officer. No-one was assaulted. The officer escorted Chris Nhike, the head of the local chapter of the Law Society, upstairs to the minister's office to deliver the petition. Mr Nhike returned in five minutes.

'Unfortunately, the minister was not there,' he said, 'so I pushed it under his door.' The lawyers cheered and dispersed, happy not to have been assaulted.

Before undertaking the action, Mr Nhike took a vote among the 100 lawyers, pointing out that the police had not sanctioned the demonstration. 'There is no risk,' he said. There were no dissenting voices. At the same time there were two human rights lawyers on trial nearby for 'public violence' in March. They were walking back to work from lunch and passed a demonstration being broken up violently, one of many squashed since the power-sharing government was formed, and got arrested.

'At one level things have changed,' said lawyer Innocent Gonese. 'At another everything is the same.'

May 2009 – About 54% of the NRZ's 164 locomotives are in working order

'The National Railways of Zimbabwe needs $150 million to fund short-term projects, The Herald reported, citing General Manager,

Mike Karakadzai. The state-owned monopoly needs the money to repair locomotives and wagons and to replace worn tracks,' the Harare-based newspaper said. 'It also needs to pay a deposit on an order for trains and wagons from China. About 54% of the NRZ's 164 locomotives are in working order,' the newspaper added.

One can't help but wonder, however, how did it get to this dreadful stage.

May 2009 – 'Between 3,000 Zimbabweans arrive in South Africa through the border posts daily'

'More Zimbabweans arriving through South African border posts is an indication that the South African government's recent visa exemptions are working,' an expert on migration has said.

Tara Palzer, a senior researcher at the Forced Migration Studies Programme at the Wits University, said it had benefited South Africa if more people arrived legally, because as more people arrived it made it easier for the government to keep tabs on who is in the country or not. However, it still does not mean how the government had any way of telling how many Zimbabweans lived within our borders.

According to home affairs statistics, between 3,000 and 3,500 Zimbabweans arrived in South Africa through the border posts daily at the beginning of the month, before the special visa exemptions applied. This figures increased by about 50% to about 4,700 last week after visa exemptions, with almost the same number leaving South Africa for Zimbabwe.

Home Affairs minister, Nkosazana Diamini-Zuma, told the National Press Club in Pretoria yesterday that there was 'not a very dramatic increase' of Zimbabweans entering into South Africa through border posts since the exemption two weeks ago. 'The majority of people just want to buy food and then go home.'

Diamini-Zuma's deputy, Malusi Gibado, added that Zimbabweans still needed valid travel documents to enter the country, which meant that not just anybody could enter the country.

May 2009 – 'Bus trip for 33 people to return to Zimbabwe from Johannesburg's Central Methodist Church'

Johannesburg – Our international migration agency says it is helping Zimbabweans who hoped to find a better life in South Africa to head home. The International Organisation for Migration arranged a bus trip for 33 people on Wednesday to return to Zimbabwe to Johannesburg's Central Methodist Church. The church was crowded with hundreds of Zimbabweans who had fled their troubled country.

Zimbabweans have arrived in South Africa seeking jobs, food and medicine. Those who left on Wednesday had been unable to find work or better shelter. South Africa officially entered a recession this week and some see that Zimbabweans have been victims of anti-foreigner violence.

Eleven

9th June 2009 – BBC News

Zimbabwe could be heading for a new wave of violence, a minister in the country's unity government has warned. Sekai Holland, a member of the former opposition MDC, told the BBC that opponents of the power-sharing government were drawing up assassination lists. She said that she believed the worst violence was being planned to coincide with elections due in 18 months.

Her comments echo earlier claims by Prime Minister Morgan Tsvangirai of ongoing political intimidation and abuses in Zimbabwe.

Ms Holland, Zimbabwe's Minister of National Healing, Reconciliation and Integration, told the BBC that she and other members of the Movement for Democratic Change (MDC), including fellow ministers, were receiving threatening phone calls every day. They had been told that the hard line members of President Robert Mugabe's ZANU-PF are adding their names to the lengthening assassination list.

'We are told we do have a list of people that they will kill,' she said. 'No one feels safe in Zimbabwe, no one, and I mean no one. We have not reached a ceasefire yet. We are still at a point where people have their guns cocked.'

Ms Holland is a senior member of the MDC and was badly beaten up by ZANU-PF supporters two years ago. She also claims that 39,000 militia men 'working inside the civil service and outside' were being paid a wage of $100 a day to beat up the MDC supported in the event of an election. This she said meant that violence in the next elections could be even worse than in 2008, when some 200 people were killed and thousands injured.

Last month, Tsvangirai, the prime minister and leader of the MDC, criticised the speed of political change in Zimbabwe. He said that although the MDC was in government, it had not succeeded in restoring the rule of law and warned his party that Zimbabweans remained hungry and afraid of political persecution. But Mr Tsvangirai, currently on a tour of Europe seeking financial aid, has insisted that the government would stabilise the situation in Zimbabwe.

He said it was 'a work in progress' but that the 'period of acrimony' between himself and Mr Mugabe was 'over'.

'Will Bashir's visit hamper Zimbabwe's pleas for aid? Mugabe couldn't care less about Bashir' – Scott Balday, ZW News

Johannesburg – Zimbabwean prime minister, Morgan Tsvangirai's job has just gotten harder. Just as he hits the road on a three-week tour to convince rich Western nations to end their sanctions against Zimbabwe and to send more aid money, Zimbabwe's president, Robert Mugabe, is back home in Harare reminding the world that he doesn't pay attention to their rules.

At a regional summit of the Common Market for Eastern and Southern Africa (COMESA) held this week in Zimbabwe's capital, Harare, Mr Mugabe has held meetings with, among others, Sudanese president, Omar al-Bashir; the first sitting president ever to face an arrest warrant for war crimes against humanity.

Since March, Mr Bashir has been under an international arrest warrant by the International Criminal Court (ICC) for war crimes committed in the Western Sudanese region of Darfur. But the arrest warrant has not stopped Bashir from travelling in the Middle East and Africa, from Qatar in the Persian Gulf to Egypt and Libya and now to Zimbabwe.

'(Mugabe) loves thumbing his nose at the international community, he is so good at it,' says John Prendergast, co-chairman of the Enough Project, a Washington-based think tank focusing on issues of genocide. Mugabe couldn't care less about Bashir. He uses him to make a point that Western institutions are irrelevant in his Africa. Mugabe, of course, is famous with his relations, but at a time when Zimbabwe is appealing for some £10 billion in development relief from rich nations, it seems a curious decision to try to put those same donor nations in their place.'

The biggest Western donor of the lot, the US, is currently debating lifting sanctions against Zimbabwe's new coalition government, which for the first time in two decades is forcing Mugabe and his party to share power with the opposition. Yet many American experts, including secretary of state, Hillary Clinton, say that the US should wait for Mugabe to leave before opening up the taps for aid.

At present, the US can only give humanitarian aid because of the US sanctions against Mugabe's regime. To date Zimbabwe has managed to secure $11.3 million in humanitarian aid relief from the European Commission, but 10% of the $1 billion it is requesting this year.

Mr Tsvangirai, once Mugabe's chief rival as opposition leader and now a coalition partner in Mugabe's government, is expected to request up to $700 million from the US government when he meets with President Obama this month. Zimbabwe's neighbours have already given the cash-strapped, inflation-ridden country up to $400 million in loans through the COMESA, which Mugabe now chairs, and the South African Development Community (SADC), which has mediated political crises between Mugabe and his opponents by inviting Bashir to a summit in Harare.

Neither Sudan nor Zimbabwe are breaking any rules and neither are one of the 108 signatories of the Rome Statute, which was created by the ICC in The Hague. In addition, Bashir enjoys a certain amount of immunity as a head of state acting in an international forum for his country's interests.

But while a few experts believe the West will punish Zimbabwe for the Bashir visit, Mugabe's message will ring clear nonetheless.

'Western policy has failed to make any real impact on changing the behaviour of the regime in Zimbabwe,' says Godfrey Musila, a senior researcher at the Institute for Security Studies (Pretoria). 'Tsvangirai is going to Europe and the US to make the case that at the end of the day it is ordinary Zimbabweans who are suffering and they need relief.'

Once officially recognised, it will be easier to prosecute

The world's leading organisation on the study and prevention of genocide has for the first time elected an African to its governing board.

At a vote on Sunday 17th June, Zimbabwean journalist and author, Geoff Hill, secured one of six places on the advisory council for the International Association of Genocide Scholars (IAGS). A total of 18 candidates competed for the board. The decision was taken by secret ballot.

The grouping, whose pronouncements on mass murder, ethnic cleansing and genocide are followed closely by both the United Nations and the International Criminal Court at The Hague, was formed in 1994 and has been denominated by academics and political analysts from the USA and Europe. The IAGS led the push to send former Yugoslav strongman, Slobidan Milosovic and Liberian dictator, Charles Taylor to The Hague.

Hill, who has repeatedly called for the Gukurahundi massacres to be officially classified as genocide, said he would 'demand that the African crimes against humanity gained the same status as those of the Holocaust and Cambodia. People now accept the 1994 slaughter in Rwanda as genocide but the previous attacks on Tutsis in that country, plus the Nigerian atrocities in Biafra in the 1960s and Gukurahundi have been completely ignored.'

Hill also said that he had already started lobbying within the IAGS for a pronouncement to be made on Gukurahundi and once it is officially recognised as genocide, it will be easier to gain support for the prosecution of those who carried out the killings.

Chihombari lives in the US and practices family medicine in Antioch,Tennessee

A niece of the prime minister is involved in an attempt to grab a farm in the Chequto district. The family medicine practioner in Antioch, Tennessee, has been actively trying to seize the De Russ Farm from Mr L J Cremer since last year.

Mr Cremer was first contacted in November 2008 by the local land officer, who produced an offer allocated to Dr Chihombari. In January 2009, Dr Chihombari's sister sent a group of unemployed youths to take the farm but the occupation only lasted three days after which the youths left, complaining they had not been paid enough.

In April, Dr Chihombari applied to the courts for an application to evict the Cremer family, producing the same offer letter as evidence, this time dated December 2009. Dr Chihombari visited the De Russ Farm in May to see her 'new' property.

Mr Cremer was born on the farm, which was originally 716 hectares in size. In 2002, 650 hectares were taken away and given to new farmers. The De Russ family were left with 60 hectares on which are the homestead and outbuildings. Mr Cremer lives on the farm with his wife, a third-generation Zimbabwean, their two daughters, their husbands and five grandchildren. Dr Russ's Farm employs 300 staff, some of whom live on the property. The state has paid no compensation for the seized land.

The Cremers used to run cattle and produce food and cotton on the seized portion of the farm but since 2002, production on that land has been minimal with no more than two hectares under crops and many now covered in thorn trees five metres tall.

In 2003, that part of the De Russ's farm still in the Cremers' hands was granted 'export processing zone' status, later turned into an Investment Licence. The status of Investment Licence gives legal protection against seizure by the state. The Cremers also have letters from the local land committee and the provincial governor recommending that they be allowed to continue farming. They grow cut flowers for export as well as vegetables for the local market. There are also plans to produce vegetable seedlings for the outgrower of a processing company. The Cremers' neighbours, who used to produce the seedlings, have been evicted.

'It is very obvious that acquisition is *not* about land reform,' said Mr Cremer in a statement. 'How can this government ask for food while they are busy removing food producers from their farms? How can they justify the unemployment rate while they are removing 300 people from employment under the guide of "land reform"? A small productive farm is being taken from Zimbabweans and given to someone who resides in America. It is all about sheer greed; people stealing our homes, lands, jobs and livelihood and hiding behind politics. The only reason for evicting us must be race.'

Dr Chihombari came to prominence in May when she was seen accompanying Mr Tsvangirai at the inauguration of Jacob Zuimba as South African president. She was born in Zimbabwe but educated in the US and has practiced there for the last 30 years. She is married to a Ghanaian, also a doctor. In 1992 she founded the Bell Family Centre in Tennessee, of which she is CEO. She is also co-owner of Mid-Tennessee Medical Associates, which is a multi-speciality centre with 16 physicians.

In 1999 her company received US$750,000 from the World Bank to fund its involvement with Ike Torwood Hospital and Redcliff Medical Centre in Kwe Kwe, which her company had taken over from Zisco, the troubled steel producer in the town.

All they have to do is claim fear for their safety and they can do whatever they want

Hong Kong – Bodyguards for the daughter of Zimbabwe's president, Robert Mugabe, who were accused of assaulting two journalists in Hong Kong, will not face prosecution, an official said on Tuesday.

'The Hong Kong Department of Justice has decided against taking the two guards to court,' a spokesman said yesterday. They were accused of attacking the journalists, who were investigating a story on Robert Mugabe's assets in Asia in February. The journalists were working on behalf of Britain's Sunday Times newspaper.

'In our review of the case, it became clear that the (guards) were genuinely concerned for the safety of Miss (Bona) Mugabe,' the Justice Department said in a statement.

The statement said that an independent lawyer had agreed that the case was 'borderline' and the public interest did not require a prosecution! The two journalists, Colin Galloway and Jim O'Rourke, said the guards had held Galloway in a headlock and grabbed one of their cameras.

The lawyer for the journalists, Michael Vidler, said his clients were most concerned about the Justice Department's move.

'This decision seems to convey the message that anyone linked to the family of Robert Mugabe, or similar heads of state, can act with impunity whenever they are in Hong Kong,' he said. 'All they have to do is claim fear for their safety and they and their bodyguards can do whatever they want, even when confronted with nothing more lethal than a camera.'

The decision comes after Mugabe's wife, Grace, was granted diplomatic immunity from prosecution over her alleged assault of a British journalist who was trying to take her picture in Hong Kong. Mugabe is reported to have bought a $5.8 million property in the city. Bona Mugabe is studying at a university in Hong Kong.

Mugabe's regime has been internationally condemned for its politically motivated violence targeting opposition and civil servants. It entered into a power-sharing arrangement with opponents in February.

Journalists barred from COMESA summit despite High Court order' – Alex Bell, SADC

Four journalists, who last week won a landmark case against the government over the legality of the Media and Information Commission (MIC), were this weekend barred from attending the COMESA summit for not being (accepted) accredited.

Two weeks ago, the Information Ministry instructed all journalists wishing to cover the event to register for accreditation with the MIC. The freelance journalists took the state to court over the issue and on Friday the High Court judge, Bharat Patal, ruled that the MIC was now a defunct body and as such, no journalist in the country was required to register with it.

The court granted the journalists an interim order barring information minister Webster Shamu and his permanent secretary, George Charamba, MIC chairman, Dr Tafalaona Mahosa and others, from interfering with the operations of the four journalists in their work. But the journalists, Stanley Gama, Valentine Maponga, Stanley Kwenda and Jealous Mawarise, were on Sunday turned away from the summit venue in Victoria Falls by security details.

The security officials insisted that the journalists, despite the production of the High Court orders, could not cover the event as they were not on the Information Ministry's list of journalists accredited to cover the summit.

Lawyers for the MIC have also announced they will appeal against the High Court ruling in a clear sign that media reform in Zimbabwe is a long way from being achieved.

Meanwhile, during the opening of the COMESA summit that alarmingly resembled a gathering of dictators and criminals, Robert Mugabe called for African countries to increase self-reliance and boost development. Mugabe, who now takes over as leader of Africa's main trading block, also said the continent must raise its international capacity by exploiting its mineral resources, rich soil and human skills!

The ageing hypocritical comments have been greeted with shock by observers as Mugabe has single-handedly destroyed development in Zimbabwe, turning the once-productive country into an aid-reliant state.

While Mugabe was lecturing his fellow African leaders on the importance of self-reliance, Prime Minister Morgan Tsvangirai embarked on a cross-continental aid-begging tour to rescue financial relationships that Mugabe's years of dictatorial abuse destroyed.

Meanwhile, outrage still abounds over the involvement of vice president Joyce Mujuru's daughter in a trade deal involving illegal gold from the DRC. Could this be the kind of exploitation of natural resources Mugabe stringently called for during his speech?

At the same time that Mugabe called for an end to conflicts across the continent, Sudan president, Omar al-Bashir, who faces international arrest for war crimes, was welcomed with open arms at the summit this weekend. The International Criminal Court (ICC) issued a warrant in March for Bashir to face five counts of crimes against humanity and two of war crimes over the conflict in Darfur.

But the Zimbabwean government defended their welcome of the Sudanese leader with Justice Patrick Chinamasa telling the media that Zimbabwe has no duty to arrest Bashir as it is not party to the treaty that set up the ICC.

'We are aware that the President of Sudan is under an ICC warrant for arrest, which he disputes. We are not a state party under the Rome Statute. We have no obligation under the statute to execute that obligation,' he said.

US has no plans to shift policy of Zimbabwe. Increasingly substantial aid is dependent upon them fulfilling the agreement they have already made.

Washington is troubled by the absence of reform in Zimbabwe and has no plans for now to offer major aid or lifting sanctions against Robert Mugabe,' the top United States diplomat for Africa said on Monday.

Zimbabwe's prime minister is set to have his first meeting with US president, Barack Obama, in Washington on Friday, part of a bid to woo financial support for the unity government he shares uneasily with rival Mugabe. But Johnnie Carson, assistant secretary of state for African affairs, said more political, social and economic reforms needed to be made before substantial US aid could kick in or targeted sanctions against Mugabe could be lifted.

'There is no indication that the US government is prepared to life economic sanctions against those in Zimbabwe who have been most responsible for undermining the country's democracy and destroying the country and its economy,' Carson said in an interview with Reuters. 'Increasingly substantial aid is dependent upon them making political concessions and fulfilling the agreements that they have already made in returning the country to more democratic rule,' he said.

The White House said President Obama was looking forward to meeting Tsvangirai, who formed a unity government with Mugabe after a disputed election last year and a brutal crackdown on the opposition.

'The two leaders will discuss the difficult road ahead in Zimbabwe, including how the US can support the forces of reform as they work together to bring the rule of law, respect for human rights and free and fair elections back to Zimbabwe,' said White House spokesman Robert Gibbs.

While 'deeply concerned' about the lack of reform, Carson said the United States would continue humanitarian assistance, particularly for health care and to boost democracy and governance in Zimbabwe.

Zimbabwe's economy is in ruins with hyper-inflation and unemployment at about 90%. Millions are in need of food and the country's infrastructure and institutions are in shambles, a situation the West blame on Mugabe's mismanagement.

16th June 2009 – 'Conditional on further democratic advances'

Berlin – Zimbabwean prime minister, Morgan Tsvangirai, welcomed re-engagement with his country on Monday, after Chancellor Angela Merkel pledged further assistance and talks in Berlin.

'I am very heartened by the fact that (Merkel) was able to express support to us,' the Zimbabwean prime minister said.

Merkel described Tsvangirai as the 'symbol of democratisation of Zimbabwe', adding that there were encouraging signs since the formation of a unitary government February.

'It is pleasing that the situation is such that inflation has regressed, schools and hospitals have re-opened, such that you can say something has got underway in the last months. Wherever possible, we will give support,' the chancellor pledged at a joint news conference, adding that German aid was conditional on further democratic advances in the Southern African nation!

Merkel stressed that German assistance – dependent also on land reform programmes – would not just take the form of financial aid but also advice and encouragement for business investment to Zimbabwe to resume.

Germany had withdrawn its development aid to Zimbabwe in light of the political meltdown under President Mugabe and provided just 10.4 million euros of humanitarian aid last year.

Tsvangirai said he was not at all disappointed that Chancellor Merkel made no concrete financial pledges and said he was encouraged by a meeting with the German development ministry due later in the day.

'There has already been an indication by Chancellor Merkel that "Yes, we realise there is progress but you need to do more" and we accept that,' Tsvangirai said after the talks in Merkel's Berlin office.

The Zimbabwean premier is touring Europe and the US in a campaign to win support for the country's new power-sharing government, as well as financial help to rebuild the country after years of political and economical turmoil.

US president, Barack Obama, pledged $73 million in humanitarian aid to Zimbabwe on Friday but said this money would bypass the government to directly benefit the people of Zimbabwe.

Tsvangirai conceded that many reforms were still outstanding, adding that potential donors were reluctant to give immediate public support and acclamation because '
suppose tomorrow it reverses? They want to be sure that this is an irreversible process of transition to democracy, and there is nothing wrong with that."

Tsvangirai entered a tense power-sharing agreement with Mugabe in January following allegations that the 85-year-old president had manipulated his own re-election.

Mugabe is largely isolated from the West and faces 'travel bans' in the US and Europe, prompting suggestions that Tsvangirai was sent on his behalf.

'I was *not* sent by Robert Mugabe or anyone else,' Tsvangirai said. 'It is my own individual initiative because cabinet has adopted the fact that we need to re-engage the world, so I am not under anybody's instructions,' the premier added.

During the European tour, Tsvangirai is also due to meet the British premier, Gordon Brown, French president, Nicolas Sarkozy, as well as leaders of Sweden, Norway, Denmark and Belgium and senior European Union officials.

The Zimbabwean premier said a huge challenge still lay ahead for the country's unitary government. 'It is to consolidate this government and to make sure this government is able to deliver on the democratisation front, on the stabilisation front and be able to go to an election afterwards. That is the biggest challenge,' Tsvangirai said.

'EU are unaware of any plans for a meeting with Mumbengegwe too early to put normalisation on the agenda' – Agnes Shaw

Harare – The warm Western welcome Prime Minister Morgan Tsvangirai has been receiving is ranking some of the governing partners, state media reported on Monday.

Tsvangirai is on a three-week trip through Europe and the US that included a meeting with President Barack Obama last week. His coalition partner, Zimbabwe's long-time ruler, Robert Mugabe, is barred by travel restrictions from visiting the stops on Tsvangirai's itinerary and the leaders with whom the premier has had cordial talks accused Mugabe of tramping on democracy and ruining a once vibrant economy.

Zimbabwe's state-run Herald newspaper reported that there were concerns among some officials aligned to Mugabe over Obama's reference to building a new partnership, not with the coalition government as a whole, but with Tsvangirai, a former opposition leader who has been beaten and jailed by Mugabe's regime.

Tsvangirai and Mugabe formed their coalition in February, pressed by neighbours to end violent political confrontation and cooperate to address their country's economic crisis. The political marriage of convenience has been rocky from the start and Western leaders say that progress towards reform has been slow.

After meeting Tsvangirai on Friday in Washington, Obama praised the premier for persevering in trying to lead Zimbabwe out of a 'very dark and difficult period'. Obama accused Mugabe of resisting democracy.

The Herald quoted tourism minister, Walter Mzembi, a Mugabe appointee as accusing Obama of being 'overtly biased' and lacking 'diplomatic courtesy'. Tsvangirai has said his three-week trip is aimed at re-engaging with the West, while officials linked to Mugabe have tried to portray it as an attempt to persuade the international community to lift sanctions.

Tsvangirai started in the Netherlands and the US, where officials demanded more progress on reforms by the coalition before aid and investment could resume. Tsvangirai was headed to Britain, Germany, France, Norway, Denmark, Sweden and Belgium.

State radio in Zimbabwe reported over the weekend that foreign minister, Simbarashe Mumbengegwi, another Mugabe appointee, has planned his own outreach visit with EU officials in the hope of discussing normalising relations but was told that Tsvangirai should take the lead. The EU said on Monday that it was unaware of any meeting with Mumbengegwi, while talks with Tsvangirai on Thursday and Friday had been scheduled for weeks.

EU spokesman, John Clancy, said it was too early to put normalisation on the agenda. 'The talks will focus on hearing out the Zimbabwean premier and how the unity government intends to meet commitments to reform and turn the country around.' Clancy also said 'the EU remains ready to offer more humanitarian aid but wants to see good progress made by the unity government before any decision can be made to lift sanctions.'

16th June 2009 – 'Shocked when the officials from the White House protocol department informed him he was barred' – Lebo Nkataso, ZW News

Zimbabwe's tourism minister was barred from meeting US President Barack Obama because he is from President Robert Mugabe's ZANU-PF party, it has emerged.

Walter Mzembi is part of a delegation led by Prime Minister Morgan Tsvangirai which is currently on a world tour to rally support for the unity government formed in February. The minister said he was shocked when the White House protocol department informed the delegation that he was barred from attending the White House meeting with Obama on Friday last week.

Mzembi and Tsvangirai met to discuss Obama's behaviour and its implications on the attempt to re-engage the West, the state-run Herald newspaper reported.

The paper quoted an unnamed official travelling with the prime minister as saying, 'No explanation was given for leaving him out. It gives rise to the unfortunate impression that President Obama is openly biased against ZANU-PF because he can't even talk to a minister from that party, even though he is representing all Zimbabweans. The oddity of this gesture was more so because earlier Minister Mzembi had audience with US secretary of state, Hillary Clinton.'

Also travelling with the prime minister is Elton Mangoma, the economic planning and investment minister. The White House had no objections to the two who are members of the MDC factions.

After a meeting with Tsvangirai, Obama said of President Mugabe, 'I think I have made my views clear. He has often not acted in the best interests of the Zimbabwean people and has been resistant to the kinds of democratic changes that need to take place. We now have a democratic change that needs to take place. We also have a power-sharing agreement that shows promise and we want to do everything we can to encourage the kinds of improvement, not only on human rights, rule of law, freedom of the press and democracy that is so necessary, but also on the economic front. The people of Zimbabwe need very concrete things: schools that are reopened, a healthcare delivery system that can deal with issues like cholera or HIV/AIDS and an agricultural system that is able to feed its people as before.'

16th June 2009 – 'Shopper's paradise for the select few'

Harare – Zimbabwe's once-deserted supermarkets are full again after the country reined in its world record hyper-inflation. But there is no wait at the tills as most people just can't afford to buy anything and what I saw for myself last Christmas was that the US dollar was being well used. People all seem to manage to get certain dollars, but never did the tills have change; they insisted they had 'the value of another item' or they would make over hand and fist!

To the poorer type, whose money had been removed from the banks, or in other words, the zeros were taken away from bank notes – my pension had been reduced to nothing following the six months I had been away – simply can't afford anything anymore.

'It is a luxury for those who have money to buy,' said Miriam Chituku, a 36-year-old mother of three holding a loaf of bread in the working class suburb of Chituku outside the capital. 'The shops are full but to us there is no difference because we cannot afford the goods. They are as good as non-existent. We only see them on the shelves.' Chituku said her family has tea without milk, in the late morning, she skips lunch and they eat dinner as their only meal in order to stretch their income from a vegetable store in the township.

But in Harare's leafy suburbs, supermarkets are a shopper's paradise. The 'select few' deciding between imported haddock fillets or full-shell mussels. 'You can get everything you want here,' said Josephine Marucchi, a housewife from the posh suburb of Mount Pleasant, pausing to choose from the various brands of cheese before completing the sentence, 'as long as you have money. It's completely different from last year (2008) when people had money and the shops were empty.'

The centre of the shop looked like a gym, stocked with modern exercise gadgets where an assistant explained to a customer how to operate a treadmill.'

Last year, supermarkets across Zimbabwe resembled empty sheds, as local manufacturers either pulled down the shutters or operated at less than half their capacity because hyper-inflation had rendered the local currency unusable. The shortages were exacerbated after the government launched a blitz (I was there) ordering businesses to slash prices, with long-ruling President Mugabe accusing some business of colluding with his Western foes to try to topple him.

Things improved after Mugabe and his one-time rival, Morgan Tsvangirai, formed a unity government in February 2009. The local currency has been abandoned and import restrictions lifted, which has erased the hyper-inflation estimated in multiples of billions last year. Now prices *all* in US dollars or the South African rand are actually declining but more than half of the population still depend on the international food aid. Workers are earning $100 a month and yet the poverty datum line is put conservatively at $437 so there is certainly a deficit of nearly $350.

Most families have to reprioritise their needs. In most cases, basics have become luxuries.

Zimbabwe's biggest employer is the government, which is paying workers only $100 a month while it tries to win international support for its plan to revive the economy and civil service, including schools and hospitals. Until the government finds a way of increasing wages, the gap between rich and poor is unlikely to change. The painfully obvious disparities have become a fact of life, creeping even into local music, 'Some die from overeating,' goes a hit song by Chiwoniso Marire called *Others Die of Hunger*.

'The Tribunal has jurisdiction over Zimbabwe, the judges do not' – Alex Bell, SADC

Justice minister, Patrick Chinamasa, has slammed a SADC Tribunal ruling meant to put a stop to the ongoing wave of farm invasions, saying orders from the human rights have no legal force in Zimbabwe.

In an interview with the Zimbabwean Times, Chinamasa warned the legal regional block's 'human rights court' against trying to lecture Mugabe on restoring the rule of law to the continuing land attacks. He also condoned the attacks that have left thousands of farm workers without jobs, saying that they are 'a justified protest against unfair land ownership by the white descendents of colonial-era settlers'.

The SADC Tribunal this month ruled that the Zimbabwean government had refused to comply with the regional court's order to allow 78 commercial farmers to keep their land. Last year the Tribunal ruled that they could keep their land and remain on it, which was targeted for resettlement under Robert Mugabe's land reform scheme.

The order was meant to offer legal protection against future land invasions and the government was also supposed to protect the farmers from future land attacks. But Mugabe unsurprisingly dismissed the November verdict and publicly condoned the renewed offensive against the country's remaining farmers. The physical attacks and fast-track prosecution of farmers intensified in the weeks that followed the dictator's speech this year and even the prime minister, Morgan Tsvangirai, went as far as to downplay the severity of the ongoing land invasions.

The farmers were forced to return to the SADC court this month to seek further action to enforce the court's original ruling and walked away victorious with a new ruling in their favour. The court ruled that the government had not only breached the November ruling but was also in contempt of the regional court. The government was also ordered to make financial compensation to the farmers affected by the land attacks, but when asked if the government would adhere to the new SADC ruling, Chinamasa responded, 'Of course not. The Tribunal has no jurisdiction over Zimbabwe. We are not party to the (SADC) Tribunal protocol.'

The Tribunal concluded its ruling by referring Zimbabwe's contempt to ZADC leaders for consideration of measures to be taken under the SADC Treaty against the government. These measures could include sanctions of expulsion of Zimbabwe from SADC.

Justice for Agriculture (JAG), John Warsley-Warswick, explained on Monday that it was not up to SADC countries to enforce SADC law, adding that SADC is responsible, with Zimbabwe as a SADC member state for the safety and human rights of Zimbabweans.

Zimbabwe, as a signatory to the SADC Treaty, is bound by law to respect the regional bloc's rulings. The government has blatantly used this relationship within the SADC to gain financial support from fellow Southern African nations. But with regard to the SADC rulings on land reform, the government refuses to respect SADC law. SADC itself meanwhile, has remained deafeningly silent on the matter.

The JAG official, meanwhile, expressed great concern for Chinamasa's comments for Zimbabwe's beleaguered farming community, saying it will 'heighten their anxieties'. He continued that there is a 'very real danger that the last of the farmers will be driven off their land' in what he fears will be 'a bloody campaign'.

'ZANU-PF doesn't want any farmers left to bear witness to what they have done and they certainly don't want any unchecked food produced,' Warsley-Warswick said. He added, 'It is very worrying, especially in a country that needs food as badly as Zimbabwe does.'

'Maybe the following will teach our 'elite' a lesson or hint!' – BBC News

Kenya ministers have been told to give up their plush cars and limit themselves to a single vehicle with a small fuel-efficient engine. All extra cars and those with an engine capacity of more than 1800cc will be confiscated and sold by September. The finance minister said their sale will be used to house those still displaced after last year's post-election violence.

Some 300,000 fled their homes and thousands still live in camps but Uhuru Kenyatta, who is a finance minister in the power-sharing government that took office in April 2008 after a deal to end violence, did not give any further details about how the internally displaced people would benefit.

The large power-sharing cabinet has come in for criticism for its cost to the taxpayer and the BBC's Nail Mwakugu in the capital Nairobi, says people are sceptical about whether ministers will actually give up their flash cars.

A similar proposal was made in last year's budget but was never carried out. However, Mr Kenyatta arrived at parliament to deliver his budget in a relatively modest Volkswagen Passat (2000cc) rather than the 3000cc Mercedes S-Class usually favoured by ministers, our reporter says. He also announced a moratorium on the purchase of government vehicles and said officials with a car would be given a monthly fuel allowance.

'I have discussed all these measures with the prime minister and the president and let me clarify, no official vehicle is exempt,' he was quotes as saying by Kenya's Capital FM.

Twelve

16ᵗʰ June 2009 – 'Vast swathes of Zimbabwe were last night plunged into darkness'

Vast swathes of the country were last night plunged into darkness after Zesa, Kariba and Hwange power stations inexplicably lost all power supplies from Mozambique's Hidroeléctrica de Cahora Bassa and from the Zambian power grid, leaving large chunks of the country without electricity.

Zesa chief executive engineer, Ben Rafemoyo, last night said that they had fallen back onto emergency supplies from South Africa's Eskom to power the southern region, which remained unaffected by last night's blackout. He said the emergency supplies were enough to power parts of the country up to the midlands only. However, he said that normal power and service could be expected some time this morning once Kariba power station was back online.

Little does the world realise, but the wonderful Zimbabweans with all their troubles have this as a regular occurrence. No electricity or water!

At the time of going to press, much of the capital, Mazai, Norton, Chitungwiza and large parts of the country going east to Mutare (Portuguese border) were still in darkness as Zesa engineers tried to restore normal power supplies.

Supplies had, however, been restored to Harare's central business district and a few suburbs in the city. Chinhoyi also did not have electricity.

The blackout occurred about two hours before hitting Harare and its environs around 8.20 am.

'We are still trying to recover but suffice to say there has definitely been a system failure that has affected Hwange and Kariba power stations. The supply from Hidroeléctrica de Cahora Bassa is also down and we have also lost supplies that come from the Zambian power grid. We are using emergency supplies from Escom in South Africa and so there is power from just after Midlands Province up to the eastern borders. Once we recover supplies from Kariba, because Kariba does not take time to bring back online, we will know exactly what has happened. I am at the control centre right now and we are also in darkness. We are rushing to bring Kariba back right now and we should be near normality by morning,' Engineer Rafemoyo said last night. With the process of recovery, more areas would have normal supplies as work progressed.

The loss of supplies from key regional partners like Mozambique's HCB and the Zambia Electricity Supply Company raised fears that Zesa had been cut off because of a mounting external debt. The utility owes its regional suppliers over US\$57 million that occurred in March last year. This is on the back of average monthly revenue collections of US\$5 million as Zesa gets customers to pay their bills, which the latter feel are unduly high. This has prompted the utility to threaten to cut off supplies to defaulters.

Zesa last week announced that the government had given it the green light to disconnect those who have not paid their bills since February this year. The power utility has announced that defaulters will be cut off from 20th June. There were also fears that the blackout could be linked to threats by Zesa workers to go on strike over a management decision to slash their allowances.

The workers gave the company up until 20th June – the same date that Zesa gave as when they would switch off defaulting customers – to reinstate the conditions of service that were unilaterally trimmed last month. However, Engineer Rafemoyo was quick to assure the public that the blackout had nothing to do with the internal administrative issues affecting the utility.

'No, it definitely has nothing to do with that. A blackout of this magnitude cannot have anything to do with internal and domestic matters such as that.'

'If Mr Rafemoyo fails to pay his bill, that cannot take out the power supplies to such large sections of the country,' the Zesa boss said.

15th June 2009 – 'No different from Poland' – Tim Reid, The Times, in Washington

Morgan Tsvangirai compared himself to Nelson Mandela yesterday as he sought to explain his decision to share power with Robert Mugabe.

Speaking to The Times before his visit to Europe this week, the prime minister of Zimbabwe, who is facing growing criticism that he has become apologist for the regime, said that he now had a 'functioning, working relationship' with Mr Mugabe, 85, the man who in recent years had him jailed, beaten and threatened with death and whose 29-year rule has led his country to near collapse.

'I can't stand up and defend his past,' Mr Tsvangirai said in his Washington hotel, minutes after an oval office meeting with President Obama. 'But I want to say here that the situation in Zimbabwe is no different from Poland where the solidarity organisation was in cohabitation with the communists in the transaction. Nelson Mandela went for two years with the former apartheid leaders in order to create the transition in South Africa. Transitions of this nature are very important because you soft-land a crisis in order to create a better basis for democratic development.'

As mentioned earlier, Mr Tsvangirai is on a three-week world tour, during which he hopes to persuade the West to increase aid to his shattered nation. In recent days, and to a sceptical audience, he has argued that Zimbabwe is now 'on an irreversible transition to democracy', a case he will make when he arrives in London on Saturday. Under the terms of his power-sharing agreement, Mr Mugabe has retained control of the police, military, intelligence service, media and criminal justice system. Opposition leaders are still being arrested and white-owned farms are still allegedly being seized.

Sitting in on the interview was a US-based representative of the Herald – the Mugabe-controlled state newspaper which has belittled Mr Tsvangirai's trip each day since he left the country a

116

week ago. The reported insisted our reciting long questions read verbatim from copious long-hand notes appeared to be an attempt to take up the time allocated for the interview.

Mr Tsvangirai insisted that Mr Mugabe now understood the dire problems facing the people of Zimbabwe, where hyper-inflation has destroyed the economy. AIDS is rampant and the country's infrastructure is in ruins.

'He is not stupid, he's astute and he is clear about what he wants to do. We both appreciate the fact that we have a national responsibility to define the destiny of the country. Only through working together are we able to respond to our people's needs.'

Such a stance from Mr Tsvangirai, who for a decade was Mr Mugabe's implacable foe, is threatening his credibility and drawing criticism from reformists, who say he should be speaking out more boldly against Mr Mugabe's abuses.

The prime minister, however, appears to believe the best way to achieve reform is from within, just as Mr Mugabe realised that.

'He needed to share power if he was going to make progress. We have shifted the arena of our struggle in order to have full democracy in our country,' he said.

Mr Tsvangirai appeared optimistic and did not talk about the death of his wife in a car crash earlier this year; an accident he survived. He insisted that the country's inflation rate had dropped from 500 billion% to 3%, a claim not supported by economists. He left the meeting with Obama with a promise of $73 million in humanitarian aid 'and no development aid', a reflection of Washington's decision to limit its assistance and keep sanctions in place until Mr Mugabe is out of power.

'I must admit when I came to Washington, I found the mood to be very sceptical,' Mr Tsvangirai said. 'But as time went on and we explained our case, I think that there has been an appreciation that Zimbabwe is in a post-conflict situation.

'Credibility of the MDC depends on targeted support' – Graham Boyton and Philip Sherwell, The Telegraph

Zimbabwe has slashed its inflation rate from 500 billion% in just three months to 3%. Mr Morgan Tsvangirai has kicked off a three-week international tour seeking political and financial support for the stricken country. He will tell Gordon Brown this week in London that his party, the Movement for Democratic Change, needs to be seen to be delivering economic progress for ordinary Zimbabweans to win the next election.

Mr Tsvangirai is the prime minister in a fractious coalition government headed by his bitter rival, President Robert Mugabe, the country's long-time autocratic leader.

Western governments are still extremely wary of dispatching more aid to a country subjected to a reign of terror by Mr Mugabe's militia and reduced to an economic basket case by the disastrous policy of seizing farms of white landowners. But The Telegraph has learned that Mr Tsvangirai will urge the US and European donors to increase their support to boost the MDC's standing in Zimbabwe. He will tell them that credibility of the MDC depends on life improving for Zimbabweans and will request 'targeted support', according to allies of the prime minister.

He will also try to assure them that continued stability before the next election will ensure a 'landslide defeat' for Mr Mugabe's ZANU-PF and that international pressure will prevent the president's allies in the military from intervening to overturn the result. Mr Tsvangirai is already arguing that the country has made dramatic economic progress since the MDC joined the coalition, to 3% currently.

'We have reopened schools, reopened hospitals, we have begun to give the people not only hope but also confidence that the future is bright and that this process is irreversible,' he said.

The runaway inflation was abandoning the worthless Zimbabwean dollar in favour of the US dollar and South African rand. Food is back on empty shelves, petrol is available again and some exiles, black and white, are talking about returning home.

Mr Tsvangirai started his world tour in Washington with a meeting with Barack Obama on Friday, where he received praise from the president.

'He is going to continue to provide us with direction and ways in which he thinks will be helpful and I am grateful to him for his courage and I'm looking forward to being a partner with him for years to come,' the US president said.

Ending a five-day visit in the US, Mr Tsvangirai told reporters that he had told Mr Obama that the country 'is coming out of a political conflict and economic collapse and the new political dispensation we have crafted is an attempt to arrest the decay.'

Through a transitional arrangement, Mr Tsvangirai will tour European capitals, including London, this week. But while the prime minister is putting the best interpretation on recent developments, there are ominous signs. Mr Mugabe has not even allowed Mr Tsvangirai to move into the official residence for his new office; land invasions of the few remaining white-owned farms are continuing, as are militia attacks on MDC supporters and there is a constant speculation about a coup by military and political hardliners. Even Mr Tsvangirai supporters fear that they are being used by Mr Mugabe simply to provide a veneer of respectability and will be dumped when the president sees fit.

The prime minister, who has frequently been in jail and beaten up, counters it is better for the MDC to be inside the government than outside. The government says it needs £6.1 billion to rebuild the shattered economy, which it forecasts will grow 2.8% in 2009. Britain announced another £15 million in humanitarian aid to Zimbabwe for health and food projects in April after the unity government was formed.

Asked whether Mr Brown would give further aid after meeting Mr Tsvangirai, a Foreign Office spokesman said, 'In principal we stand ready to help Zimbabwe's new government and administration to bring about much needed change. But the extent and nature of this support will be determined by the actions the new government and administration takes on the ground to reverse the political, economic and social decline. In particular, we and the international community will be looking for full and equal access to humanitarian assistance, commitment to macroeconomic stabilisation, democratic process and respect for internationally accepted standards of human rights.'

15th June 2009 – 'Assess foreign exchange and the state of international reserves'

The head of the International Monetary Fund team arrived in Zimbabwe on Monday to assess the coalition government's economic policies and the country's still-enormous humanitarian needs.

'The IMF staff mission will look into the country's economic performance since the setting up of the inclusive government in February,' an official close to the delegation told AFP.

The delegation will, among other things, hold meetings with officials (government) and representatives of industry. The IMF mission is the third this year and follows the Fund's decision last month to resume technical aid to Zimbabwe, which for years has barred any assistance. The rest of the IMF team will arrive in a week's time and the mission is to wrap up its work on 29th June, officials said.

According to the IMF team, it will assess foreign exchange inflows and the state of international reserves and will meet with the World Food Programme about the country's food needs. The mission will also discuss the United States's $718 million humanitarian appeal that includes food aid for six million Zimbabweans, about half the population.

In February, long-time rivals President Robert Mugabe and Prime Minister Morgan Tsvangirai, formed an inclusive government following a deal brokered by former South African president, Thabo Mbeki. The new government is seeking $8.5 billion dollars to revive the shattered economy and the civil service, including schools and hospitals, but major Western nations have withheld aid demanding to see more significant political reforms.

Tsvangirai met on Friday with the US president, Barack Obama, at the White House, but left with little new aid. To date the new government has raised over $1 billion coming from African organisations, but that includes little direct financial support of the government. The South African country currently owes the IMF US$133 million, according to the Fund.

Zimbabwe's economy has been shrinking for years, contracting by 6.1% in 2007. This year the Finance Ministry predicts the economy will grow by at least 4%.

Interactive Forum

Prime Minister Morgan Tsvangirai plans to use the internet to promote transparency and inform the country's citizens of the activities and initiatives of the newly created coalition government.

The launch of the website coincides with the swearing in with Morgan Tsvangirai becoming a member of parliament in Zimbabwe's House of Assembly.

In his address to parliament, Mr Tsvangirai said, 'In this spirit of openness, today we are launching the prime minister's website, which will not only serve to keep the people informed about the activities of our government, but will also provide an interactive forum for the people to participate and contribute to the affairs of government. The address of this website is: www.zimbabweprimeminister.org.'

The website will be made interactive and will encourage citizens to actively participate and share ideas and opinions.

'Highlights: The chaos, violence and thuggery of land reform' –Bulawayo

A Zimbabwean judge has ordered the eviction of top government official, John Nkomo, from a lucrative 'safari lodge and farm' which he seized from another man several years ago.

Justice Francis Bere, sitting in the High Court in Bulawayo last Thursday, ordered the deputy sheriff to evict Nkomo, who is also chairman of President Robert Mugabe's ZANU-PF party, from Jizima Lodge in Matabeleland, North Province, to pave the way for businessman Langton Masunda.

'You are required and directed to eject the said John Handa Nkomo and all persons claiming through him, his goods and possessions whatsoever from and out of all occupation of the said ground and/or premises,' Bere said in the order.

Jizima, a farm seized from a white farmer during the height of Mugabe's chaotic land redistribution programme, had been the subject of an ownership wrangle after Nkomo, then land reform minister, allocated the form to Masunda about five year ago, only to try to grab the property allegedly after discovery at a later stage that the farm had a successful safari lodge on it.

The dispute between Nkomo and Musunda over the lodge nearly turned fatal a month ago when the young brother to Masunda was shot five times by a security officer employed by Nkomo. The security officer, Eddie Sigoge, was charged with attempted murder and unlawful possession of a firearm and was granted bail when he appeared in court in Bulawayo last month.

In ordering Nkomo's ejection, Bere upheld an earlier ruling he made in 2006 where he found the attempts by Nkomo to cancel his original offer of the lodge to Masunda illegal. The wrangle over Jizima Lodge only helps to highlight the chaos, violence and thuggery that have characterised Mugabe's land reforms, which were to benefit poor black peasant farmers deprived of arable land in 2000 'on paper' by former colonial governments, but most of the best farms seized from whites ended up in the hands of Mugabe's officials, their relatives and friends.

Land reform has led to hunger after Mugabe's government failed to provide blacks resettled on former white farms with inputs and skills training to maintain production. Poor performance in the mainstay agricultural sectors has also had far-reaching consequences as hundreds of thousands of people have lost jobs, while the manufacturing sector starved of inputs from the sector is operating below 15% of capacity.

'Patience is wearing thin' – David Smith in Harare

'Things are getting a little better,' Tsvangirai tells the US and Europe. At home they are not so sure.

Three months ago, Davidson Makhado took his first job as a teacher to play the part in reopening schools in Zimbabwe. The 35 boys in Makhado's class at Ellis Robbins School in Harare are eager to learn African history but only have a single text book between them, so before each lesson, Makhado makes extensive notes, which he then painstakingly dictates.

'It is very difficult to teach,' the 25-year-old said. 'The children complain about it a lot.'

The stuttering revival of the education sector is a litmus test of Zimbabwe's faltering and fragile progress since President Robert Mugabe and Prime Minister Morgan Tsvangirai's inclusive government was formed in February.

Teaching used to be a well paid profession when Zimbabwe's schools were the envy of Africa. Not any more. Like all civil servants, teachers are now earning an allowance of $100 per month. Some are still waiting for their first payment to come through.

'$100 is very, very little,' Makhado said. 'If I was in my own home paying $60 rent and electricity and water bills, I certainly couldn't afford it, so I'm having to stay with my brother.'

Zimbabweans seem willing to give the government a chance of compromise but patience is wearing thin.

'The unity government at the moment is running at 80% failure,' Makhado said. 'The things we want to be addressed are not yet addressed. The salaries of civil servants are pathetic and not enough for servants and people with families and extended families. Morgan Tsvangirai still has a lot to do to prove he can deliver something to us!'

The price of failure will be the loss of people like Makhado from the country's schools.

'If the salary remains like this, I'll be sorry and I will see to it that I resign and change profession to do something better than this. I'll give them 18 months at most.'

Tsvangirai, leader of the Movement for Democratic Change, set off yesterday for a tour of Europe and the US seeking to persuade Barack Obama, Gordon Brown and other heads of state that this tormented nation is now on an upward trajectory.

Yesterday he said in The Netherlands that he was not touring with a begging bowl but with a base of rock bottom, it could hardly be getting worse. Last year Zimbabwe, once the region's biggest economy after South Africa, stared total collapse in the face: hyper-inflation was at a world record 500 billion%, unemployment at more than 97%, shops and supermarkets empty, five million people in need of international food aid and nearly 5,000 dead from the worst cholera outbreak in 15 years.

A superficial normality has since returned to the streets of the capital, Harare, with traffic flowing, people actually shopping and children walking to school again in smart uniforms. The city hosted a jazz festival at the weekend and is striving to rebrand itself as a tourist destination during next year's football World Cup in neighbouring South Africa.

'Mugabe's Zimbabwe', however, is a place where appearances can be deceptive.

'If you're confused about Zimbabwe, you haven't been here long enough,' said Eddie Cross, Policy Co-ordinator General for MDC.

On the surface it looks pretty civilised but look beneath the surface and the human situation is still very grim. Hospitals have reopened with up to 90% of doctors and nurses, many of them receiving top-up wages from the British government aid. But half of basic drugs are unavailable. Pregnant women who need caesarean sections in rural Bulima must walk 12 miles to the nearest hospital, according to the development agency, CAFOD.

Inflation has been neutralised after the US dollar and South African rand were adopted as national currencies and food is back on the supermarket shelves, but the economy is broke, agriculture is in crisis and many people still can't afford a loaf of bread, they now buy individual slices.

Incidents of cholera have been curtailed, after a huge effort by aid agencies, but access to clean water is limited, sewage pipes continue to burst and Oxfam warns of an 'eight in ten chance' of a fresh cholera outbreak this year.

Rumours abound of dissent in the army and police amid signs that Mugabe's grip on the state apparatus might finally be weakening but invasions and beatings on white-owned farms have accelerated and there is no respite from the arbitrary arrests of journalists and human rights activists.

Schools, of which only 10% were open last year, are back to 100% with 12,000 teachers having returned to their jobs! But one textbook is shared on average by 30 children in rural classrooms, which are often in disrepair. Universities are in even worse condition and effectively closed.

'Teachers are in school but the truth is they are not teaching,' said one head who did not wish to be named.

'They maintain a presence because they don't want their allowance to be cut off but real teaching is not taking place,' Raymond Majongwe, secretary general of the Progressive Teachers' Union of Zimbabwe said. 'The teachers are there but there is nothing in terms of teaching and learning materials.'

But he also struck an upbeat note in that the unity government has brought back food and smiles for many Zimbabweans.

'In the past six months we have smelt democracy. As a union we have been able to go to places where we have never been before without being arrested, but we can be optimistic only if the correct people ultimately take the reins.'

The chief concern for most Zimbabweans is money. Just 6% of the workforce has a job. The US dollar and South African rand have stabilised the economy but excluded many citizens, especially in rural areas. Oxfam believes that currencies have caused poverty to increase possibly even double and forced companies to close with banks also.

Stephen Maengamhuru, 60, a pastor in the city of Mutare in Eastern Zimbabwe, said, 'Scratch the surface and people in the rural areas certainly have no chance to get dollars. I had to give my grandmother dollars to go to a grinding mill because she couldn't get any money anywhere. Most people are relying on a son and daughter working in town to pitch up with money. The unity government was our hope for survival but we have a lot of principals dragging their feet and throwing spanners in the works.'

Families cannot even afford to bury their dead. Hospital mortuaries, intended to store 20 corpses, have become overcrowded with five times that amount. Some bodies have reportedly been nibbled by rats. Harare hospital was recently forced to clear its mortuary of corpses unclaimed for up to six months and give them paupers' burials.

Some women have turned to prostitution. Vanessa, 22, standing at a notorious pick-up point in the daytime, said 'We want to survive with our children, pay rent and take care of our children. Some days I can earn $40 – $50. Other days I earn nothing. I have a three-year-old daughter and I need the money for her.'

Many people see the unity government as their last hope. It remains delicately balanced between Mugabe's ZANU-PF party and Tsvangirai's MDC. A trial of strength is underway between Mugabe's hard power, the army and the police and Tsvangirai's soft power with ministries such as education and health.

David Coltart, the MDC education minister, said 'If we can deliver our health and education then in the mind of millions of parents, the MDC will be associated with delivering. The counter to that is if we fail, we will be seen as no different from ZANU-PF. There is no doubt in my mind that there are elements trying to set us up to fail.'

He added, 'We are dealing with a partner that doesn't know what democracy means and has been dragged into this process is almost irreversible.'

'Optimists hope the ZANU-PF hierarchy will accept an amnesty and pay-off from Tsvangirai to step down. Pessimists fear that they will lash out, but they see power ebbing away,' Eddie Cross of the MDC said. 'The people who have run this country as a military junta, killing and maiming thousands and marginalisation. They are going to fight back from a near-death experience. The patient is recovering slowly but remains in a critical condition and the danger of a relapse is real.'

21st May 2009 – 'Mugabe suffers rare setback in power struggle with MDC' – Daily Telegraph, UK

President Robert Mugabe suffered a rare defeat on Thursday when his opponents in the Movement for Democratic Change won control of key positions in Zimbabwe's government.

The new coalition between Mr Mugabe and Morgan Tsvangirai, the prime minister and MDC leader, has suffered paralysis and deadlock. In particular, the two sides have clashed over provincial governorships, all five of the vacant ambassadorial posts and control of the Power Reserve Bank.

Yesterday, the dispute was partially resolved in favour of the MDC. Mr Tsvangirai announced that the parties of the two factions will have six of the ten governorships and all five of the vacant ambassadorial jobs. In addition, Mr Mugabe has agreed to allow Mr Bennett, the MDC Treasurer, to become agriculture minister and the IMF to assist Zimbabwe for the first time since 2003.

'We recognise that progress has been made and continues to be made with respect to rebuilding Zimbabwe and having a positive impact on the lives of the people,' said Mr Tsvangirai.

But the two sides remain deadlocked over the most important matter – control of the Reserve Bank, which has the key to responsibility for economic policy. Last year Mr Mugabe reappointed its controversial governor, Gideon Gono. His policies are blamed for Zimbabwe's collapse into hyper-inflation and economic ruin. Western donors have demanded Mr Gono's removal before any aid can be released. One diplomat in Harare called Mr Gono, 'the destroyer of Zimbabwe's economy'.

Mr Mugabe, however, has insisted on keeping him in office. The president is also protecting another notorious ally, Johannes Tomara, the attorney general. He is overseeing a new wave of land seizures and the arrest of MDC activists and journalists.

Mr Tsvangirai wants both men removed. The dispute will now go to the regional African bodies who serve as guarantors of Zimbabwe's power-sharing agreement.

Mr Gono is fighting back by trying to have Tendai Biti, the finance minister from the MDC, sacked for allegedly breaking foreign currency rules.

In a letter seen by the Daily Telegraph, Mr Gono accuses Mr Biti of 'endangering my life and that of my children and family' by 'harassment, false justifications, victimisation, malice and misrepresentations'.

In an interview with the Daily Telegraph, Mr Biti dismissed all these accusations. Despite his appointment as finance minister, he still does not feel confident enough to work in his own office in Harare, fearing the rooms may be bugged. Instead he meets visitors in a small office.

'I will not be diverted from what I am doing. I have a job to do and not in half measures,' he said.

Mr Biti urged the West to support Zimbabwe's new government with financial aid.

'The West is being unscientific and historical,' he said. 'What needs to be understood is that if this experiment fails, we have no cheaper alternative, no cheaper option. If the West doesn't come in, the price of undoing the mess will be much higher. We have seen this in places like Liberia and look at the cost of Somalia? How will anyone reconstruct Somalia?'

Article by Constantine Chimakure

The war of attrition between finance minister, Tendai Biti, and Reserve Bank governor, Gideon Gono, has taken a dramatic twist with the Central Bank boss accusing the MDC secretary general of pursuing a vendetta against him after the bank probed allegations of 'rampant' externalisation of foreign currency money laundering in the law firm where Biti is a senior partner.

Gono, in a letter of complaint dated 11th May about personal victimisation and vilification by Biti, alleged that the Central Bank investigated Honey and Blankenberg and uncovered that it had externalised over US$1 million between October 2005 and May 2006. The Central Bank chief said that he was convinced that Biti's fight to have him removed as governor of the Reserve Bank had its background in 'self-interest and protection'.

The governor said the case against the law firm was before the courts, adding that the team members who investigated the matter were now reluctant to testify after seeing the victimisation he was going through.

But yesterday, Biti denied his fight with Gono was personal.

'I have not seen the letter but I want to say I do not have a personal fight with anyone,' Biti told the Zimbabwe Independent. 'I was given a mandate by the government to carry out a job and that job will be done.'

Prime Minister Morgan Tsvangirai also denied seeing the letter, which is addressed to him and was copied to former South African president, Thabo Mbeki and other SADC leaders.

Biti said his mandate was to stabilise the country's macroeconomic fundamentals. 'I must put food on the table of Zimbabweans and I will not be diverted from doing my job by those who think I am fighting for a personal war.'

He said the law should take its course if Honey and Blackenberg externalised large sums of money 'or should I say "foreign currency" as alleged by Gono,' adding that the law firm was known for its reputation and standards.

Documents in the possession of the Independent show how the Central Bank's Financial Intelligence Inspectorate and Evaluation Division and the police investigated the law form, including searches at its office.

The Financial Intelligence Division was called by a whistle-blower on Friday 23rd June 2006, alleging that the law firm was externalising all legal fees charged in foreign currency for mostly external clients. There were fees for registration of trademarks and patents for corporates domiciled outside Zimbabwe. On 27th February 2006, a certain bank team met the whistle-blower again, who insisted that the law firm had external clients who paid in foreign currency that was banked externally and the documentation relating to the transactions were in the form of emails.

The whistle-blower, the documents reveal, claimed the law firm was earning US$30,000 weekly from such services and that a password to a computer programme with the data was only known by Barry Brighton, a lawyer with Honey and Blackenberg. The whistle-blower claimed that every month the law firm deleted records of the transactions from the computer.

Owing to the 'nature and severity' of the alleged offences, the Central Bank called in the police to concentrate on the criminal element of the dealings and the Financial Intelligence Division on the money laundering aspects. It was agreed that the raid on the firm had to be well timed, given that it was 'manned by lawyers whose lifeline depending on defending criminals and hence were expected to firm up against any move with potential to expose them', read one of the documents.

The same day the offices of the firm were searched, it was discovered, among other things, that all documentation for application and registration of patents and trademarks were under the custody of Brighton and Chris Kimberley and that the law firm had been registering patents and trademarks for companies domiciled outside Zimbabwe. This firm levied fees in foreign currency which they diverted to an off-shore account in the Isle of Man.

The documents reveal that law firm wrote two letters to the Central Bank on 31st May 2006 in relation to the payments received abroad. The firm argued that the fees were received on behalf of an external company, Vernon Consultancy, under a sweeping arrangement where funds would be moved from their external accountant. But the Central Bank did not buy the explanation and insisted that available documents showed that they were in full control of the funds.

The firm also argued that they were subcontracted to register trademarks and patents by Vernon Consultancy, but the Central Bank insisted that emails it retrieved reveal that the legal practicalities had registered the patents and trademarks as principals and not agents in a memorandum dated 12th June 2006 to the Central Bank Financial Intelligence Division head, the principal legal advisor.

Thirteen

July 2009

Having just returned from Zimbabwe, it is truly difficult to believe what is going on. Certainly there is food in the shops and most rubbish in our beautiful shopping centres has been removed. Vendors who made the mess seem to have disappeared.

Farmers were still having trouble and the odd murder is being performed.

The heavenly blue skies and climate (which like the rest of the world) is changing slightly – dark evenings at all times and 'sundowner time' at 6.00 pm.

People call for drinks, the servants get the ice buckets filled and the laughter starts and the many heartaches and worries vanish for a while. 'Colonial living' is still in Zimbabwe. Everyone works hard and plays hard the best they can.

'It's not a grant, it's a loan, it attracts interest' – source?

Harare – The International Monetary Fund said on Friday that it had allocated a $510 million loan to Zimbabwe but finance minister Tendai Biti said that the government cannot afford to take the loan.

The allocation follows an agreement by the G20 group of the world's leading economies in April to increase to $750 billion the IMF's support to economies stricken by the world's recession.

But Biti told German Press Agency, DPA, 'It's not a grant, it's a loan and a loan attracts interest. We would be contracting debt when our balance of payment and our debt is very fragile. We have less than US$2 million in import reserves. Our arrears account for 150% of gross domestic product. There is no way we can take that (loan) up in the context of the arrears and the deficit. It would be very imprudent.'

The loan would have been the IMF's first payment to Zimbabwe since 1999, soon after which Robert Mugabe launched a campaign of violent repression, mass seizures of white-owned farms, commercial farmland and economic policies that plunged the economy into chaos and saw the country fall steadily back on its payments to international creditors.

A power-sharing agreement between Mugabe and Morgan Tsvangirai, his pro-democracy opponent but now prime minister, was inaugurated in February and Biti abolished the worthless national currency and introduced the US dollar as legal currency. The action promptly stabilised the country's economy.

'Chinamasa neglected to say that those requirements for ratification were made redundant'

Justice member, Patrick Chinamasa, missed the public this week when he announced Zimbabwe had pulled out of the SADC Tribunal, arguing that the panel was not properly constituted and therefore illegal.

Zimbabwe Lawyers for Human Rights (ZLHR) have said Chinamasa misinformed the public that the Tribunal was illegal and not properly constituted because it was not properly ratified by two thirds of SADC members.

ZLHR argues that Chinamasa's interpretation is wide of the mark because the articles he was relying on have been repealed by an amendment to the SADC Treaty. Article 16 repealed articles 35 and 38 and overrides article 22 of the Treaty, which deals in part with the need to have ratification by two thirds of SADC members. What Chinamasa fails or neglects to mention, or address, is the fact that in 2001 the SADC Treaty was amended so as to make the SADC Tribunal an integral part of both the Treaty and the institution of SADC.

'The said amendment to the SADC Treaty specifically established the SADC Tribunal and incorporated it into SADC as an integral organ. The amendment went on to refer to the Tribunal Protocol and categorically excluded it from the usual requirements for ratification by two thirds before it could come into force and effect,' ZLHR said.

ZLHR added 'Honourable Chinamasa and/or his legal advisors neglected, or failed, to appreciate that these requirements for ratification were thus made redundant by the said SADC agreement on the amendment to the Protocol at their meeting in Lunda, Angola on 3rd October 2002.'

SADC member heads of state and government and/or their duly authorised representatives agreed that it was not on Wednesday.

The state-controlled Herald newspaper reported that justice minister Patrick Chinamasa had delivered a letter to the registrar of the SADC Tribunal to formally withdraw Zimbabwe from any legal proceeding involving the Regional Court.

Chinamasa said, 'There was never any basis upon which the Tribunal could seek jurisdiction on Zimbabwe based on the Protocol, which has not been ratified by two thirds of the total membership of SADC.'

It is widely believed this is happening because ZANU-PF is very unhappy with recent Tribunal decisions in favour of white commercial farmers who are fighting the government against the acquisition of their farms. But on Friday the MDC said that it was not aware that a decision to pull out of the Tribunal had been made.

Gordon Moyo, the Minister of State in Prime Minister Morgan Tsvangirai's office, told SW Radio Africa that he only heard about it in the press and revealed that neither the prime minister nor the cabinet were consulted on the matter.

Moyo said, 'If a decision had to be made, the decision had to be taken either through the Council of Ministries and I was at the last two or three meetings and nothing of that nature was brought up to the cabinet to make a decision on. You are talking about the policy in relation to other countries, more so in the sub-region. All members of government should be aware of that and should be consulted on such issues.'

The minister said, 'Until there is proper communication on this matter by the justice minister, to me it remains something that is not true. It is too ghastly to be true.'

The MDC said it expected all members of the government to act in unison and bring important issues to the cabinet, or the principals.

'The principal that I work with is not aware of this,' added Moyo.

A second ruling showing the Zimbabwe government in contempt has also been ignored. The Regional Court has now asked the Paragon body to consider enforcement against Zimbabwe at the forthcoming SADC Summit in the DRC.

Fourteen

25th September 2009 – ZW News (the world's leading website on Zimbabwe)

The following address was delivered by Ian Smillie of the Development Diamond Initiative during the Rapaport International Diamond Conference in New York on 10th September 2009:

Less than a month ago, the chair of Kimberley Process told an Agency France Presse reporter in Angola that 'The Kimberley Process is not a human rights organisation. That is what we have the United Nations for.'

Is this true? I suggest that it is not. Human rights and the diamond industry is not new and it cannot be divorced from the Kimberley Process and the effort to halt conflict diamonds. It is worth reviewing the history of conflict diamonds because from the very beginning, the Kimberley Process was all about human rights. Let me go through the not-so-distant history.

The war in Angola – much of it fuelled by diamonds and half a million dead. The wars in DRC – heavily fuelled by diamonds and 3.3 million dead, if not more, from direct and indirect causes. In Liberia, Charles Taylor took control of his own country's meagre diamond resources and then fostered a proxy war in Sierra Leone, a war characterised by banditry and horrific brutality waged primarily against civilians and fuelled almost entirely by diamonds. 75,000 people or more lost their lives. Rebel butchery left thousands of women, men and children without hands and feet, disfigured physically and psychologically for life.

No human rights issues here?

The second paragraph of the Kimberley Process preamble speaks of 'the devastating impact of conflicts, fuelled by the trade in conflict diamonds', of the peace, safety and security of people in affected countries and the systematic and gross human rights violations that have been perpetrated in such conflicts.

I start with this because it is important to remember why the Kimberley Process was created. It was created first and foremost to end the phenomenon of conflict diamonds and to prevent it from returning. The ending of those conflicts was clearly about human rights. That did not need to be spelt out beyond the Kimberley Process preamble because nobody imagined at the time that some governments in pursuit of the internal controls required by the Kimberley Process also aimed to protect the legitimate interests of the diamond industry and the millions of people who depend on it for a livelihood, most of them in very poor countries, and it offered a hope. A hope that diamonds might, in the war-torn countries, be transformed from a negative to a positive – into something that might provide revenue, jobs and hope.

The Kimberley Process has accomplished a lot. The very fact that the Kimberley Process negotiations helped choke diamond supplies to rebel movements in Angola and Sierra Leone and contributed to the end of hostilities. The Kimberley Process has the best diamond database in the world and the KPCS is credited by several countries with the growth in legitimate diamond exports and thus of tax revenue.

The Kimberley Process is discussed as a model for other extractive industries and as a model of participation and communication between governments, industry and civil society, all of which play an active and meaningful role in its management. But there was no provision in the Kimberley Process to do what all regulators must do. There was no provision to plug holes, tighten loose bolts and fix the parts that were not working.

A fundamental part of law enforcement is the need to keep one step ahead of the crooks as they figure out new ways and rules and regulations but in the Kimberley Process, there has from the very beginning been a prohibition against 'opening the document'. This is like saying that there can never be any additions to the Magna Carta. We will live in the 13th century for ever.

Problems

Despite these handicaps, for a while there was optimism. Today, almost seven years on, in my view (Ian Smillie) the Kimberley Process is failing badly and would not rate a four out of ten from any serious independent observer.

Accountability is the primary issue. There is no Kimberley Process central authority. Problems are shifted from one internal 'working group' to another. Debates on vital issues drag on for years. There is no voting in the Kimberley Process, all decisions are reached by 'consensus', which in the real world means 'general agreement'. But in the Kimberley Process it means 'unanimity'.

Individuals can, and frequently do, hold up forward movement on anything and everything. Nobody takes any responsibility for action .or inaction, failure or success and nobody is held responsible.

The KPCS peer-reviewed mechanism, which I helped to design, is a disaster. Some reviews are thorough and recommendations are heeded. In many cases, however, recommendations are ignored and there is little or no follow up. Some reviews are completely bogus.

In 2008 a bloated, nine-member team visited Guinea, a country whose diamond industry is beset by corruption, weak diamond control, rotten statistics and almost certain smuggling. Over the last two years, official Guinean diamond exports have increased by a staggering 600%. The Kimberley Process team spent less than two hours outside the capital city and its reports remained unfinished for almost 11 months. This is a parody of effective monitoring and sadly it is not an exception.

Angola has obvious human rights problems. Hundreds of thousands of illicit Congolese diamond diggers have been expelled over the past two or three years to the accompaniment of serious human rights abuse. Miners are beaten, robbed, raped and force-marched hundreds of miles. The Kimberley Process has had nothing to say about this because it's not a human rights organisation!

Zimbabwe, rife with smuggling and gross diamond-related human rights abuse, has consumed months of ineffectual internal Kimberley Process debate through 2009. Let me dwell on this for a few moments because it is indicative of so much.

Late in 2008, between 80 and 200 illicit diamond miners were killed by the Zimbabwean armed forces. This was widely reported in the media and by Zimbabwean human rights organisation, Partnership Africa Canada reported on it in March this year (2010) and human rights issued a report in June.

The Kimberley Process was finally shamed into sending a review mission! It found evidence of serious non-compliance with minimum Kimberley Process standards as well as dramatic human rights abuse. The testimony of some victims was so poignant that the Liberian team leader left one of the meetings in tears. The team's interim report recommended inter alia suspension of Zimbabwe from the KPCS, but the suspension recommendation was quickly denounced by the Kimberley Process chair, who told reporters in Harare, before the team's report had even been completed, that the suspension would never happen. Under pressure he has since denied that he ever made the statement.

It is obvious that regional politics are at work and that vetoes are being lined up. Australian diplomats paid quiet visits to the government's team members, recommending against any action that might damage the interests of a diamond mining company with Australian connections in Zimbabwe. For these governments and the others that are currently active behind the scenes, business and politics trump human rights and the very purpose of the Kimberley Process. They trump good management; they trump common sense and decency and the long-term interest of the entire diamond industry.

Other cases of flagrant non-compliance have been ignored until they become media scandals; fraud and corruption in Brazil, Ivorian conflict diamonds smuggled through neighbouring countries. In two of Africa's largest diamond producers, Angola and DRC, internal controls are so weak that nobody can be certain where half of the diamonds really come from. Venezuela has a record of shooting artisanal diamond miners, but this has never been discussed in the Kimberley Process, in fact, elaborate measures were taken in 2008 to allow Venezuela to remain a

Kimberley Process participant despite its flagrant non-compliance, on the understanding that it would suspend exports and imports until it had regain control of its diamond industry.

A study by Partnership Africa Canada in May 2009 corroborated by a BBC team that visited Venezuela in August, found that Venezuelan diamonds are still being openly mined and openly smuggled. The Kimberley Process, however, accepted the official Venezuelan position. As a result, for more than four years the Kimberley Process has implicitly sanctioned.

The cost of the Kimberley Process collapse would be disastrous for an industry that benefits so many countries and for the millions of poor countries who depend, directly and indirectly, on it. A criminalized diamond economy would undoubtedly re-emerge and conflict diamonds could soon follow.

The budget of the UN peacekeeping mission in Liberia this year is $561 million. Over $200 million more than the budget of the entire Liberian government. The United Nations peacekeeping operations in Côte d'Ivoire and the DRC have a combined budget of $1.8 billion on peacekeeping but, after seven years, the Kimberley Process can't get anywhere near or close to proper diamond tracking in Angola and the DRC.

The KPCS is too important to fail and it is too important to other countries, companies and people for making believe. Its problems are not insurmountable. They can be fixed. They can even be fixed without a major overhaul, but it will require a degree of honesty, commitment and energy that has so far been absent.

The solutions are straightforward; the Kimberley Process requires explicit reference to human rights in the management of diamond resources. It requires an independent, proactive and efficient body with expertise that can analyse problems and act quickly to correct them, applying meaningful sanctions where necessary. It needs an independent review mechanism. It needs a conflict of interest policy that will refuse parties with commercial or political interests. It needs a good dose of transparency and it needs a voting system instead of a vetoing system.

Too much to ask? Some governments might think so. The industry might think the ideal is not worth fighting for. But remember where we came from. Remember the death, destruction and warfare that was fuelled by diamonds. Remember how this industry, whose product is held by so many as a symbol of love, fidelity and beauty, was tarnished by smuggling, tax evasion, theft and sanctions busting. And remember we already have a global agreement that involved 78 governments, an agreement with a box full of tools that with some fine-tuning are more than capable of dealing with the issues.

Things can change if governments and the industry really want to turn the Kimberley Process from the 'talk shop' it has become into the shining example of responsible management that we thought it would be when we first began to talk about it ten years ago.

16th September 2009 – 'African Consolidated wins Zimbabwe court ruling'

African Consolidated Resources said the High Court yesterday confirmed the company's right of title to claims on the Marange diamond field.

The Zimbabwe government seized ACR's Marange diamond field in October 2006 and allocated the claim to the state-owned Zimbabwe Mining Development Corporation. The seizure, backed by Zimbabwe's military, took place after thousands of illegal miners descended on Marange. African Consolidated Resources had held the claim for less than a year before its confiscation.

ACR has attempted to work with all elements of the Zimbabwean government in order to agree a joint venture with the government or parties nominated by them.

The company said in a statement released in the UK today, 'The Zimbabwe government has never given a formal reason for the seizure of ACR's diamond claim in Eastern Zimbabwe.'

They added that following the group's success in the Zimbabwe High Court, they remain committed to dialogue with the government.

At least 200 people, mainly illegal miners, have been killed by Zimbabwean security forces in Marange. New York-based Human Rights Watch, said in a report on 26th June, 'The Zimbabwean military use the forced labour of children and adults and are torturing and beating local villagers on the diamond fields.'

They added that 'some' income from the sale of diamond fields was going to senior members of President Robert Mugabe's ZANU-PF party. Zimbabwe's mining minister, Obert Mpofu, a member of ZANU-PF, has repeatedly denied wrongdoing in Zimbabwe's state-controlled Herald newspaper.

The Kimberley Process, a diamond industry self-regulating body, has visited Marange twice this year. The Namibia-based body told the Herald on 30th July that Zimbabwe should 'refrain' from selling diamonds for six months or more until minimum standards are met in Marange.

UK-based African Consolidated Resources is listed on the London Stock Exchange AIM markets.

The specification of Kingdom Meikles Africa Ltd took a new twist on Thursday when riot police blocked the company's shareholders from meeting to decide on the future of the group's CEO, Nigel Chanakira.

The shareholders arrived at Meikles Hotel at 10.00 am but found the doors of the conference room locked and guarded by riot police. The chairman of the company, John Moxon, told SW Radio that Chanakira was in hospital in South Africa. Moxon, speaking from South Africa, said the shareholders had called for a meeting to remove Chanakira and his close associates, Callistus Chikonye and Busi Bango. He said the board had resolved they were to be removed from any of the subsidiary boards of the company. They were to be removed because the board felt they were obstructing the process of demerging the (Kingdom) bank from the rest of Meikles.

Moxon said that when the company executives assembled, they were told there was a court order organised by Chanakira and the government to postpone the meeting for two weeks.

'Mr Chanakira,' the chairman said, 'is in Johannesburg. He is allegedly ill, which one of the reasons for the court order. In other words, they were suggesting that for compassionate reasons, the meeting should be postponed. How ill he is I do not know, but I do know from people who spoke to him yesterday, that he managed to conduct his business quite satisfactorily from wherever he was in hospital, so he can't be that ill.'

According to Moxon, Chanakira is in Milpark Hospital in Johannesburg and is believed to be suffering from flu.

The government recently specified Kingdom Meikles as one of the country's largest companies for allegedly externalising foreign currency. The authorisation for the seizure was made by the two ministers of home affairs, Giles Mutsekwa and Kemba Mohadi.

Mutsekwa told SW Radio Africa last week that he authorised this because Moxon had committed a serious crime by externalising US$21 million from Zimbabwe, but Moxon denies externalising the funds and says his lawyers will be taking action against the ministers. He said money was invested outside the country with the approval of the Reserve Bank and the money went through the Reserve Bank into the banking system and then out of the country.

The embattled businessman said he had written evidence about this, although the approval was done years ago, he said.

'These approvals are currently in the hands of the Zimbabwe state president and I am not sure what he is doing with them in terms of advising his people that the approvals were proper. As far as the co. minister is concerned, his comments or his accusations are defamatory and I have handed that over to my lawyer and I imagine they will be taking action against him.'

Fifteen

24th September 2009 – 'Mugabe denies blame for Zimbabwe's woes' – CNN

Zimbabwe president, Robert Mugabe, in a rare interview on Thursday, depicted himself as an African hero battling imperialism and foreign attempts to oust him rather than the widespread perception of a dictator clinging to power at the expense of the welfare of his people and country.

The 85-year-old Mugabe, the only leader of Zimbabwe since it became independent from Britain in 1980, rejected repeated assertions by CNN's Christiane Amanpour that his policies have driven the nation, once known as Africa's 'bread basket' to virtual collapse. Instead Mugabe accused Britain and the United States of seeking to oust him by imposing economic sanctions, saying it grew enough food last year to feed all its people and defended policies that have driven white farmers off their land as properly restoring that land to indigenous Africans.

'The land reform is the best thing (that) could have ever happened to an African country,' said Mugabe, a former revolutionary leader who came to power when white-ruled Rhodesia became black-ruled Zimbabwe. 'It has to do with national sovereignty.'

It was Mugabe's first interview with a Western television network in several years and he appeared to get frustrated with some of Amanpour's direct questioning, repeatedly denying widely accepted evidence and reports on his nation's woes.

Mugabe denied that his ZANU-PF party 'lost' the elections in 2008 that forced him to accept a power-sharing agreement with his chief rival, Morgan Tsvangirai, who is now prime minister.

Violence surrounding the disputed election, much of it against opposition supporters, further damaged Zimbabwe's standing, but Mugabe rejected any blame on Thursday.

'You don't leave power when imperialists dictate that you leave,' he insisted. 'There is regime change. Haven't you heard of the regime change programme by Britain and the United States that is aimed at getting Robert Mugabe out of power and his party out of power?'

He also waved off Amanpour's assertion that the power-sharing arrangement was not working and that political opposition figures are continuing to get harassed and arrested.

Asked about Roy Bennett, a white opposition figure who has yet to be sworn in as agriculture minister a year after formation of the power-sharing government, Mugabe stammered before saying that Bennett faces charges of 'organising arms of war against Zimbabwe'. He had heard that the prosecution lacked evidence in the case, but said he wouldn't agree to swearing in Bennett until after any charges were dropped.

Mugabe also denied any responsibility for harm to the nation from his economic policies, instead blaming what he called 'unjustified and illegal' sanctions that he said were intended to bring regime change and which should be lifted.

'We should have no interference from outside,' Mugabe said.

He continued, saying that most of the sanctions were directed at individuals rather than economic entities. When Amanpour challenged Mugabe by saying most of the sanctions were directed at individuals, Mugabe said she was wrong.

'The US sanctions are real economic sanctions. Have you looked at them?' he said.

Amanpour tried to push the point, saying that outside observers blamed his policies and not sanctions.

'Not everybody says so,' Mugabe cut her off. 'It's not true.'

He also rejected criticism from South African Archbishop, Desmond Tutu, a Nobel Peace Prize winner for his role in the anti-apartheid struggle and who has accused Mugabe of turning Zimbabwe into a 'basket case' and for 'repressing his own people'.

'It is not a basket case at all,' Mugabe said. He later called Tutu's comments 'devilish talk' and added, 'He doesn't know what he's talking about, the little man.'

On the takeover of white-owned farms, a policy blamed for undermining the agriculture section, Mugabe displayed the African nationalist fervour of his revolutionary days.

'Zimbabwe belongs to the Zimbabweans, pure and simple,' he said, then adding that white Zimbabweans, even those born in the country with legal ownership of their land, 'have a debt to pay. They occupied the land illegally. They seized the land from our people.'

When Amanpour pressed him on white farmers being forced off their land, Mugabe shot back, 'Not just off their land – our land. They are British settlers,' he said, later calling them 'citizens of colonisation seizing land from original people, indigenous people of the country.'

Asked if he would run the elections likely to take place in 2011, Mugabe refused to answer but denied he feared defeat and again rejected charges of past electoral wrongdoing.

'Elections don't go smoothly all the time in many countries,' he said, tossing a jab at the United States. 'Look what happened elsewhere. They didn't go smoothly here. Look what happened during the first term of Bush.'

'Swazi king says Harare is on track' – Hivos: People Unlimited website

Peter Fabricius, ? Swaziland's King Mswati III, says, 'Things are going well so far in Zimbabwe and the Southern African Development Community has received no complaints that would require it to intervene.'

He was speaking at the end of an extraordinary summit of the SADC in Sandton on Saturday. The summit was called to seek solutions to the crisis in Madagascar. It decided to appoint former Mozambican president, Joaquim Chissano, to head a high-level team to intensify mediation efforts in Madagascar and to move them outside the country so that ousted president, Mark Ravalomanana, may take part.

Before this, the SADC executive, Tomas Salomao, had said Zimbabwe may also be discussed because a letter written by the prime minister, Morgan Tsvangirai, and deputy prime minister, Arthur Mutambana, to SADC chairman, Jacob Zuma, was to be considered by the SADC ministerial troika on security, which might then refer it to the summit.

In the letter, the two MDC leaders asked Zuma to get the SADC to intervene in their dispute with President Robert Mugabe over several issues, including the appointment of senior officials. But Zuma and Mswati said afterwards that Zimbabwe had not been discussed.

'The Zimbabwe issue is a different issue,' Mswati said. 'But we dealt with that a long time ago and things are going well so far. I went there for a visit not so long ago and saw great progress so it was moving on the right track.'

When a journalist asked how Mswati could say that when there were daily reports of people being abducted and jailed, the Swazi king said 'nothing official'.

'If the SADC were informed officially, it would take up these issues.'

When journalists tried to ask more questions, Zuma said Zimbabwe had not been on the agenda for the summit.

Salomao had said earlier that the Zimbabwean unity government's multi-party Joint Monitoring and Implementation Committee would have to decide, it was unable to deal with the dispute between Mugabe and his two rivals before it would be referred to the SADC.

While the summit was taking place, Tsvangirai was being heckled off the stage in London by disgruntled Zimbabwean expatriates who he had urged to return home to rebuild the country. They were unhappy about his decision to share power with Mugabe and Tsvangirai was on a world tour to drum up support for the unity government.

He told the BBC there had been no choice for Zimbabwe but the unity government and that reform was inevitable and would lead to an election in two years. For his efforts to win support for Zimbabwe, he was greeted with cheers from his erstwhile supporters and threats from Mugabe's ZANU-PF party, which said it would take action against him for undertaking an unauthorised trip.

The Sunday Mail, a pro-Mugabe weekly newspaper, yesterday quoted information secretary, George Charamba as saying his department was investigating whether Tsvangirai had broken the law by going overseas without consulting his fellow cabinet members. British secretary, David Miliband, said Zimbabwe was in desperate need of investment and economic development. Tsvangirai had taken talks with the British prime minister on this day.

24th June 2009 – 'Politics, economy, the land rule of law, corruption, human rights, environment and DRC' – ZW News

Zuma's office had insisted the generals never reported back to Mbeki in writing.

Cape Town – 'NGOs have taken further steps to force the presidency to publish a report by retired army generals into state-sanctioned violence in Zimbabwe, the South African History Archive (SAHA) said on Friday.

They had submitted an internal appeal to President Jacob Zuma's office in terms of the claim Promotion of Access to Information Act, disputing the claim that the document does not exist.

The SAHA, the South African Litigation Centre, the Southern African Centre and South Africa for Survivors of Torture last month invoked the act to get the report, which was commissioned by former president, Thabo Mbeki, into the team to assess the extent of the army's involvement in the political crisis in Zimbabwe. The NGOs said they were convinced that the six generals produced a hard-hitting report that influences the power-sharing deal that Mbeki brokered between Zimbabwe's political rivals last September.

But Zuma's office had insisted the generals never reported back to Mbeki in writing.

Frank Chikane, the Director General in the presidency under Mbeki and Trevor Fowler, who currently holds the post, produced affidavits in which they said there was not only no report, but no supporting documentation on the general's mission. The SAHA said it was hard to believe that they were not asked to document their findings as the mission cost R650,000, according to the Foreign Ministry and this cost the South African Ministry or taxpayer.

'To suggest that this amount of money could be spent and the admitted investigation conducted merely for a one-off oral briefing to be made to the president beggar's belief.'

Consequently the NGO's last resort to obtain the report.

Human rights groups accused President Robert Mugabe of unleashing a systematic campaign of violence on opposition supporters after his ZANU-PF party lost control of parliament to the Movement for Democratic Change in the elections in March 2008. MDC leader Morgan Tsvangirai claimed at least 100 of his supporters were killed.

Friday 4th September 2009 – 'Lacking any legal foundation' – source?

Lawyers for the Zimbabwean farmers who took their cases to the SADC Tribunal have dismissed as 'lacking any legal foundation' the government's move to no longer recognise judgements handed down by the court.

The lawyers, Jeremy Gauntlett and FB Pelser, both South Africa advocates, and constitutional law expert, Professor Jeffrey Jowell, concluded in a written legal opinion that there is no bona fide basis for the contention that the rulings by the Tribunal do not bind the government of Zimbabwe.

Two days ago, the Herald newspaper reported and made public a letter written on 7th August by Justice Patrick Chinamasa, informing the Tribunal that Zimbabwe has formally withdrawn from any legal proceedings involving the court.

Justifying the action, Chinamasa wrote, 'There was never any action or basis upon which the Tribunal could seek or purport to have found justification on Zimbabwe based on the protocol which has not yet been ratified by two thirds of the total membership of SADC.'

'Not true,' say the lawyers. 'Zimbabwe is a signatory to the SADC Treaty and the protocol setting up the SADC Tribunal in terms of article 16 (2) of the Treaty is binding on all SADC members, rendering ratification unnecessary. Further,' argue the lawyers, 'the current attorney general, Johannes Tomara, and his deputy, both formally accepted the jurisdiction of the SADC court earlier this year under oath and in writing.'

'And finally,' they say, 'the government has seconded a senior Zimbabwean judge to serve on the Tribunal, illustrating its acceptance of the Tribunal's legal standing. We note that it is made ten months after the main ruling by the SADC Tribunal in favour of the applicant, Zimbabwe farmers, their workers and families and some three months after the finding by the Tribunal that the Zimbabwe government is acting in defiance of the main ruling and awarding costs against the government of Zimbabwe. It also follows on a Tribunal ruling in favour of a black Zimbabwe farmer, whose land had also been seized under Land Bank legislation, also with a costs order against the government of Zimbabwe.'

The statement, significantly, is made just days in advance of the SADC summit meeting which has been asked by the Tribunal in terms of the latter orders to consider enforcement steps against Zimbabwe as a SADC member.

5th September 2009 – 'More than three million Zimbabweans were placing a huge strain on South Africa's resources' – ZW News

South Africa wants long-running power-sharing negotiations in Zimbabwe to move ahead more quickly, a senior member of South Africa's ruling ANC has said.

Thandi Modise, deputy secretary general, wanted to see a recovery in Zimbabwe that would allow millions of Zimbabweans, who have fled economic meltdown in their country, to return home. She said more than three million Zimbabweans who had crossed the border were placing a huge strain on South Africa's healthcare, education and housing resources.

Zimbabwean president, Robert Mugabe, and his long-time rival, Prime Minister Morgan Tsvangirai of the MDC, formed a unity government in February, but are still wrangling over a power-sharing agreement that could pave the way for reforms.

Years of economic crisis, characterised by record rates of inflation, forced millions of Zimbabweans to seek work in South Africa, where there were bloody clashes last year between economic migrants and South Africans worried about their jobs.

South African president, Jacob Zuma, went to Zimbabwe last week to press Mr Mugabe and Mr Tsvangirai to resolve their differences so that economic aid can flow. As mediator, Zuma has been expected to adopt a more robust line with the feuding Zimbabwean leaders than his predecessor, Thabo Mbeki, who advocated quiet diplomacy but was criticised for being too close to Mugabe.

Modise said South Africa wanted the negotiations between Mugabe and the MDC to pick up pace.

'South Africa as a whole wants to see a Zimbabwe that is beginning to work and to put its citizens first,' she said, 'and that is why we are encouraging the talks between President Robert Mugabe and the MDC to be more positive and to be faster because all of us want to see our countries working as well as they can do,' she told Reuters in an interview on Wednesday during a visit to London.

'Particularly to begin to see a situation in Zimbabwe which will enable Zimbabweans in South Africa and elsewhere in the world to come back to Zimbabwe to rebuild their country,' she said. 'I think there are more than three million Zimbabweans in South Africa.'

She said South Africa could not repatriate the Zimbabweans and 'you cannot turn your back on Zimbabwe. President Zuma will do what he can to mediate, to make sure things are working in Zimbabwe,'

Modise said that last Tuesday, Tsvangirai said he wanted next week's summit of regional leaders to push Mugabe to fulfil the power-sharing agreement and to speed up reforms. Tsvangirai said the South African Development Community meeting in the Democratic Republic of the Congo on 7th September should remove obstacles in the unity government.

Modise was in London to launch the ANC's first foreign branch since the party came to power in 1994.

5th September 2009 – 'EU sees improved relations with Zimbabwe. "It's moving very slowly and we want it to speed up!"' – Nelson Banya, ZW News

Harare – Zimbabwe's relations with the European Union are improving but there will be no direct funding for the Harare government until political talks with the block are concluded, an EU official said last Wednesday.

The EU, one of Robert Mugabe's staunchest critics, imposed sanctions on the veteran ruler and his inner circle and suspended direct aid in 2002 over charges of rights abuses and electoral fraud. Mugabe accuses the EU of punishing him for seizing white-owned farms to resettle landless blacks.

Mugabe and long-term foe, Prime Minister Morgan Tsvangirai, formed a power-sharing government in February in a bid to end a political crisis that followed last year's disputed elections. The new government is working to re-engage the EU and the United States. Western donors have demanded broad political and economic reforms before giving direct aid to the government. The donors currently provide only humanitarian assistance.

Dominique Davoux, the EU Head of Economic Co-operation and Food Security in Zimbabwe, told a business conference in Harare that efforts to restore ties were being made.

'Zimbabwe's international relations are on the mend with bilateral and multilateral re-engagement efforts taking centre stage, starting with the prime minister's visit to Brussels in June,' Davoux said.

'It's moving very slowly and we want it to speed up to deal with areas of concern on both sides.'

The talks between Harare and the EU are meant to resolve the dispute over Harare's and Zimbabwe's human rights records, political reforms and sanctions slapped on Mugabe's previous ZANU-PF government, as well as the resumption of aid.

Davoux said any possible financial assistance to the new unity government, which says it requires about $10 million to rebuild the economy, dependent on the successful negotiations.

'Opportunities for Zimbabwe within the EU-ACP (African, Caribbean and Pacific) partnership framework are premised on normal relations,' Davoux said. 'However, until the political dialogue concludes favourably, our areas of concern to the EU, our current co-operation.'

Tsvangirai's Movement for Democratic Change (MDC) accuses Mugabe's ZANU-PF of not doing enough to convince the Western allies to remove sanctions.

5th September 2009 – 'Partners in the coalition government would have to learn to demonstrate the ability to share power equally'

Harare – A United States Congress delegation visiting Zimbabwe this week has said Washington would only consider removing travel and economic sanctions against President Robert Mugabe and his elite upon the full implementation of Global Political Agreement.

Congressman Gregory Meeks, who is leading the five-member delegation, said partners in the coalition government would have to demonstrate ability to share power equally as agreed in the Global Political Agreement before asking for the removal of sanctions.

Speaking after meeting parliament Speaker, Lovemore Moyo, and leaders of the parliament-driven constitution-making process, Meeks said the regional Southern African Development Community (SADC) should push for the resolution of outstanding matters.

'There are issues in regards to outstanding matters. These are issues which have to be resolved and I am hopeful that SADC and both sides will sit down and resolve the issues agreed upon the GPA and once that happens then I think we will be in a better position to review the matter. That is the challenge for the government,' said Meeks.

Meeks's team, comprising four Democrats and one Republican, is the largest congressional delegation in close to a decade, in what could signal Washington's desire to be more accommodating to Harare. The delegation met Robert Mugabe on Thursday afternoon but both sides did not comment on the discussions. Although the coalition government has stuttered on for the past five months and seems to be in no immediate danger of collapse, tensions have built up over disagreements on the appointment of senior officials and the issues of US and EU sanctions on Mugabe and his inner circle.

Mugabe has recently been accusing former opposition leader and new prime minister, Morgan Tsvangirai, of failing to do enough to campaign for the removal of sanctions. Tsvangirai met the delegation yesterday and made assurances that the coalition government presented an opportunity 'to a new day'.

Sixteen

5th September 2009 – 'A crisis driven by greed' – Anthony Pambazuka News (published 3rd September and online 5th September)

Dewa Mavhinga wrote: 'I had not realised the true extent and impact of the Zimbabwe crisis on ordinary Zimbabweans until last weekend when I embarked on a four-and-a-half hour drive from Johannesburg to Kabokweni, a tiny, far-flung township situated in a valley near Nelspruit in South Africa's Mpumalanga province.

'I was visiting my two brothers, a cousin, a nephew and an uncle, who now, due to circumstances back home, are trying to eke out a living there. To my utter amazement, I soon discovered there are literally hundreds of Zimbabweans there, perhaps without a thought of returning home soon.

'Commenting on how he has been forced to put away his degree certificate and resort to doing odd and often degrading jobs just to survive, all my uncle said to me was, "Look what Mugabe has done to us."

'I felt a deep sadness in the depths of my soul and began to agonise over the root cause of the crisis on Zimbabwe.

'This morning, while taking a shower (that is usually my time of greatest inspiration), it suddenly occurred to me that the primary driver of the crisis in Zimbabwe and the consequent misery and suffering of the people, is just greed on the part of those in authority. For the avoidance of doubt, authority in Zimbabwe resides with ZANU-PF and its allies – the so called "war veterans", green bombers and security forces. Greed has so consumed those in authority, so much so that they have ceased to care about anything except their excessive desire to accumulate massive wealth, which they neither deserve nor need.

'Political power for them is the vehicle through which they can satisfy their greed and therefore they would be prepared to shed blood to acquire and retain that political power. In their twisted sense of logic, they are therefore justified in unleashing waves of electoral violence and coerce people to "vote" them into political power or to use other fraudulent means to attain political office.

'Understanding that greed is the primary driver of the Zimbabwean crisis would lead to a better understanding of the paradoxical situation of Zimbabwe that, in the midst of all this suffering, you find multi-millionaires, in United States dollars terms, on the streets of Harare.

'Chinotimba, a mere municipal guard (no offence to this humble profession intended), who was virtually penniless before he discovered the benefits of ZANU-PF membership, can claim that due to loss of his mobile phone for just a week, he had lost business worth US$19 million and this is not one of these Chinotimba jokes doing the rounds. What business is he into? Clearly there are a few people who are directly benefiting from the suffering of millions of Zimbabweans. That same group of people is reaping where they did not sow.

'Again this is not just a figure of speech, scores of those aligned to ZANU-PF are currently on an invasion spree of white-owned farms and are reaping where they did not sow. Zimbabwe has enough resources to support all those who live in it and also to support the region, but a few politically connected and greed people are busy plundering Zimbabwe and eating everyone's share. I would not be surprised if there are people in Zimbabwe whose daily prayer is that the crisis never ends.

'Greedy political leaders, who do not care about the people they purport to represent, invariably breed misery and suffering. The breed of political leaders often having the following distinctive characteristics:

'One – Leaders, although generally incompetent and lacking in business acumen.

'Two – They measure their political achievements by the wealth accumulated by cars they own.

'Three – They publicly speak against the West and pose as pan-Africanists while privately sending their children to school in the West and drink their wines from the West and do not miss out on their monthly satellite television subscriptions.

'Four – All their ill-gotten wealth is derived exclusively from their political connections.

'Five – Their lavish and outlandish lifestyles are at odds with their professional salaries. For example, it is not surprising in Zimbabwe to come across a mere journalist working for state media but with powerful political connections, owning several properties that he can never acquire on his journalist's earnings.

'The breed of political leaders is beyond redemption and cannot be expected to reform and be like the biblical Zacchaeus, the chief tax collector who repented and gave away his ill-gotten wealth. Politicians of this kind, who unfortunately at present dominate the political scene in Zimbabwe, must be removed from office and mechanisms put in place to make sure this breed become extinct. This legacy of leaders who doggedly pursue self-serving interests must be broken.

'Without such a paradigm shift, charting a new political direction for Zimbabwe will remain a pipe dream. It is well worthwhile noting for political leaders in government, particularly those in the MDC who so many of us look up to for hope, that greed is not a trait confined to leaders from one particular political party.

'Zimbabwe desperately needs political leaders with integrity, who deeply care for others and have the ability to self-transcend. Political leaders are judged not on the basis of the political party they belong to but on content of their character and their service to humanity. I am absolutely convinced that if we had leaders who really cared, then Zimbabwe would not have gone through the horror, pain and suffering which has characterised the past decade and continues. It is not an act of God, neither is it a freak of nature that Zimbabwe finds itself in this multi-layered socio-economic, humanitarian and political crisis!

'The issue boils down to want of able political leadership; want of leaders who have already distinguished themselves in their private and professional lives who now take up private life ownership roles to serve, deriving satisfaction from putting a smile on an old woman's face.'

Dewa Mavhinga is a human rights lawyer based in Zimbabwe.

2nd September 2009 – 'Chombo's kingdom revealed' – The Zimbabwean

Everybody knows that ZANU-PF ministers have risen from humble beginnings to incredible power and wealth from beyond their legitimate earnings, but proving it has been almost impossible.

Given the web of deception surrounding their dealings, the result of painstaking research by The Zimbabwean reveals the details of man's journey to eye-watering riches. This is the first in a series of revelations:

The Zimbabwean can exclusively reveal the rise of a complete non-entity from material and political obscurity to a position of incredible wealth and influence through alliances with politicians, fixers and bureaucrats.

Our investigations have revealed that local government and rural development minister, Ignatius Chombo, who owns dozens of houses and luxury cars, has become hugely wealthy during his years as one of Robert Mugabe's cabinet ministers.

Chombo has become hugely wealthy with his residential stands in almost every town and city in Zimbabwe. He also owns 11 luxury cars, 17 tractors, three combine harvesters and hundreds of other farming implements and assets. This is confirmed by a material deed in the MDC's possession.

There is no way his official salary, even including the generous allowances enjoyed by top officials, could over the years have brought him a fraction of these assets.

Hidden shelf complaint

The investigation also revealed that ownership of the housing stands Chombo has accumulated have been concealed through the use of shelf companies. This was facilitated by attorney general, Johannes Tomana, who masterminded the transfer of the properties to some of Combo's sons and investment vehicles. This is available to view on our website at www.thezimbabwean.co.uk.

Chombo's letter also advised Tomana to transfer 100% shareholding of Growfin Investment, his major vehicle, to Chombo Family Trust. He also advises the AG to transfer the new Allan Grance Farm, subject to dispute between Chombo and his first wife, Marian, to the trust.

The letter further states: 'Bus to be requested in the company of Enock Chombo, Nimrod Chombo and Ignatius Chombo Jnr.' The contents of other documents in our possession bear witness to Chombo's incredible property empire, stands in Epworth, Chirunda, Kariba, Ruwa, Chinhoyi, Mutare, Chegutu, Binga, Victoria Falls, Zuimba, Chitungwiza, Beitbridge, Harare and Bulawayo. Most of the stands are hidden under investment vehicles created by the minister. More information on the particulars of the stands owned by Chombo is available on our website.

Chombo has also made headlines for his involvement in the Joshua Mgabuko Nkomo Expressway Project which was awarded to a Ukrainian investment company without going to tender. The city of Harare has begun an investigation into the project.

Investigation by the Financial Gazette

It was established recently that a caretaker council, The Harare Commission, unelected and handpicked by Chombo, approved the sordid deal. In terms of the Urban Councils Act, the Minister of Local Government, Urban Council and Rural Development is the ultimate authority who must approve council contracts and projects.

Michael Machachi, an old associate of Chombo, wholly owns Classique Project Management, a consultancy appointed by the Commission and handpicked by the same ministers to manage the project.

As part of its resolutions adopted during its last full council meeting, held on 7th August 2009, The Harare Commission ordered Machachi to produce in chronological order a full report of the procedures that were followed to award the contract for the design, construction and dualisation of Joshua Mgabuku Nkomo Expressway to Augur Investments.

27th September/3rd October – 'Government loses battle over diamonds' – The Standard

The government last week lost its three-year-old battle to wrestle control of the Marange diamond fields from the British-registered African Consolidated Resources (ACR) in a landmark High Court ruling.

The ruling could have far-reaching implications for the government, which had profited from the sale of diamonds from the Chiadzwa area in Marange.

ARC approached the courts in 2006 after the Zimbabwe government, a year after the company had been granted mining rights in the area. The government then started mining the precious stones through the Zimbabwe Mining Development Corporation (ZMDC) but mayhem quickly ensued in the diamond fields as government officials, police and army officers joined illegal panners in plundering the gems.

The scale of the looting and violence that occurred in Marange was unprecedented. This alarmed human rights groups who started campaigning for Zimbabwe's ban from the international trade in diamonds. The campaign prompted the Kimberley Process to launch investigations into how diamonds were mined in Zimbabwe.

But the tables turned against the government on Thursday in what was lauded as a landmark ruling. High Court Judge, Justice Charles Hungwe, ordered the ZMDC to stop its mining activities and directed the government to restore ACR's rights to mine in the area.

'It is hereby ordered that the ACR's claims—within the area previously covered by EPO 1523 are valid and that they have been valid since originally pegged,' Hungwe said, delivering judgement in the case that began in October 2006.

'The rights granted to ZMDC by virtue of the special grant shall not apply in respect of the ACR claims area and ZMDC must cease its prospecting and diamond mining activities in the ACR claims area.'

Hungwe also ordered the Minerals Marketing Corporation of Zimbabwe (MMCZ) to return to ACR all diamonds seized from the company and all precious stones it bought from ZMDC that were mined on the ACR claims.

'Alternatively, MMCZ can account for the proceeds of any such diamonds which it has sold,' Hungwe said.

About 40 foreign companies are estimated to have been buying diamonds at Marange daily before the military moved in. It is estimated that ACR lost about US$6 billion in the past three years.

Thousands of people from both within and outside the country invaded the area in the diamond rush which ensued.

Last year, the government deployed soldiers to seal the area, arguing that it wanted to stop the illegal mining activities. But review teams from the Kimberley Process Certification Scheme said they discovered that the army committed serious human rights violations and smuggled diamonds.

Judge Hungwe also ordered the law enforcement agents to stop interfering with ACR activities.

Mines and mining development deputy minister, Murisi Zwzwai said yesterday that he had not yet seen the judgement. His boss, Obert Mpofu, was said to be attending a funeral. Mpofu recently said the government had identified investors to help it exploit the diamonds commercially.

ACR welcomed the ruling, saying it wanted to discuss a joint venture with government. In a statement on Friday, the company said, 'Following the group's success in Zimbabwe's High Court, the group remains committed to dialogue with the Zimbabwe government with a view to establishment of a joint venture which will operate for the benefit of the company and the people of Zimbabwe.'

As soon as the joint venture achieves physical procession of the claims, its immediate priority will be the establishment of full security as soon as it is practicable. Thereafter, the company hopes to make further announcements in respect of its intentions to establish a mutually beneficial operation as the situation develops.

ACR lawyer, Jonathan Samkange, said Hungwe's ruling showed that the country's judiciary was independent.

'This ruling also comes at the right time,' he said. 'We are happy it came after a few days of the Mining Indaba, where President (Robert) Mugabe promised investors that property rights will be respected and also that the rule of law will prevail and that indigenisation law will not affect mines.

'This judgement will allow the inclusive government to demonstrate to the world it upreparedness to abide by these promises. We hope the government allows my clients to fully implement the order.

'Majority shareholders in the company are Zimbabweans, although, of course, they are different races. What the government does with the order will either make it walk with their shoulders high up or mess it up.'

'AG orders fresh probe of Nkoma sodomy scandal' –

The attorney general's office has ordered fresh investigations into allegations of sodomy involving ZANU-PF chairman, John Nkomo, and a 31-year-old man.

Last month, the state refused to charge Mncedisi Thwala for allegedly making a false report, after claiming that Nkomo sodomised him at a local hotel in 2002.

Police were ordered to carry out further investigations but there were fears the matter would be swept under the carpet. But Simon Nleya, the senior public prosecutor at the Tredgold Magistrates Court last week said that both Nkomo and Thwala were still technically under investigation.

'It is true that there is an investigation,' he said in an interview. 'The last time the matter was brought to the courts, the police were told to carry out further investigation into the matter and as we speak right now, the investigations are going on. Technically, both sides of this whole issue are under investigation.'

Thwala was arrested the day after he made a police complaint that he was sodomised by Nkomo. There were reports that the police wanted to charge him with making false reports and perjury for allegedly lying under oath in relation to the Nkomo complaint.

However, the investigation will have to establish if the complainant told the truth in his report to the police and the investigations are also under instruction to check whether the accused really committed the said offence.

Police spokesman, senior assistant commissioner, Wayne Bvudzijena, on Friday would not say whether police were investigating the matter.

'So far I am not sure whether an instruction for new investigations has been sent. If it has, we are obliged to carry out the instruction as given by the attorney general's office,' he said.

Nkomo has refused to comment on the allegations, but supporters say they are part of a smear campaign to try and stop him from succeeding the late vice president, Joseph Msika, following his death in July.

Thwala, who claims that he once escaped to South Africa, says he unsuccessfully tried to report the alleged sodomy on numerous occasions.

The co-minister responsible for national healing is clear favourite for the Vice Presidency.

Seventeen

While all these ups and downs are going on and while the unity government is in power, we find that Air Zimbabwe is broke. It took me three days to get to Zimbabwe. Engine trouble and 2.50 am and we were transported to a hotel leaving early the next morning. Arriving again at Gatwick, another delay, no wheelchairs and very few staff to assist us. God knows how I am going to return home in December! I have a three-month ticket!

On another occasion in Zimbabwe during October 2009, 17 MPs were accused of murder and violence. Will we ever be normal again in our beautiful Zimbabwe?

October 2009 - Murder and Violence

The police and the attorney general's office have failed to press murder and violence charges against the 17 ZANU-PF members of parliament say the MDC.

The charges arise from violence committed during the election period last year. In its latest publication, the changing Times says the MDC has accused the law enforcement authorities of persecuting 'innocent' officials belonging to the party while ignoring serious crimes committed by Zimbabwean strongmen, Robert Mugabe and his senior officials.

The MDC said it had evidence that the ZANU-PF had committed a wide range of offences, including murder, but it did not name the officials.

However, human rights groups have named Murehwa MP, David Parirenyafwa among the perpetrators of some of the worst cases of violence against MDC supporters last year.

The accusation is among a number of charges the MDC has used to disengage from further involvement with Mugabe and ZANU-PF in the transitional government.

MDC security chief, Kisimusi Mudzingwa, recently sent to the attorney general's office a complete dossier of evidence collected by the party concerning violence against its members during 2008. He was subjected to a hostile interrogation by the police shortly afterwards but no further action has been taken against the perpetrators named in the dossier. As far as we know, they have not even been interviewed.

Last month the MDC accused notorious Masvingo-based Major General Engelbert Rugefe of drawing a pistol and threatening to shoot Tichaon Chiminya, one of its MPs.

The party said the MP met Rugefe at the Chevron Hotel in Masvingo at the weekend, where the soldier queried why Chiminya had not saluted him. Rugefe is then said to have pulled out his pistol and threatened to shoot him.

October 2009 - Problems, Problems, Problems

Then Mutambana states that Mugabe must shape up or shut up! Zimbabwe deputy prime minister, Arthur Mutambana has warned Mugabe and ZANU-PF about stalling the progress of the inclusive government, saying that Mugabe must shape up or shut up and ship out!

Addressing a press briefing ahead of a meeting with Mugabe on Monday (9th October), Mutambana, who is one of the principals of the Global Political Agreement (GPA), blamed Mugabe and his party for the constitutional crisis gripping the country following the suspension of government duty by the MDC, led by Prime Minister Morgan Tsvangirai.

'I will tell President Robert Mugabe in our meeting today that you are president because of negotiations and the GPA. If this inclusive government collapses, you cease to be President of Zimbabwe and you will be an illegitimate leader,' Mutambana said. 'No one in SADC or AU (African Union) will accept you as leader so you better shape up or ship out. You have limited options. Let us find ways of working together.

'The SADC communiqué issued in January before the formation of the inclusive government is clear on the appointment of the Central Bank governor and the attorney general. That document is binding,' said Mutambana.

ZANU-PF has of late been arguing that the outstanding members of other parties are not part of the GPA.

Mutambana said the country was in a constitutional crisis after the unwarranted arrest of Roy Bennett last week and urged SADC to engage with the Zimbabwean crisis immediately.

October-November 2009 – 'To engage with the Zimbabwean crisis immediately' – SADC

During the last nine months of the unity government, there have been so many problems for Tsvangirai, with murders still being committed. The poor MDC were tackled by ZANU-PF in many ways, which caused a great rift between ZANU-PF and MDC. Tsvangirai even appealed to Western donor countries to reward the good work for his unity government by widening support to include development assistance.

'People must recognise and reward progress,' Tsvangirai told journalists in Harare on Sunday evening in October 2009.

He also added, 'There is no dispute in everyone's assessment that there is indeed progress being made in Zimbabwe. And how do you reward Zimbabwe and that progress? By moving away from just humanitarian aid to economic growth, development aid and to ensure that any restriction that are there to be removed.'

Western countries that provide the most aid have maintained the most humanitarian assistance but refused to provide direct financial support to the unity government, demanding more democratic reforms, including freeing the media and upholding human rights.

'I know that a lot of people are sceptical of the history. I am not going to defend what has happened. What is important is that we have opened a new chapter, which we have agreed upon in Zimbabwe,' said Tsvangirai.

Meanwhile, Tsvangirai, who last week received two international human rights and democracy awards from the International Bar Association and the Spanish Fundación Cristóbel Gabarrón, said the accolades were a recognition of Zimbabweans' fight for a just and democratic society. Tsvangirai had also been in the running for the Nobel Peace Prize that went to the American US president, Barack Obama, last week (October 2009).

October 2009 – More Farming Problems

Farm seizures are still going on in spite of the unity government. Some were actually caught on film last week.

Ben Freeth, who was beaten and his house burnt down, has been in Washington to ask Obama to help stop the Zimbabwean government from seizing the remaining write farms by force.

His father-in-law, Mike Campbell, shot footage of the campaign of harassment against them and it forms part of a film to be released in London.

The South African Development Community (SADC) Tribunal in Namibia ruled last November that the farm seizures were illegal and ordered the Zimbabwean government to pay costs, but Robert Mugabe's regime allegedly sent thugs to set fire to both men's farms while they were at church, destroying everything they owned as well as the homes of their owners.

Freeth said he had written four times to Prime Minister Morgan Tsvangirai, but his letters were never acknowledged.

In desperation, he decided to take his case to Washington. He spent Friday on Capitol Hill telling his story to legislators and hopes to meet Hillary Clinton, the secretary of state, this week.

September 2009 – 'Mugabe blames US and UK for Zimbabwean crisis' – CNN

Last week, 24th September 2009, Robert Mugabe granted an interview to CNN's Christiane Amanpour at the United Nations.

Amanpour: What are you going to ask? Are you going to ask President Obama to lift the sanctions that are imposed on you?

Mugabe: Not really, I haven't come here for President Obama to address the United States alone. I've come here to address the General Assembly, which is part of the United Nations structures and we are entitled to discuss matters that affect us in the global environment and the matters that affect us in a particular way in Zimbabwe and this is what I am going to do.

Amanpour: But you obviously are calling for sanctions to be lifted.

Mugabe: Yes, that I will do certainly. The sanctions are unjustified, illegal and they are meant for regime change to address the illegal principal.

Amanpour: You say for regime change, but it really is about trying to get the political situation stabilised and for the last year you've been in a power-sharing agreement with the leader of the opposition, Morgan Tsvangirai. What does power-sharing mean to you? Many people say that it is name only right now.

Mugabe: No, it is really power sharing and that power sharing is encapsulated in an agreement we call the Global Political Agreement and this was arrived at through the facilitation that we got from South Africa and specifically through the facilitation by former president, Thabo Mkebi.

Amanpour: The problem, though, Mr President, is that many people are saying that you and your party are still trying to reduce the MDC majority or their officials in parliament. There are MPs who are being arrested. They're being charged with alleged crimes to prevent them from being able to take office. Why is this happening?

Mugabe: First, may I point out and make it quite clear, the Global Political Agreement was arrived at after a series of meetings, which involved not just ZANU-PF and the MDC, as represented by Tsvangirai and Professor Mutambara and their negotiators, and these provisions in the Global Agreement were reached after many strenuous discussions had taken place.

Amanpour: Right, but the question really is—

Mugabe: And so they were not forced upon us, we came to an agreement.

Amanpour: No, but the question really is—

Mugabe: We came to them deliberately.

Amanpour: All right, so if you say you arrived at them deliberately, why then are their MPs and officials still being harassed?

Mugabe: Because the issue of those being arrested is a different matter altogether. Some of them have committed crimes before the Global Agreement, crimes such as rape and kidnapping. You couldn't let people who have committed such crimes get away with it merely because there is a Global Agreement.

Amanpour: Has Roy Bennett committed a crime? Why is he not sworn in?

Mugabe: Roy Bennett has been charged and on the face of it, the charges are very serious, but I am told by the leader of the MDC that the prosecution is addressing no evidence. There are no witnesses. If there are no witnesses, the prosecution will arrive at a time when they will say so.

Amanpour: So charged with what?

Mugabe: But let's not read that for them. Let them read that conclusion on their own.

Amanpour: Do you think that he will be appointed?

Mugabe: Yes, yes, yes, if he's acquitted he will be appointed.

Amanpour: But charged with what?

Mugabe: Charged with—charged with—you know, tried to put— I think he was found to be responsible for organising arms of war against Zimbabwe.

Amanpour: Well, we will obviously have to ask him about that, but—

Mugabe: And—and—and that, this—these are the charges that are being made on the face of them.

Amanpour: Well—

Mugabe: But if the prosecution cannot prove that, in fact he did so, that in fact, he's guilty of, you know, trying to organise—you know—

Amanpour: Mr Mugabe, that is certainly the first I have heard of it and we will obviously put that to them. But can I say this, there are a lot of people, as you heard in that report, that considered you an African hero back in 1980. Some of my friends, Rhodesians, some I have worked with in the Rhodesian army and then became journalists in Rhodesia, were stunned by the conciliatory nature of the addresses you gave back in 1980.

Mugabe: Yes.

Amanpour: Describe how your politics for ten years led to prosperity, led to successes in mining and agriculture and all sorts of things, and then over the last ten years things have really gone sour in a bad way, a big way. Why is it that that has happened?

Mugabe: Over the last ten years?

Amanpour: No, no, since land reform. And remember that the presidents of Mozambique and Tanzania, when you took the country to liberation, said to you, 'You have the Jewel of Africa in your hands, now look after it.'

Mugabe: Yes, we are looking after it.

Amanpour: Did you look after it?

Mugabe: Yes, in a very big way. Over the last ten years we have had the sanctions imposed on us by the United States, plus sanctions imposed on us by the European Union over the last ten years.

Amanpour: Right, but they were specifically targeted sanctions.

Mugabe: No.

Amanpour: Against individuals not against the trade or development.

Mugabe: Zimbabwe, no, no, no, no. The US sanctions on us are real sanctions, economic sanctions. Have you looked at that? Look at them and you will satisfy yourselves that they prevent companies from having any dealings with us.

Amanpour: But they are very specifically targeted?

Mugabe: They prevent any financial institutions—

Amanpour: But how do you account—?

Mugabe: —from having any relations with us.

Amanpour: —for these incredible statistics? Where since you took over, life expectancy has dropped, manufacturing has fallen—

Mugabe: But I'm just telling you—I'm just telling you—

Amanpour: One in fourteen people are malnourished—

Mugabe: I am just telling you the reasons. It is because of the sanctions, mainly.

Amanpour: But everyone is saying it is not because of sanctions but because of mismanagement.

Mugabe: Not everybody says so.

Amanpour: Most people do. Most independent observers say that.

Mugabe: In Zimbabwe—it's not true.

Amanpour: Now, to get out of this —how to get out of this? Do you think—for instance, right now—?

Mugabe: The sanctions, the sanctions must be lifted and we should have no interference from outside. The continued imperialistic interference on our affairs is affecting the country, obviously.

Amanpour: I would like to play one sound bite from a neighbour of yours. A Nobel Prize winner, Archbishop Desmond Tutu, who said the following: 'He's destroyed a country that used to be a bread basket. It has become a basket case itself. But I think now—I mean that the world must say, look you—you—you have been responsible with your cohorts, you have been responsible for gross violations and you are going to face indictment in The Hague unless you step down.' How do you respond to that? First, that you have turned the bread basket of Africa into a basket case?

Mugabe: No, it's not a basket case at all. Last year we managed to grow enough food for us all. We are not a basket case anymore.

Amanpour: One in fourteen people are called malnourished.

Mugabe: No, no, no, no.

Amanpour: Your country is practically dependent on humanitarian aid.

Mugabe: Just now you're not talking of the present.

Amanpour: I know things have got better in the last year.

Mugabe: They have got much better in terms of food.

Amanpour: But it is still like a war-zone.

Mugabe: People have grown enough food for themselves. We have had years, continuous successive years of drought. Don't forget that. And in addition—

Amanpour: I've seen the drought figures. I've got all the statistics here—

Mugabe: —sanctions as well.

Amanpour: Yes.

Mugabe: And combine the effects of sanctions and what do you get?

Amanpour: Well, the effect of what many people are saying is the land reform that really created this huge discrepancy in your ability to farm.

Mugabe: The land—

Amanpour: We are going to go to a break and we'll talk about that when we come back. All right?

Mugabe: Yes, but the land reform is the best thing that could have happened.

Amanpour: The best thing?

Mugabe: Yes, to an African country.

Amanpour: We will talk about that in a second.

Mugabe: It has to do with national sovereignty.

Amanpour: OK, let's talk about it in a second.

Mugabe: I will never, never, never surrender. Zimbabwe is mine. I am a Zimbabwean. Zimbabwe is for Zimbabweans. Zimbabwe is never for the British. Britain is for the British.

Amanpour: Is that just political rally rhetoric or did you mean that? What did you mean?

Mugabe: That Zimbabwe belongs to the Zimbabwean people.

Amanpour: Right, do you consider—?

Mugabe: Pure and simple.

Amanpour: And everybody believes that?

Mugabe: Yes, all people believe that.

Amanpour: So do you consider white Zimbabweans?

Mugabe: Those who are naturalised and have citizenship, yes.

Amanpour: Those who have been living there for year and years and years?

Mugabe: But historically—

Amanpour: Right.

Mugabe: Historically, they have a debt.

Amanpour: The people who contributed to farming historically, they have a debit to pay?

Mugabe: Yes, yes, their land. They occupied the land illegally. They seized the land from our people.

Amanpour: Look—

Mugabe: Therefore the process of reform, land reform, involved their handing—having to hand over the land. We agreed upon this with the British people, by the way.

Amanpour: Some 80% of that land was taken after you took office. Some of the farmland, and with the very certificates that mean government approval. Why are these people being hounded out of the country? Why are they being—?

Mugabe: They are not being—they are not being hounded.

Amanpour: Hounded off their land, then!

Mugabe: No, no. They are not being hounded out of the country.

Amanpour: We have just done reports about it.

Mugabe: Those who are in industry and manufacturing and mining are not being—

Amanpour: The farmers I am talking about. Why is that?

Mugabe: —are not being affected.

Amanpour: Wonderful farmland and why are they being—?

Mugabe: What are you talking about? We are getting land from them and that's all. They are not being hounded out of the country at all.

Amanpour: They *are* being hounded off their land.

Mugabe: [inaudible] their land is not theirs [the British].

Amanpour: Even though they bought it with the certificate of approval from the government?

Mugabe: But haven't you heard of the Lancaster House discussions and the agreement of the British government? Because they are British settlers and we agreed at the Lancaster House that there would be land reform.

Amanpour: But they are citizens aren't they? And isn't the farming disaster contributing to your—?

Mugabe: Citizens by colonisation, seizing land from the original people of the country.

Amanpour: But how did that all go so wrong?

Mugabe: You approve of that?

Amanpour: How did that go so wrong? Because when you came in it was about reconciliation.

Mugabe: They knew about it. They knew we had this programme of land acquisition and land reform. They knew about it.

Amanpour: What about the blacks, then?

Mugabe: And the British knew about it.

3rd October 2009 – 'MDC appeals to SADC again' – The Standard

Frustrated by the snail's pace at which the Global Political Agreement (GPA) is being implemented, the MDC has once again appealed to the Southern African Development Community (SADC) to expeditiously deal with the outstanding issues threatening to tear apart the unity government.

SADC earlier this month failed to deal with the outstanding matters and teething problems facing the unity government and referred the disputes to the track on peace and security.

The regional body and the African Union (AU) are guarantors of the shaky seven-month government of national unity, which MDC-T says is threatened by the failing, or rather, failure to resolve the outstanding issues!

The MDC's appeal comes barely a week after the party started consulting the grass roots on the wisdom of its continued participation in the inclusive government in light of ZANU-PF's transigence.

Chamisa spoke to The Standard and said the MDC-T has employed a two-pronged strategy in dealing with the outstanding matters.

'We are consulting with our constituencies around the country and at the same time we have written to SADC appealing to them to urgently deal with the outstanding matters,' he said.

Chamisa spoke to The Standard after the party's extraordinary national executive council meeting, held on Friday to review the future of the troubled unity agreement.

The outstanding issues include Mugabe's unilateral appointment of Reserve Bank governor, Gideon Gono, and attorney general, Johannes Tomana, as well as the swearing-in of the Deputy Minister of Agriculture designate, Roy Bennett.

This is not the first time that the MDC has appealed to the regional body to intervene. In May the MDC sent a letter to SADC seeking an urgent resolution of the crisis.

The MDC spokesman said his party has already lined rallies across the country to consult its stakeholders on the wisdom of remaining in the unity government.

He pledged that the party would seriously consider the outcome of the people's views in the consultations as they were the real owners of the agreement.

10th November 2009 – 'Beaten and buried alive: JOMIC hears torture ordeal' – The Zimbabwean

Nine months of procrastination, deceit and dishonesty. Tortured MDC official, Pascal Gwezire, has revealed the horrific ordeal he underwent at the hands of his abductors.

Gwezire told the Joint Monitoring and Implementation Committee (JOMIC) that he was abducted in front of his wife and children by a team that included intelligence operatives and police offers in riot gear.

He was first taken to Marimba police station, where he was blindfolded and driven to an unknown place.

Gwezire said he was viciously beaten and that one of his captors actually bit off a piece of his ear (left). He was hit with one-metre batons and his genitals were pulled with string during his interrogation. He was also buried alive in a grave.

JOMIC has now opened a full-scale investigation into the refusal by prison authorities to allow Gwezire, the MDC transport manager, to receive medical treatment for injuries and torture sustained during his abduction.

Gwezire was abducted on 27th October and held incommunicado until 31st October, when he appeared in court badly injured.

He is accused of stealing rifles and a shotgun and of undergoing military training at Soroti Training Camp in Uganda back in 1999. On 31st October, he was remanded in custody, although the wounds on his legs were infected. Three days later, JOMIC sprang into action, opening a full-scale investigation into why Gwezire had been denied a doctor whilst in prison.

Harare magistrate, Archie Wochiunga, on Friday threatened to charge prison authorities with contempt of court for wilfully defying his earlier order to grant medical attention to Gwezire. Officials say the prison doctor has been ordered not to give medical attention.

The Zimbabwean newspaper understands the JOMIC secretariat visited Harare Remand Prison on 4th November and also met Senior Assistant Commissioner Chisora at his offices. He is said to have vehemently denied that Gwezire was being refused treatment. JOMIC was absolutely shocked to see Gwezire's left leg getting septic, a source said.

He said the wound was infected by handcuffs as he was being tortured using the 'bridge method', read JOMIC's report. He said he could no longer hear with his left ear after he was slapped many, many times during his torture, which he said lasted for about five days. 'He also showed us scars on his lower back and black marks over his body.'

MDC activist, Peter Munyanyi, who escaped from his captors after six months of imprisonment and torture, has spoken of his terror.

Munyanyi, who was among hundreds of MDC supporters who went missing following last year's post-election violence, said he did not know where he was after being locked up by state security agents in a dark room without blankets, clothing or toilet facilities.

During the six months of his imprisonment, Munyanyi, from Shana village in Gutu South, says he was also given very little to eat. He lived in continual fear that he would never see the outside world again, let along his wife, Jacqueline, and three-year-old son, Malvern.

His six-month ordeal started on the afternoon of 13th December at Ustida Business Centre in Gutu, where three men, driving a white single-cab CAM truck, pounced on him. They assaulted him and tried to force him into the vehicle.

'I managed to escape from them and ran away. One of them started firing shots at me and when the third shot was fired, I panicked and fell to the ground. That is when they started kicking me very hard with booted feet until I collapsed. From then on, I don't know what happened,' he said.

When Munyanyi regained consciousness, he found he had a broken arm and a missing tooth and was locked in a dark room. Unknown to him, this was going to be his home for the coming six months.

'I never received any treatment for my broken arm and I had to use the t-shirt I was wearing when I was abducted as a sling. I received excruciating torture during this period,' said Munyanyi.

'I would sleep on the floor and every two weeks I was given a bucket of water to wash my body.'

13th November 2009 – 'Plot to oust Tsvangirai revealed' – Itai Dzamanas

The battle for the presidency of the MDC. For many within the party, as well as even observers, investigations by the news leader completed recently have proved that MDC-T president, Morgan Tsvangirai, has been fighting hard to conceal and manage what our investigations have revealed to be deep power battles involving senior party officials. Insiders point at secretary general, Tendai Biti, as well as organising secretary, Elais Mudzuri, as being the architects of what we have confirmed to be a serious plot towards taking over the party presidency.

Our investigations into the thick succession plot have shown that behind-the-scenes battles have been based mainly on a bid to oust Tsvangirai through changing the party constitution. It has emerged that the Tsvangirai camp in the party is on the edge of another possible clash with the camps believed to be behind Biti and Mudzuri.

We have in the past weeks been reporting about the mystery and confusion with MDC-T over alleged secret constitutional amendments that were believed by some to have been made to protect Tsvangirai from losing the presidency at the party's next congress.

Our latest investigations have brought a new dimension and twist to the whole issue. Top sources at Harvest House, the MDC-T headquarters, and within the leadership (the party's) opened up on the battle believed to be involving Biti and Mudzuri, both understood to be trying to use the route tried before by former secretary general of the original MDC, Welshman Ncube, through bringing a constitutional amendment to effectively rule out Tsvangirai from contesting for another term at the next congress.

The original MDC constitution of 1999 has a somewhat controversial clause on the issue of terms of the party president. Firstly, it says that the leader of the party must be limited to two terms but specifies that this applies to the national presidency. This means that limit is only applicable in the event that the party president becomes the country's president. Secondly, the original constitution interestingly remained quiet on the issue of terms for the party president at the party level. That, therefore, means in that case the party president could run for as many terms as possible, as long as re-elected.

Ncube tried to change the constitution when he fought his battles against Tsvangirai, which culminated in the chaotic split of 2005 and the new leader confirmed it was one of the reasons he was once physically assaulted at Harvest House by Tsvangirai's followers.

Now we have it on good authority that Biti has also been trying to include a provision in the constitution to impose a limit on the party president's terms to a maximum of two, which would see Tsvangirai being ineligible to contest at the next election.

'Biti has ambitions to become the party president and has been trying to make that amendment,' a top party official involved in the goings-on said this week. 'He has been trying to do it the smart way, the same way Ncube attempted previously, but Tsvangirai has his people and they have been making sure to block those plans.'

Biti has previously denied to this writer about harbouring ambitions to become the party president, but our efforts to contact him for comment over the latest information failed this week.

We have it on good authority that as the alleged plans to conclude the constitutional provision by Biti and his colleague in what MDC-T insiders call 'the Biti faction' has been in place, on the other hand the Tsvangirai camp has also been hard at work. Our sources say the Tsvangirai faction has been scuttling and even pre-empting the plans to change the constitution and recently even went further to effectively and decisively deal with the matter.

'Tsvangirai has even got rid of the whole clause regarding limits for the party president and the constitution you will get today if someone agrees to give it to you is totally silent on these matters and subjects,' a senior party member said on condition of anonymity.

The goings-on and battles over the control and manipulation of the constitution are so complicated and deep to the extent that concerted efforts by this power over the past weeks to obtain copies of the latest version of the MDC-T constitution were met with various responses and attitudes from the party leaders. The MDC website also has nothing on the link under the title of 'constitution' and insiders say it is 'work in progress on the constitution'.

MDC-T spokesman, Nelson Chamisa, on Tuesday strenuously denied that there is a succession crisis in the party but went on to confirm the controversial existence of the provisions on the president's terms and how it is linked to the national presidential terms.

'There are no succession problems in the party. We are a happy family,' Chamisa said. 'We are not infected by this ailment and it is elements in ZANU-PF, where they are grappling with succession problems, who try to export the problem to us.'

He denied there have been amendments to the constitution. 'It's not true that the constitution was amended. The MDC as a party is an organisation and party with a structure and we hold congresses where we elect our party leadership. The constitution has a clause that says the party president automatically becomes the candidate for national elections and goes further to say he or she will be limited to two terms as national president. It doesn't put any limit on the terms as party leader. It is not explicit but by inference it says the terms must be a maximum of two in the event of he or she becoming national president.'

Chamisa confirmed that Tsvangirai is serving his second term as leader of the MDC but went on to say, 'We held our congress in 2005, which was a fire-fighting one after we had been ambushed by the plotters of a split.'

During our investigation, we also gathered that Mudzuri is understood to have expressed a desire to succeed Tsvangirai. 'He has been mobilising support behind the scenes and believes he is capable of taking over from Tsvangirai if the opportunity is availed,' a top source said.

We failed to reach Mudzuri for comment.

Fears of a coup plot crippled the ZANU-PF side of the unity government after the discovery of a massive disappearance of guns from army reserves, which the above paper has established is believed to have been an inside job.

Details show that a massive manhunt was launched within the Zimbabwe National Army and Air Force ranks following the looting of guns, which led to arrests and abductions, as well as kidnapping of MDC members and activists.

Senior army officials this week revealed to this paper that the ZANU-PF regime of Robert Mugabe, which is the dominant force in the fragile coalition government, developed serious fears of another coup plot possibly being mulled. It has emerged that they initially suspected MDC-T leader Morgan Tsvangirai's party as being architects of the strange happenings.

MDC Treasurer Roy Bennett's name is said to have cropped up from the intelligence as being the possible person behind the plan, but the sources say it was dismissed after they discovered it involved inside people.

Further investigations have said to have shown the security and intelligence chiefs that the looting and guns and whatever ultimate plan of the organisers was orchestrated from within the top echelons of the army and air force, raising the possibility of a coup plot being considered by some security chiefs.

A very senior army chief based at the KGVI barracks in Harare told us in confidence that it was established that the looting of guns 'was an inside job and in fact involved very senior officials within the security system'. He added that the emergency of that fact sent shockwaves within Mugabe's system because it pointed to a possible plan to stage a coup or even spark an armed revolt.

The News Leader understands that the state security system deployed in its might has been failing to trace the whereabouts of most of the missing guns and ammunition more than two months since the disappearance, again raising fears they could be taken across the border.

Mugabe's intelligence came up with a possibility of the destination having been South Africa or Botswana and reliable sources say there have been deployments to the neighbouring countries to try and investigate.

'One thing that is clear is that there is a plan being considered by the organisers of the looting guns and ammunition,' another top intelligence source said. 'It seems the earlier suspicions that it could be the work of Tsvangirai's party failed to sustain due to what emerged from the investigations, especially the fact that some members of the army at the barracks stole the guns and ammunition and were working as part of a huge, seriously organised plot involving powerful individuals.

The News Leader hears that many, many army officers, especially of the rank of captain, were behind the disappearance of the arms.

'There are many who are believed to have been apprehended for the disappearance of the arms and it is not clear what their fate is,' one of the sources said.

Defence minister, Emmerson Mnangagwa, declined to comment on the saga, saying, 'that is not a story. I will not comment.'

But a ZANU-PF government minister speaking to us on condition of anonymity revealed that, 'Mugabe now suspects the looting of the arms to have been organised by senior security chiefs who could be working with some politicians to possibly organise a coup or armed revolt against his hold on power. He fears a coup and it seems there are people he is suspecting who are being watched,' the minister said.

Our sources from the MDC side of the GNU said they only learnt of the disappearance of the arms through the media reports with one insisting, 'It is an inside job.'

A lot of uncertainty has been hovering around the Mugabe regime over the past couple of years. In June 2006 a coup plot was foiled and serving, as well as former, army officials were arrested who implicated Mnangagwa, as well as being the organiser of the plot.

Last year uniformed soldiers ran amok and ransacked shops in Harare protesting against poor living conditions but also trying to mobilise the masses to stage a possible uprising.

The News Leader established that following the latest incidents of disappearance of arms from army barracks and fears of a possible coup plot or an armed uprising, Mugabe has put security forces on high alert.

Eighteen

We worry, we battle, we keep cheerful and all help each other while friends and others have been forced to leave the country, no longer receiving their pensions and having had noughts taken off our savings and relieving our bank accounts of millions.

How can we help the country we all built up when Ian Smith and others were in power? The mining world with diamonds, gold, platinum, copper, you name it. Our emeralds were the best in the world. I could go on and on. Where has it all gone?

The farmers were called the 'bread basket'; today, through murder, riots etc, they took the farms from us. For what? We were without food. If we could, we would get it on the black market or pay the earth for it while all the shelves in the supermarkets were empty. Why, when we'd had it all?

We had everything when Ian Smith was in power. Then the Jewel in the Crown was given to Mugabe and we have had nothing but heartache, riots and murder ever since!

ZANU-PF, leader of the fragile coalition government, this week took an entourage of over 50 members to a food summit in Rome, Italy, at the expense of the taxpayer and gobbling up US$400,000! This amount could have purchased 400 tonnes of maize (the African basic diet) seed or fertiliser, which could have gone a long way towards solving the shortages affecting the majority of the farmers this season, a situation which poses the danger of a recurrence in food shortages.

Mugabe, in a very characteristic and highly predictable fashion, took the occasion at the food summit to lash out at the West and blame it for Zimbabwe's problems.

The News Leader heard from a very highly placed diplomatic official based in Rome, that the aged leader and his entourage were a spectacle in the Italian capital as other dignitaries wondered about the logic of Mugabe, who has presided over the economic meltdown of the former bread basket of South Africa, taking a huge delegation to a food summit.

It is also said by the source of The News Leader that Mugabe also created a lot of interest with the many security details he moved about with. 'He had about 20 security agents on his delegation and it left many people stunned.'

Our source at the Reserve Bank of Zimbabwe headquarters in Harare said that Mugabe's entourage received in excess of US$250,000 from the Central Bank for allowances during the trip, while another total cost of US$150,000 is estimated to have been spent on their travel and accommodation expenses.

Efforts to get comment from Mugabe's spokesman, George Charamba, failed before going to press.

Mugabe has over the years developed a penchant for international trips and always attends meetings and summits as they present him with an opportunity to travel abroad, especially now after being slapped with travel restrictions by the European Union, Australia and the United States of America.

Just before the Rome jaunt, Mugabe briefly stayed in the country after returning from an Africa-China summit held in Egypt, again taking a huge entourage and gobbling huge amounts of funds.

Most Zimbabweans are struggling with economic hardships that are underlined by high unemployment, food shortages, crumbling education as well as health sectors, caused by the bad policies of Mugabe and his ZANU-PF party during their reign in power.

The formation of a coalition government with the MDC last year, after his party lost to the MDC in the elections, has failed to extricate the country from the myriad problems.

Four months have gone since I arrived again in beautiful Zimbabwe on 3rd September 2009. An absolute shock – three days in Gatwick Airport. Air Zimbabwe, apart from being broke, developed engine trouble and was waiting for a new part.

I was on my way to see Alistair, whom I mentioned in my autobiography *Never a Dull Moment* (ISBN: 1-4196-6896-x, ISBN-13: 978-1419668968) and who, having just returned from one month with me in the UK, was now dying in St Ann's Hospital, Harare. I cooked for him for four of the most terrible months of my life, only to find out that he had always planned to return to a previous relationship. He is now back on his feet but has lost my love, for many years the greatest love a woman could give a man!

While I was in Zimbabwe from 3rd September until 11th December, there were so many activities on the political side and all so very sad! When we had one of the most beautiful and peaceful countries in the world, all the noughts were taken off the Zimbabwean dollar and our banks were emptied; nothing from my pension at all until the bank told me one day that the government would give me US$37 per month, which would not buy enough food for half a week. It was worthless.

Then the US dollar came into power, which truly saved the nation in many ways. Britain did help their British to fly home and got them little homes. What heartache for so many. I myself used to save every penny of my state pension to see my lovely friends at least once or twice a year.

I stayed a few times with a wonderful friend, Maria Dias, who owned a hairdressing salon. How she carried on is a miracle; phoning up clients daily to say sorry, there was a power cut. No electricity was a common thing. People would wash their hair at home if their electricity was on, or sit in Maria's garden in the beautiful sunshine to dry it, or return home with their curlers in until dry and then returning them the next day.

Everything was in the Rhodesia logo – 'It is but a pleasure'. There was no class distinction; everyone knew their place and everything was 'but a pleasure' to help anyone and everything. Now, unfortunately, it is a case of 'I'm all right, Jack' and can one blame them? While in Zimbabwe in 2009, it was nothing to have no water or electricity for day after day. One just accepts the fact that the phones were not working either!

I remember in December 2009, the headline in the Sunday Zimbabwean about Biti, the finance minister, read 'Biti decries political landmines'. He was presenting his 2010 national budget to parliament, which Zimbabwe's coalition government has had to operate since its formation in February 2009 and describing it as a political minefield littered with 'landmines' meant to derail plans to restore sanity in the troubled country.

Biti said the greatest challenge facing Zimbabwe at the moment was a 'Balkanised' coalition government where the constituent members of the new administration pursued 'politics of the past'.

President Robert Mugabe and former opposition leader, Morgan Tsvangirai, joined forces to establish a coalition government ten months ago.

Movement for Democratic Change (MDC) leader, Tsvangirai, became prime minister under the compromise regime formed with the assistance of the Southern African Development Community following disputed polls last year.

Biti, who is from Tsvangirai's party, said the new Harare regime lacked a common vision among the three parties represented in government.

'We have to speak with one voice and if we have a balanced government in respect of which the government is a mirror image or an asymmetrical reproduction of the politics of the past and attrition, murder and dishonesty, then that is a landmine,' he told the very latest edition of a weekly newsletter published by the prime minister's office.

Another booby trap was the slow pace of political reform, which was costing the country dearly in terms of winning over crucial Western aid to revive the country's economy.

Hardliners in Mugabe's ZANU-PF have been working to derail the fragile unity government, which they see as a threat to the patronage system they had become used to during the past decade. They are resisting reforms such as the repeal of tough security and media laws and the roll out of the process towards the creation of a new democratic constitution.

Biti said that all parties to the power-sharing agreement, which led to the formation of the unity government, should comply with guidelines and timelines with regards to crucial democratisation processes like the constitutional-making process.

He said the booby traps could 'curtain and smother' Zimbabwe's investment potential and affect the implementation of the 2010 national budget that he presented last week (December 2009).

Then there are big problems with Chinamasa protesting over food aid. Chief negotiator, Patrick Chinamasa, in the ongoing power-sharing talks, has protested to the Joint Monitoring and Implementation Committee (JOMIC) over what he said was the 'politicisation' of food aid by Prime Minister Morgan Tsvangirai's MDC-T party.

Last Sunday's news in the Zimbabwean reported that MDC sources said Chinamasa, who is also Zimbabwe's justice minister, last month wrote to JOMIC to complain about alleged politicisation of non-governmental organisations (NGOs) food distribution programmes in Manicaland Province by Tsvangirai's party. But after investigating the alleged politicisation, JOMIC discovered that there was no substance to Chinamasa's claims other than pure paranoia on the part of ZANU-PF. What they called politicisation of the NGO food assistance programme was, in fact, the presence of the MDC newsletters at the distribution points in one of the areas.

JOMIC is a special multi-party task force mandated with supervising the implementation of the Global Political Agreement (GPA) signed by ZANU-PF and the two MDC leaders and formations last year. It handles all complaints, grievances, concerns and issues relating to compliance with the GPA.

While I am writing, human rights groups have accused ZANU-PF of using food aid as a political weapon on which it punishes known MDC supporters.

The Zimbabwe peace project last month (November 2009) accused Mugabe's party of falsifying records to deny known opponents' assistance from the Department of Social Welfare and NGOs.

The group said that public access to food and humanitarian assistance was being denied through co-ordinators, volunteers, village heads, councillors and chairpersons linked to ZANU-PF.

We have also heard that Zimbabwean children are rescued from traffickers and also two young teenage children are missing from home. The public and the police are searching for them. Let's hope this is not the start of more tragedy!

South Africa's president, Jacob Zuma, is still to this day (13th May 2009) trying to sort out the mess since the coalition government was formed with Robert Mugabe and Morgan Tsvangirai. Will there ever be understanding and peace? It will be interesting to see how the UK progresses with their brand new coalition government!

Mbeki failed (last SA president) and Zuma's presidency seems to have moved away from Mbeki's 'quiet diplomacy' to a more robust and open mediation effort. Although to the average suffering Zimbabwean, there seems little to suggest anything has changed, as they are denied access to information about the many, many, many talks they have had.

Zuma has had meetings with the chairperson of ZADC, Gwebiza, also at this movement in May 2009 and in December he admitted there is a need to have a full SADC summit to deal with the many continuous issues. We shall see what the future will bring!

Roy Bennett is, to this day, still in the news! Here we are in May 2009 and Roy is in the headlines and I quote from The Zimbabwean: 'PM is nothing, we are in charge', 'Cop tells Bennett "Our job is to cut your throat."'

Senator Roy Bennett was last weekend stopped by intelligence operatives from complying with a legal order to repossess his personal property from his grabbed Charleswood Estate in Chimanimani. The estate, which I so often think of, is in the beautiful mountainous region in Eastern Zimbabwe, which has long been an MDC stronghold, was grabbed from Roy and is now run by ARDA.

On 26th March 2009, Bennett was harassed with his wife, Heather, by intelligence operatives who had mounted a roadblock along the road to Charleswood. Bennett was complying with an order to retrieve his personal belongings from his residence on the estate, including his dead father's ashes, after receiving a letter from ARDA lawyers, Jakachira & Company, instructing him to retrieve his property.

Bennett has a pending court action against ARDA over his illegal expulsion from the property. In a letter to the Joint Monitoring and Implementation Committee (JOMIC), a special multi-party taskforce mandated with supervising the implementation of the inclusive government, Bennett said on arrival in Chimanimani town at the turn off to Charleswood Estate, at approximately 1900hrs on 26th March, he encountered a police roadblock. He was travelling in two seven-tonne trucks he had hired to load with his property.

'It was quite obvious that they were waiting for me as there was a reaction with people covering my vehicle shouting "NDI Bennett! NDI Bennett!" and a person dressed in civilian clothes ran to the headlights in front of the vehicle and knelt to take my number place,' Bennett said in his report lodged with JOMIC.

'I moved the vehicle forward and forced him to move out of the way. I then got out and asked him what the problem was and why they were taking my number and reacting in the manner they were.'

Bennett said the officers answered in a very aggressive manner, demanding to know what he wanted and why he was there. All other vehicles were passing through; none were being stopped.

'I answered that I was in Chimanimani to recover my property and they asked under whose authority. I answered by asking why there were questioning me and what had I done wrong. They answered that they were under instructions and said "you may not question us". I produced the lawyer's letter and was then directed to the member in charge, one Inspector Browned, who I introduced myself to, shook his hand and handed him the letter. I then asked him what the problem was and he said, "Do not talk to me."

'I said, what is the problem? I am a senator in the upper house and the agriculture minister designate, did he not know that there was an inclusive government and that harassment of the MDC officials should not be taking place? He replied that there was no inclusive government and said "Who is the prime minister? I only know the president and act on instructions,"' Bennett says in his report to JOMIC.

Bennett says he was forced to wait 30 minutes after the officers took the lawyer's letter. He managed to identify Sergeant Majumbati from police security intelligence and said the officer harassed his wife in the presence of a uniformed police officer.

'His actions were aggressive but I could not hear what he was saying,' the report said.

'My wife later informed me that he was demanding her ID. She refused to give it to him as he was in civilian clothes and would not identify himself. He instructed the uniformed police officer to instruct my wife to give her ID (but then) this officer just walked away. He then called another police officer, who demanded my wife's ID, which she immediately gave him.'

Bennett then said the officer told his wife 'Do you know we will kill you? Our job is to cut your throat'. My wife appealed to the uniformed policemen for protection and he told her to 'F*** off, they can do what they want'.

'It was at this stage that the member in charge returned and gave me back the letters and said "You can go now". I again questioned him as to the aggression and hostility displayed by the police. I said that I would call the prime minister and he said "Do what you want. He is nothing, we are in charge" and he then got in the police vehicle and left.'

Bennett said in his report to JOMIC, whose role it is to receive any reports and complaints in respect of any issue relating to the implementation of enforcement and execution of the GPA.

'The whole incident left me feeling very threatened and I was sure that the incident was being instructed from a higher authority as the member in charge was always talking on the phone whilst walking away. My wife was completely traumatized and it took some 60 minutes for her to stop shaking. I also heard from my drivers that they had been threatened and grabbed by the front of their shirts and asked "What are you doing here? Do you want to die?"'

Bennett told JOMIC that he stayed the night with friends and a CIO vehicle he identified drove past the house two or three times during the night.

'I decided to return with the truck at 0400hrs, feeling extremely threatened due to the threat level,' he said in his report. 'I decided not to go to Charleswood.'

Bennett returned to Zimbabwe in January 2009 after spending two years in exile in South Africa. The MDC Treasurer General was arrested last year, accused of plotting against the Mugabe government. The charges were that he illegally possessed arms for the purposes of committing terrorism and banditry. Bennett fully denies the charges, which carry a possible death threat or prison sentence.

Yesterday a High Court judge was expected to rule on an application by the defence team that the case be thrown out because the state had dismally failed to provide a prima facie case against him. Time will tell. Poor old Roy Bennett had had more than is fair share of wrongs in Zimbabwe.

Nineteen

Now we return to one of Zimbabwe's many heartaches for the Zimbabweans.

The last few years have been impossible. Before the Zimbabwe dollar left us, all the noughts were taken away and our bank accounts were empty. My pension did not appear in the bank for over a year, until I asked the bank to please give me something and they gave me US$37 a month. That would not buy me a week's groceries!

I wrote to Mr Biti, MDC Finance Manager since February 2009. It's not what you know, it's who you know and being the widow of the last white attorney general, I thought he might give me an introduction to someone who would help me in the pensions office to let me have a little more of what was rightfully mine.

Brendan must be turning in his grave! Not even a reply. Maybe the letter never got as far as his desk! It does not look as though I will see my friend on a yearly visit this year. Nothing is reasonable or fair but then I cool off when I think of so many incidents that should never have happened.

At least the British government came to the rescue on 8th May 2009.

8th May 2009 – Information in England, Scotland and Wales – EWSNI

The government is offering assistance to all British people who have been resident in Zimbabwe for at least the last five years and who wish to resettle in the UK. The help is available to British

Citizens aged 70 and over and to others who are vulnerable for other reasons other than their age.

They will be interviewed by British officials in Zimbabwe to meet eligibility requirements and immigration controls and will be allowed to bring spouses, partners and dependents with them. Once they reach the UK, they will be offered social state benefits and support, subject to a means test.

Up to 1,500 elderly and disabled British citizens have received letters from the UK government offering this help.

The Department of Health has announced that British citizens arriving from Zimbabwe under the UK Borders Agency Resettlement Scheme are exempt from charges and should not be asked to pay for any hospital treatment they require. Further information is available from the British Embassy in Harare on 00 263 (0)4338795 or 00 263 (0)912124341 (Mon – Thurs, 8.30 am to 2.30 pm) and on the Foreign and Commonwealth Office website at www.fco.gov.uk

After the Lancaster House talks, the Jewel in the Crown was given to Mugabe. Before this occurred, even when the Rhodesian war was on, we wanted for nothing! Yes, we battled over certain things. As a matter of fact, my own son was wounded three times.

I devoted my life to the troops and my clients in my hairdressing salons were all busy with knitting needles, bless them. Some clients had never held a knitting needle before in their lives, but after I had taught them pearl and plain stitches for scarves, they kept going. Some of the scarves could have reached Kariba. We gave hundreds of mittens, balaclavas, socks, you name it.

The Rhodesians have a saying 'It is but a pleasure' and my God, they meant it. It was nothing to have cake sales. I developed showers for the troops and collected $1,500 on my own, leaving my clients to the staff and going round hospitals to see what they needed and went out collecting in the factories etc. Every boy got his wish but everybody gave and all were happy, not like now. Murders, hunger, strikes; you name it, the poor Zimbabweans have got it.

I produced so many troop shows. Forty-two were cast in one; school children, doctors, dentists, servants, we all got stuck in while our wonderful men were being killed and wounded.

Some of the wives told of some terrifying happenings, for example when one farmer's wife went missing. Most white farmers put up with the most dreadful hair-raising incidents. The whites put notices up in supermarkets, post offices, garages and loos – anywhere public – just no sign of her. When they were in her beautiful home checking everything for the estate, they found her in the loo. Her eyes were wide open, legs and arms cut off and sticking inside the loo.

I was doing a regular client one day and noticed her cheerful smile and conversation was indeed lacking. She suddenly looked up at me and broke down. Her lovely husband had been in hospital at least six weeks and she used to visit him after having her hair done, so it wasn't her hair do. She put her arms around me, sobbing her little heart out. I took her into the staffroom, dried her eyes and gave her a coffee. I dashed to the girls and asked them to cope with my clients – they were all regulars, so I knew they would understand – dashed back, put my arm round her waist and guided her through the staff entrance to my house. (Thank God I had just moved. I'd sold my house and moved into a townhouse – Tudor style – three minutes' walk from the salon.) I took her into my bar and gave her a neat brandy to sip. She then poured her heart out to me amongst the sobs.

She had been to see her husband. He had been very badly wounded in the bush. On arriving home, she noticed her electric fence was down and the gates (electric) were wide open. She could see smoke on her land in the distance. Very calmly, she picked up her gun and in a complete daze, started to walk towards her house. There was not a sound of tractors or payloaders; no workmen about, not even the police boy on duty. With her heart in her mouth, she kept going, pointing her gun at every sound. Then she was there. The front door was open and all the windows around her beautiful home were smashed. Her cook boy was lying on the kitchen floor in a pool of blood, dead. She had had him all her married life, over 35 years. There was no sign of the houseboys or gardeners, so with trembling hands, she opened door after door in her mansion. Every drawer had been emptied on her beautiful Persian carpets; blood was on the wallpapered walls and all the photographs smashed on the ground.

She felt sick but it had to be done. She checked her gun for bullets and in a daze walked outside and got hold of her cell phone and called her neighbours. Not a word would come out of her mouth. Thank God she managed to shout 'Help me, help me'.

They filled their Jeep with workers and after a five-mile dash, they arrived with guns, got back in their vehicles and slowly went to see what the rest of the nightmare held in store for them.

There was a long, long ditch, which the workers had dug at gunpoint – it was a mass grave! There must have been at least 20-odd men shot and thrown into the grave.

Wondering where the rest of the staff were, they slowly got into their armed Jeeps again – don't forget the farms out there have thousands of acres and hundreds of staff, most of the vehicles were machines for farming use. In the distance there was a black object it seemed, but on arrival they found that the terrorists had attacked dozens of workers (I've forgotten the name of the machine, but it is like a long comb or teeth). Every man had been tied by the balls and driven across the land until they were left to die in sheer agony in the blazing sun. This was nearly a whole gang of workers.

Then, back in the Jeep to check their son's property another couple of miles away on their land.

What a shock! The son was on his honeymoon. His house had been burnt to the ground and all his wedding presents were gone. His place was not there and all the petrol pumps were burnt out. No wonder my poor client was in shock.

Oh yes, we had a lot of problems during the war but somehow we expected it. None of us expected starvation and murders and our beautiful Zimbabwe to be utterly ruined, although it looks very much that way.

Now I will jump to May 2010.

12th May 2010 – 'Urgent Help is Needed' – ZW News website

They are sending us a message to show the Zimbabwean government that there are certain consequences to their abuse of human rights.

AfriForum seized a Cape Town property belonging to the Zimbabwean state, saying that the move is a start of a 'civil sanctions campaign' against President Robert Mugabe's government.

'This is a process aimed at helping the people of Zimbabwe in a way that creates hope and shows that it is possible for civil society to institute civil sanctions against a regime that does not help its people,' Willie Spies, a lawyer for AfriForum said outside the offices of the Sheriff for the District of Cape Town.

The process started in November 2008 when the SADC ruled in favour of Michael Campbell and 78 Zimbabwean farmers that the land reform programme in the country was 'racist and unlawful'. Mugabe described the ruling as 'nonsense and of no consequence to Zimbabwe'.

The tribunal followed up its ruling with a contempt ruling and costs order in June 2009. On 25th February, the North Gautent High Court in Pretoria registered the tribunal's rulings. Four Zimbabwean properties in the Cape Town suburbs of Zonnebion, Kenilworth and Wynberg were initially identified. AfriForum agreed only to attach the Kenilworth property located in Salisbury Road at this stage, as its value was estimated at around \$2.5 million was sufficient to cover the cost of the order.

Zimbabwean justice minister, Patrick Chinamasa, dismissed the High Court's move as 'null and void', calling the attempts to attach assets nothing more than 'political grandstanding' and the properties were under diplomatic immunity.

Spies said that Zimbabwean farmers, workers and ordinary citizens had asked AfriForum for help in taking the legal process further in South African last year.

What happened today (12th May 2010) is the attachment of a property situated in Kenilworth. It is being leased to a third party tenant. The fact that it is being leased makes it a commercial property, which makes it liable for attachment as a result of a court order.

Spies said that the attachment was not a recovery for damages for farmers who had lost their land. It was, they said, 'a symbolic gesture to show it is possible to enforce legal principles against the Zimbabwean government in South Africa'.

'We see it as a way to send out a message to show the Zimbabwean government that there are certain consequences to their abuse of human rights.' They said the South African government committed itself last year to upholding the SADC tribunal ruling.

'The message we are getting from the Zimbabwean people is that they are encouraged by this. It gives them hope to be able to see things are happening with their neighbours' help. The process we are following here is the only hope they have got. We do that to encourage them and to tell them that there are people out there still fighting.'

Spies said that AfriForum was aware of other commercial creditors of the Zimbabwean government who were interested in joining the civil proceedings.

2010 – 'Under current circumstances, Zimbabwe is a no-go area for foreign investment' – ZW News, Harare

A German business delegation has cancelled a visit to Zimbabwe, put off by Harare's controversial plan to force foreign-owned firms to give a controlling state to local blacks.

The German African Business Association (GABA) said the trip had been called off because Zimbabwe has become a 'no-go area' for foreign investors following promulgation of the empowerment laws that give foreign-controlled business up to 2015 to sell majority state to indigenous Zimbabweans or face punitive levies and taxes from the government.

'Under the current circumstances, Zimbabwe is a no-go area for foreign investment,' said Andreas Wenzel, Regional Manager for Southern Africa for the GABA that was helping organise the visit.

Wenzel held out hope that the delegation investors from Hamburg and the German Southern African Chamber of Industry and Commerce in Johannesburg could still go to Zimbabwe at a later stage this year, but said this would depend on the outcome of consultations within the Harare power-sharing government over the empowerment laws.

Cancellation of the German visit comes a week after Norway announced it was putting a hold on a US$1.5 million project to assist Zimbabwe's agriculture sector because of the indigenisation law.

Zimbabwean Saviour Kasukuwere announced last month that all foreign-owned businesses, including banks, mines and factories, must offload at least 51% of their shareholding to locals by March 2015. Mugabe gave companies orders to submit him plans showing how they will transfer shareholding to black Zimbabweans.

The indigenisation rules have been a source of controversy and foreign investors have further divided Zimbabwe's shaky coalition government with Prime Minister Morgan Tsvangirai's MDC party pushing to have the laws repealed or drastically changed, while the coalition government has said it is reviewing the indigenisation laws.

Mugabe and his ZANU-PF party, who still wield greater power in the unity government, insist the empowerment drive must go ahead, ignoring warnings that this could scare away foreign investors whose funds Zimbabwe needs to rebuild its shattered economy. Critics fear Mugabe's ZANU-PF wants to press ahead with transferring majority ownership of foreign-owned companies as part of a drive to reward party loyalists with thriving businesses.

Back to poor Roy Bennett. Today on 12th May 2010, he was back in court again, arriving at the High Court to hear whether his application for a dismissal of the state's terrorism trial against him was successful.

Authorities moved to slap him with new charges, this time for possession of a large amount of maize.

Bennett was summoned to appear in court on 6th April on charges of being in unlawful possession of 109 tonnes of maize on his farm in October 2001. Authorities had seized the maize, which Bennett said he grew on his farm for stock feed and to feed his workers, but no charges were laid until now.

'It's preposterous, absolutely preposterous,' said the MDC politician, who was nominated by Prime Minister Morgan Tsvangirai for the post of deputy agriculture minister in the country's unity government.

'These people, President Robert Mugabe's ZANU-PF party, which controls the attorney's office, have not the will to move this process forward and bring democracy and making a better life for the people,' he said angrily.

The development came when the High Court was due to rule on Bennett's application to have charges of terrorism against him thrown out in a case that has drawn out over a year. Bennett was arrested a few days before he was due to be sworn in as deputy minister last year and charged with terrorism, banditry and sabotage for allegedly plotting to blow up a radio communications mast east of Harare. Charges he emphatically denies.

The MDC sees the case as an attempt to keep Bennett, whose farm was expropriated by Mugabe loyalists, out of government.

The hearing has seen the state's case collapse on its key claim that Bennett and Michael Hitchman, a French-born local firearms dealer and trader, exchanged emails planning the alleged sabotage. Mugabe has been using the case against Bennett as a reason for refusing to swear in Bennett, one of the main sticking points in negotiations between the MDC and ZANU-PF on implementing their 2008 unity accord.

What chance has Morgan Tsvangirai got when the headlines along tell the battle is a huge problem? Meeting after meeting, international trips and advice from South Africa. Zuma has still not settled the differences of the unity government. Where will it all end and when? Murders and corruption seem never ending.

I remember last May (2010) reading in ZW News that President Robert Mugabe was digging his heels in again so negotiators from Zimbabwe's three main parties are expected to have little progress in kick starting their stalled unity government to report back to President Jacob Zuma.

Mugabe and his ZANU-PF were still insisting they will implement none of their outstanding commitments to the 18-month-old Global Political Agreement (GPA) until targeted Western sanctions against him and his cronies are lifted.

Zuma visited Harare for two days of intense discussions with the three parties and others two weeks ago and extracted from the parties an agreement that they would implement their outstanding GPA commitments and report back to him by that same day. Despite the lack of progress, the negotiators from the three parties in the unity government – ZANU-PF and the two MDC factions were expecting to work very late the night before to have something to show Zuma.

Zuma is the official Zimbabwe talk's facilitator of ZADC, so he is obliged in turn to report to the chairman of the SADC troika on defence and politics, President Armando Guebuza of Mozambique, who is the official supervisor of the talks.

A government official close to the talks said in Harare yesterday (11th May 2010), 'Negotiators have to finish discussions at the end of the day so they can send the report to the principals and simultaneously to Zuma. But the implementation is proving to be a problem because ZANU-PF is still insisting they will not give in on the issue of sanctions. But there is a slight movement in that the MDC seems to have relaxed their demands to have the Reserve Bank of Zimbabwe governor, Gideon Gono, and the attorney general, Johannes Tomana, removed from their jobs. In return, the MDC is getting favourable concessions on issues around media reforms and the electoral environment, otherwise on the main issues like provincial governors and Roy Bennett, there is no movement,' he said.

After his talks in Harare a couple of weeks ago, Zuma told the press that the parties had agreed on many outstanding issues and said that negotiators had been instructed to implement the agreements. Sources in the talks had reported after Zuma's visit that Mugabe had agreed to remove Tomana and the MDC had accepted that Gono could stay, largely because it felt he had been neutralised by the transfer of most of his power to the Finance Ministry, now controlled by the MDC member, Tendai Biti.

It was also told that Mugabe would drop the treason charges against Bennett, which held up his appointment as deputy agriculture minister and that he would be appointed to a different government position. But soon after Zuma travelled back to South Africa, Mugabe told his officials nothing had been agreed upon and yesterday evening no signs of the compromise which Zuma appeared to have affected were visible.

Twenty

In the meantime, we return to our diamond troubles, which have caused many deaths, violence and much corruption on so many occasions to this very day.

May 2010 – Diamond Troubles

Zimbabwean parliament committee members opened a fact-finding mission to the Marange diamond fields of Manicaland Province on Tuesday of the first week in May but immediately ran into resistance from one of the firms developing the resource in partnership with the government.

Local activists meanwhile declared they are increasingly concerned about the continued presence of the Zimbabwean military controlling the area.

The Chiadzwa Community Development Trust voiced its concerns on Monday in a meeting with lawmaker, Shuwa Mudiwa, and the environmental lawyers. The group said the presence of soldiers in the Marange district of the Chiadzwa area, as it is also known, promotes corruption. Activists charged that syndicates have been siphoning diamonds from Marange to sell in nearby Mozambique.

The community group said that local miners should be able to obtain licences to dig for diamonds alongside the government's joint venture partner firms.

Mbada Diamonds and Canadile Mining, Farai Maguwa, Director of the Centre for Research and Development in Mutare, told VOA that the government should immediately order the military out of Marange district because soldiers continue to abuse residents.

Meanwhile, members of the parliamentary committee on mines were stuck in Mutare late Tuesday evening after being barred from the offices of Canadile Mining, a firm mining diamonds in Marange under a joint venture with a Zimbabwean government entity. Canadile officials told the lawmakers that they could not enter the offices because they lacked proper police authorisation. The committee, en route to Marange to look into a wide range of alleged abuses, had a letter from the Zimbabwe Mining Development Corporation, sources said. They wanted to inspect Canadile's facilities for the storage of diamonds, among other aspects of the operation.

Committee chairman, Chindon Chininga, a member of the ZANU-PF party of President Robert Mugabe and a former mines minister, was said to have been livid when his team was barred from Canadile's premises on Tuesday, armed with a letter from the police. Before proceeding to Marange itself, Mbada barred journalists from accompanying the panel members into the alluvial diamond zone.

I think it is so very sad to read old newspapers at times. When all is said and done, Morgan Tsvangirai is trying so hard to prevent all the violence and have peace in our nearly ruined Zimbabwe. What a job he has when time and time again everything seems to be against him.

As a prime minister and a pillar of the government, he agreed to open an exhibition commemorating victims of political violence. The police were quick to defy Mr Tsvangirai. A day before he was due to speak at the event in Harare, police seized the exhibition's 65 photographs, all of which were graphic images of violence before Zimbabwe's 2008 elections.

Although the prime minister and his Movement for Democratic Change are theoretically equal partners in the coalition government with Robert Mugabe, the president, the reality is indeed very different. Mr Tsvangirai lacked the authority to prevent the police from sabotaging an event he had chosen to open. Only a High Court order compelling the police to return the photographs allowed the exhibition to go ahead.

'There is nothing at all new in this story. It reminds us of the trauma we all went through as a nation,' said Mr Tsvangirai, saying that such exhibitions were a necessary part of the 'healing process'.

Analysts believe that he and his party are in office but not in power. Mr Tsvangirai's growing number of critics accuse him of being co-opted by Mr Mugabe to lend a sense of respectability to the government.

'When the president speaks, people sit up and take notice because they know that his is the voice of authority,' said a leading businessman. 'People applaud Morgan's promises of change, but they do not believe them.'

Mr Tsvangirai's actions have fed the suspicion that he has been reduced to serving Mr Mugabe's agenda. Last week, the prime minister was reported to have urged Western countries to lift the restrictions they have imposed on Mr Mugabe and his allies, which ban them from visiting the US and the European Union and freezes their overseas assets. Then Mr Tsvangirai said that he supported Mr Mugabe's opposition to giving gays legal protection in Zimbabwe.

While Mr Tsvangirai or the prime minister's handlers have sought to clarify his remarks, some fear that he is becoming a convenient stooge to Mr Mugabe.

Jacob Zuma, the South African president, set a deadline today (12th May) for the three parties in Zimbabwe's government to settle their differences. In particular, Mr Tsvangirai wants to dismiss Gideon Gono, the Central Bank governor, who is accused of undermining the economy, and Johannes Tomana, attorney general, who is allegedly protecting powerful figures from prosecution. But Mr Mugabe has refused to get rid of either.

Last weekend he insisted that EU and US restrictions must be lifted before other issues could be addressed.

Here we are in June and no better off with agreements between Morgan Tsvangirai and Robert Mugabe.

In general: Army and copy join Chiadzwa syndicates, which is only a worry. More than 500 people were arrested in the Chiadzwa diamond fields during the month of April this year alone under the security forces' Operation Hakudzokwi Phase VII (a place of no return).

According to a briefing note by Assistant Commissioner Mawere to the sub-national Joint Operations Command (JOC) dated May and which was leaked to several media organisations by a well-connected ZANU-PF source, this was an increase of 121 over the March figures.

It is understood that Kimberley Process Certification Scheme's diamond monitoring, advisor for Chiadzwa, Abbey Chikane, has also seen the memo which states:

'The period from 23rd March 2010 to 5th April 2010 witnessed an increase in gweja (illegal panners) population and activities in the area of Chiadzwa primary and Muchena areas. This was attributed to connivance with gwejas by the outgoing contingent of 22 Infantry Battalion. The unit formed syndicates with illegal panners towards the end of its tour of duty.'

Fourteen soldiers, including an unnamed commander, were 'expelled' from operating Chiadzwa, but the report gives no detail whether they were disciplines in any way.

It highlights the problem of indiscipline and greed on the part of members of the security forces, supposedly keeping order in the diamond fields, and indicates that there is gross indiscipline within the forces.

Observers say this puts a large question mark over the validity of the government's promises to the Kimberley Process to put its own house in order.

The brief note also talks of problems at Chirasika panning sites and for the first time officially confirms the involvement of a Chinese company in partnership with the Zimbabwean government in Chiadzwa.

The company, named Angin Investments, is one of three companies mining the diamond fields. The others being Canadile and Mbada.

Concern is gathering of people at the Chinese concession seeking employment. Some of these job seekers end up doing illegal panning in the area, says the report.

It also confirms the murder of Herbert Gwiriri, who is referred to as 'a suspected gweja' by a Lance Corporal Marida of 4.2 Infantry Battalion on 10th April 2010.

During the disarmament, he shot and injured Constable Bhiseki Emmanuel of headquarters troop Fairbridge, on the finger and lower leg. 'Lance Corporal Marida is being charged with Murder and attempted murder,' reads the briefing note.

It also confirms The Zimbabwean's previous reports about the military wanting to move more than 120 facilities from the area.

There is no progress on the ground since the last visit by the sub-national JOC on 26th March 2010. 'The following number of families need to be relocated immediately to ARDA: Transan Mbada – 49, Canadile – 44, China Zimbabwe – 49' says the report. The ARDA property is believed to be a farm outside Odzi.

Under the headline 'Challenges' the briefing note says that all the pits and shafts in the area must be refilled. It also states that there is a need to provide adequate food rations to security forces to avoid cases of armed robbery and indiscipline, transport for commanders, food and lubricants in order to increase VOs by commanders and to pay 'I' and 'S' to (security forces) members to minimise cases of syndicates and armed robberies.

The police believe there is still a residence population of about 400 gwejas in the area.

The memo also confirms the continued existence of the JOC and its tentacles around the country, which was supposed to have been dismantled under the terms of the GPA and replaced with a National Security Council. This body has only met once since the GPA was signed in February 2009. The JOC comprises the heads of the army, police, air force and CIO and reports only to President Robert Mugabe.

When I was in Zimbabwe in September 2009, the thing that stood out in my mind was all the police blocks. They were booking people and taking bribes off the public for all sorts of different reasons. So much so, the public were given little cards saying:

Useful contacts for when you feel the police
are trying to harass you or solicit a bribe from you.

0912 719730/011 769768 Superintendent Ncube
011 415491 Superintendent Kangware
0912 273 286 Superintendent Bodbo
0912 965 030 Inspector Chigome

One wonders how bad things really are. For days and days we had no water and the electricity would be off with no warning, usually when we would be in the kitchen cooking a meal or watching the news. Even the washing machine would stop and the telephones would go off. God, what a life! Things are getting worse, not better.

Twenty-one

I am now writing on 3rd June 2010. Headlines in the newspapers are quite frightening: 'Thugs roam free', 'Government backs down in Kingdom Meikle case', 'Pits meant for supporters of MDC revealed as torture bases', 'No rush on elections', 'Houses Director fired', 'Radios confiscated', 'ZANU strengthens ties with Chinese'.

Well, I do know that Robert Mugabe bought property in Hong Kong and his wife had a wonderful shopping spree, insulting and shouting at the reporters, which was hushed up, and to hear she had amnesty in Hong Kong so she could say and do as she wished. It only seems a couple of years ago, if that, when a boat from China arrived in South Africa full of war material, guns etc and was refused docking. Whatever was Mugabe up to then?

It makes me shudder when I think of all the wealth of agriculture, mining, cotton, coffee, tea, sugar, diamonds and emeralds; you name it, we used to grow it. And the tourism: the famous Victoria Falls, Kariba, the lakes, the fantastic colours overlapping our beautiful tarmaced road from flamboyant jacarandas to many, many more blossoms of purple, pink, yellow and red. Oh, what a magnificent country, all ruined through war, murder, corruption and lies. Will it ever be the wonderful country it was again? What did Mugabe do to his Jewel in the Crown that we were all so happy and content with? To say nothing of our royal blue skies without a cloud. It has been proved to be one of the best climates in the world.

11th June 2010 – The Return of the Blood Diamond

The international human rights group Global Witness (GW) has painted a negative image of Zimbabwe's diamond industry ahead of next week's meeting of the Kimberley Process Certification System (KPCS) in Israel to determine the future of its so-called 'blood diamonds'.

In a report entitled 'The Return of the Blood Diamond', GW said this week that the army must be withdrawn from the diamond fields and the Zimbabwean government must not enter into any new joint-venture agreements with potential diamond miners until the current dispute was resolved.

'Zimbabwe must immediately withdraw the army from the diamond fields, hold rights abusers to account and suspend imports and exports of rough diamonds until the diamond section meets international standards. It should also suspend the introduction of new investors into Marange until the legality of current joint ventures can be established and effective oversight implemented,' GW said.

The US-based organisation said the role of Mugabe's top military brass and the involvement of senior officials of his ZANU-PF party must also be probed.

At the weekend, mines and mineral development minister, Obert Mpofu, expressed optimism that Zimbabwe's diamonds would be allowed to trade on the international market following a positive preliminary report from the South Africa Diamond Council chairman and KPCS monitor, Abbey Chikane.

Chikane is said to have expressed reservations about some of Zimbabwe's practices, in particular the continued presence of the army in the diamond fields. Human rights abuses and theft, but it is likely to authorise Zimbabwe's intended sale of four million carats' worth of diamonds from Marange.

GW alleged that Zimbabwe's military and political elite were bent on selling the diamonds and gaining control of the diamonds through violence.

'Zimbabwe's ZANU-PF political elite and military are seeking to capture the country's diamond wealth through a combination of state-sponsored violence and the legally questionable introduction of opaque joint-venture companies,' GW said.

'The Return of the Blood Diamonds' critics, the KPCS, set up to end the trade in conflict diamonds for its alleged repeated failure to react effectively to the crisis in Zimbabwe.

Blood diamonds – the case against ZANU-PF

Over the past three years, the National Army has visited appalling abuses on civilians in Marange's diamond fields. Nobody has been held to account for these crimes and now it turns out the joint-venture companies normally brought in to improve conditions, are directly linked to the ZANU-PF and military elite.

'Thanks to the impunity and violence in Zimbabwe, blood diamonds are back on the market (international),' said Elly Harrowell, a GW campaigner.

The GW report accuses Mpofu, a ZANU-PF stalwart, of being at the forefront of efforts to block parliament's oversight of the joint-venture companies. Canadile Mining and Mbada Diamonds. The watchdog says Mpofu has imposed his allies as board members and sidelines the state mining company, ZMDC. Mbada Diamonds is chaired by Robert Mhlanga, a former top Air Force officer and witness at Morgan Tsvangirai's treason trial.

'The investment deals have been done with scant regard to legal process against a background of utter violence and intimidation and are dangerously lacking in transparency. This leaves the door wide open for state looting and the usual corruption and raises the very real possibility of internationally certified diamonds financing renewed political violence in Zimbabwe,' said Harrowell.

Harrowell said that instead of suspending Zimbabwe for flagrant breach of its code, members of the KPCS have settled on 'a weak compromise agreement' which Zimbabwean authorities have repeatedly breached.

'Mpofu and his cronies have demonstrated a flagrant disregard for the scheme's rules. They seem intent on pursuing their violent, self-serving exploitation of the country's diamond wealth. Nobody should be under the illusion that this is about anything other than lining the pockets of ZANU PF and their allies, who are being squeezed by economic sanctions,' she said.

17th June 2010 – 'Dirty diamonds special report: This is ugly, so what do we do?' – The Zimbabwean

The level of direct involvement of individuals, companies and institutions of Europe, South Africa and the Middle East in the looting and perversion of justice within our much-maligned Zimbabwe beggars belief.

The dirty secret needs to see the light of day and the governments of these states need to confront the ugliness head on.

The most glaringly obvious case in point is the Chiadzwa diamond debacle and as we speak the international involvement in this rape of Zimbabwe's birthright gathers pace.

We ask, or rather *must* ask, what the UK, South African and Mauritian authorities are doing about this? They ring their hands in terror at the lack of respect for law in Zimbabwe, but do nothing in their own jurisdictions to reprimand or investigate their own corporate badies wilfully exploiting Zimbabwe's lawlessness to profit from blood diamond money. Why? (Oh, God, if only my darling husband were alive, the last white attorney general, who resigned under national interest! He must be turning in his grave!)

It just seems inconcievable that those people have not read the international press about the court orders and ownership issues.

While it is not yet known how many diamonds were successfully bought and by which companies, these participants obviously must know the risk that the owners of these diamonds will track them down and demand compensation.

Another issue – what are the governments of India, Belgium, Israel, Brazil, the United Arab Emirates and Dubai doing about these rogue companies of theirs?

What can the public do? Many of these bidders are allegedly ethical suppliers and traders in gems. How can they possibly know that there will be no consumer backlash against the products?

It is time for the retailers like Tiffany and Cartier to stand up and demand an end to the trade in unethical or stolen goods. Rosy Blue's business would collapse under such a boycott.

This is similar to the threatened boycott on Nestlé products when they were supporting stolen milk from Zimbabwe but is far, far more important.

Trade in stolen goods is an international crime. Any activity in contempt of a very specific court order is a crime in Zimbabwe. The mining of these diamonds is therefore a crime, regardless of the actual alleged ownership by one party or another. So what do the bidders possibly see as their defence to allege they were buying in good faith?

The Kimberley Process has failed miserably in trying to assist transparency in Zimbabwe's murky underworld-ruled diamond sector. They have failed to identify the corruption and criminality of current mining. They have failed in their purpose and the failure must surely reside at the door of KP monitor, Abbey Chikane, whose behaviour and non-disclosures have led to increasing scepticism about his impartiality.

Suffice to say that yet another international body has failed to condemn the lawlessness and breakdown of society in Zimbabwe. Instead they seem to have whitewashed the appalling perversion of justice and are recommending an endorsement of the diamonds that are clearly the proceeds of criminality. No doubt this will be the cover behind which the buyer at the latest auction will hide to justify their trade in these contraband goods.

This dirty secret needs to see the light of day and the governments of these states need to confront that ugliness head on.

I need to let you know what the Kimberley Process is. I think I did mention this at the beginning of the book but it is important to remember as there will be further news regarding diamonds later on.

The Kimberley Process was introduced in 2003 by the United Nations and was designed to certify the origin of rough diamonds and ensure diamonds could not be used to finance war and human rights abuses. It is a Certification Scheme (KPCS).

The role of the KPCS is to act as a watchdog on companies and countries involved in the diamond trade and to stop 'blood diamonds' from entering the mainstream rough diamond market. It involves both industry and government representatives of the major diamond producing and diamond consuming nations.

The impetus to set up the process came largely from the revelations of terrible war crimes and atrocities in Liberia and Sierra Leone, which ultimately led to the current trial of Charles Taylor in The Hague.

'Secret deals and shady companies: The filthy business behind the diamond trade'

In May, Mbada Diamonds is alleged to have held a major diamond viewing without the knowledge of the Kimberley Process (KPCS) agent in Harare, Abbey Chikane. Sources said Mbada, a recently formed company with no background in diamond trading, deliberately misled the KPCS.

It has now been confirmed that Mbada Diamonds has closed and finalised the awards in a tender that has exceeded US$150 million, as revealed in a source.

The sale appears to have been with the full blessing of the Minister of Mines, Obert Mpofu, in spite of his assertions that he had banned diamond exports as directed by cabinet.

Robert Mhlanga, the Robert Mugabe-approved chairman of Mbada Diamonds and South African, David Kassel, are said to have staged this secretly held diamond tender.

Mbada invited a number of major diamond firms to view the diamonds at Harare Airport from 15th to 30th May. However, all the participants were asked to leave on 24th May when Abbey Chikane went to see Mbada.

Mbada hope to gain Kimberley press papers for the 3.56 million carat lot of rough diamonds, estimated to be worth US$150 million, but had told participants that they had planned to sell the diamonds with or without KP papers.

Companies that attended the pre-auction viewing of the diamonds included Rosy Blue, Radam and Samir Gems from Belgium, Diaryrio from Brazil, Kesru Gems, Sunrise from India, Zar Diam, Pure Diamond, Amani Gems, Akshar International from Dubai, Super Gems from Belgium and Dubai and LLD from Israel.

Mbada, who's alleged right to mind derives from a disputed right held by ZMDC, is believed to be a front for a variety of elites, but is financed and controlled by the New Reclamation Group Ltd, known as Reclamation and South African Scrap Metal Trading Company. The holding is fronted by a Mauritian tax-haven company called Grandwell Holdings Ltd.

Reclam's chief executive officer and chairman, David Kassed, signed the diamond tender documents. Also involved in the group is his friend and business partner, Robert Mhlanga, former vice marshal in the Zimbabwe Air Force, now living in Sandton, Johannesburg, who allegedly began his diamond trading during active service in the Democratic Republic of the Congo war.

The shareholders register of Reclam makes for interesting reading and includes Old Mutual and Capital works. Old Mutual holds 5% of the company and has appointed a director to the Reclam board, Zwinton Dicks. Old Mutual is a listed London company worth £6 billion.

Capital works have 15% of Reclam's shares. It is a South African private equity company made up of many of the South African yuppie set that formerly worked for Brait Capital, two of whom sit on the Reclam board. These are all supposedly legitimate and clean organisations.

The newspaper is in possession of company documents that directly show a resolution by the Reclam board to enter into diamond mining in July 2009. Even the name of Zimbabwe is concealed in the minutes of this meeting.

Why did the directors of this meeting from Old Mutual and Capital works not insist on transparency in the matter? Were they aware that these operations would be in Zimbabwe and on rights owned by another company altogether? If so, why did they allow the company to hide the facts? Either way, why was there no due diligence by the directors themselves? Why have Capital works and Old Mutual not sued Reclam and the chairman, David Kassed?

'The only possible answer is it seems they were fully compliant in this well-orchestrated plan to lawlessly loot from Zimbabwe in what amounts to be organised crime,' said Andrew Cranswick of African Consolidated Resources plc (ACR) in 2009.

It is well know that in September 2009 the High Court ruled that the ZMDC and obviously their partnership companies (Mbada and Canadile) were mining illegally and that the rights still belonged to the original owner, ACR, and that all diamonds ever derived from that place should be returned to ACR. Most importantly, it was ordered that appeal against the court judgement would not delay execution of the order which was to have immediate effect.

The High Court order was ignored by Mbada, Canadile, ZMDC and the police, who were supposed to enforce it.

The chief justice of the Supreme Court, Godfrey Chidyainsuku, in February 2010 further clarified this order. He ruled that pending the appeal, all the diamonds should be held in safe keeping in the vaults of the Reserve Bank of Zimbabwe (RBZ) while all mining should cease pending the outcome of the main appeal.

It never ends! Who on earth can we trust in Zimbabwe?

17th June 2010 – 'Rights activist claims diamond watchdog linked to ZANU-PF' – The Zimbabwean

Farai Maguwu, the Director of the Centre for Research and Development, was arrested last week after describing human rights abuses, illegal panning and diamond smuggling in a supposedly confidential meeting with the Kimberley Process monitor, Abby Chikane.

Maguwu said his problems started after a meeting with the KP monitor last Tuesday. He said he had been assured that information discussed in the meeting was 'confidential'.

In the meeting, Maguwu told Chikane what his organisation had observed at the volatile diamond fields, where he said human rights abuses were continuing alongside illegal gold panning and the smuggling of diamonds without KP certification.

Maguwu said he was shocked to hear that the day after the meeting, Chikane's emails and itinerary had been stolen, but believed he had been 'set up' by Chikane.

Maguwu said he was being charged with giving Chikane a state security document drafted by the army and was prejudicial to the state.

'I did not give Chikane anything, but in the conversation, Chikane himself mentioned this document and asked me about it,' said Maguwu.

'Little did I know that the meeting was to set me up so that Chikane could create a story out of the meeting, resulting in all these problems that we are now facing, emanating from a meeting that I had with one person and in close confidentiality.'

In an interview with SW Radio, he accused the KP monitor of complicity with ZANU-PF, saying he was part of the gravy train.

'There must be something that is going on behind the scenes between Abbey Chikane and the ZANU officials who are plundering Manage diamonds.'

Maguwu continues, 'Even if this case goes to court, he (Chikane) is going to be a witness against me and him being an interested party means that he is now working to advance the interest of one party against the other.'

'This is the latest in a series of attempts by the Zimbabwean authorities to intimidate human rights activists and stop them from investigating and publicising ongoing abuses in the Marange diamond fields,' said Bernard Taylor, executive director of partnership Africa Canada.

Andrew Cranswick, chief executive officer of African Consolidated Resources plc is in hiding, afraid too that he will be arrested by the authorities. ARC's lawyers and a senior company executive, Ian Harris, have already been arrested on undisclosed charges.

ACR is the company locked in the much-publicised legal battle over the ownership of the Chiadzwa Marange diamond fields.

Cranswick Marange, born and bred in the mining town of Shurugwe, echoed Maguwu's suspicions that Chikane was not impartial and therefore an unacceptable KP monitor who had been tainted by corruption.

'It is alleged that he was shortlisted for the position with only two other candidates and was handpicked for the position through the influence of Namibia (the current KP chair) and ZANU-PF Minister of Mines, Obert Mpofu,' said Cranswick.

He said when he took up his duties as KP monitor, Chikane failed to objectively listen to all his stakeholders. Cranswick alleges that ACR was given no hearing and had to initiate a meeting to air their views. ACR showed The Zimbabwean a letter they had written to Chikane to clarify their concerns. Chikane was reluctant to discuss Marange.

'Basically, we wanted the KP monitor to impartially consult with all shareholders in an open and transparent manner,' said Cranswick.

This, however, seemed impossible and Cranswick mentioned an incident in which Chikane scrambled to hide his face when some well-known ZANU-PF appeared in a public place where they were having an informal meeting with Chikane.

'Chikane's credibility is further compromised by his being the brother of Frank Chikane, who was closely linked to Thabo Mbeki's pro-ZANU mediation mission to Zimbabwe during the Global Political Agreement negotiations,' said Cranswick.

'Frank Chikane is said to have facilitated a joint venture between Patrice Motsepe's African Rainbow Minerals and Darrendale Platinum Project, whose owner is suspected to be Grace Mugabe but is fronted by Cross Global Hong Kong's Jack Hsieh.

Chikane is also related to Kagiso Chikane, who is named as the chief executive of African Renaissance Holdings, one of the mining companies with ties to Rich Rewards Ltd in Mauritius and Rich Rewards is partly owned by Obert Mpofu and allegedly was a recipient of a US$1.25 million bribe in exchange for a joint-venture application in the Marange deal.

'Smuggling, greed and corruption uncovered' – The Zimbabwean

A new Partnership Africa Canada (PAC) report 'Diamond and Clubs – The Militarised Control of Diamonds and Power in Zimbabwe' describes the smuggling, greed and government-sponsored human rights violations of the country's diamond trade.

The 32-page report criticises the Kimberley Process for losing direction and credibility and makes recommendations to deal with the crisis in Zimbabwe and in the Kimberley Process, including Zimbabwe's suspension from the KP and a new boundary definition of 'conflict diamonds'.

Zimbabwe is not the only country failing to meet some, or all, of the basic requirements asked of diamond-producing nations by the Kimberley Process (KP), but Zimbabwe sets itself apart from the others because of the government's brazen defiance of universally agreed principles of humanity and good governance expected of adherents to the KP, says the report.

While the KP monitor, Abbey Chikane, found the country to be compliant with KP's minimum requirements, PAC claims that government officials and representatives of two new exploration companies, Mbada and Canadile, have gone through the motions of presenting themselves as legitimate partners in their efforts to mine diamonds in the Marange region.

PAC called the monitor's positive report 'a whitewash' and urged the immediate release of Farai Maguwu, the leading Zimbabwean human rights activist monitoring the abuses in the diamond fields (by The Zimbabwean special correspondent).

Going back to the end of last March 2010, I remember reading that the mines minister, Obert Mpofu, having said he had done his research and found that people in the diamond business globally were drug traffickers, smugglers or just plan crooks. What chance has one got in the true decent business world? So much crime and corruption.

25th March 2010 – 'The Corruption of Diamonds' – The Zimbabwean

Mines minister, Obert Mpofu, has admitted that some officials of the two companies contracted to mine diamonds at the controversial Marange fields, might be 'crooks'.

Mpofu went on to tell a parliamentary probe into irregularities in the mining sector that it was 'virtually impossible to get clean people in the industry'.

Giving evidence to the parliamentary committee investigating operations in Marange, Mpofu said he was aware that some of the directors of the two firms, Canadile and Mbada Diamonds, were involved in shady business deals but challenged the committee to identify any investors in the diamond industry who were clean.

'He said he had done his research and found that people in the diamond business globally are drug traffickers, smugglers or plain crooks. He said this was the trend worldwide and the committee was fooling itself by thinking that they could get a clean diamond investor,' said a source who attended the briefing by the minister. The hearing was held behind closed doors.

The government-owned Zimbabwe Mining Development Corporation (ZMDC) last year partnered little-known Grandwell of South Africa to form Mbada Investments, which is mining diamonds at the Marange field. The ZMDC also partnered another little-known South African firm, Core Mining and

214

Minerals, in a joint-venture operation mining and trading as Canadile Mines. All these firms I have mentioned before.

But parliamentarians have accused some members of the boards of the two firms, whose names have not been mentioned or disclosed, have been former illegal drug and diamond dealers in the Democratic Republic of the Congo (DRC) and Sierra Leone.

Under the law, Mpofu can appoint a chairperson and deputy of the ZMDC board but has no authority to name people to sit on boards of joint-venture companies formed by the state mining corporation and other entities.

One of the appointments is former Zimbabwe Air Force helicopter pilot, Robert Mhlanga, who has interests in Grandwell but was named by Mpofu to represent the ZMDC on the Mbada board as chairman.

According to diamond.net, Mhlanga was Zimbabwe's first black helicopter pilot and worked as a courier to Mugabe's first wife, Sally.

Mhlanga is said to have made a fortune through various projects in Africa and was active in the DRC diamond trade when Zimbabwean troops fought there.

The Mbada chairman is known to have close ties with Zimbabwe's military establishment that is accused of stealing millions of dollars worth of diamond's from Marange and selling them on the foreign black market.

The committee accused Mpofu of failure to diligently vet people before forming a partnership with them to mine in the Marange diamond fields.

Mpofu admitted that he did not follow laid down procedures when he licensed Canadile and Mbada to mine diamonds at Chiadzwa (no smoke without fire!).

Sources said that under fire, the minister vainly sought to explain away his actions by arguing that the country badly needed money.

I could go on and on about the diamond world, but let's write about what is happening now!

Twenty-two

In March 2010, the Germans bust Mugabe's sanctions. This could only happen in Zimbabwe! Just in a down and out country crying out for food and other help.

March 2010 – 'A US$13.5 million dairy plant for Zimbabwe' – The Zimbabwean

A plant is being built in South Africa for the Mugabes by a subsidiary of the German-owned Guth Ventiltechnik.

A German company with a branch in South Africa has actually busted the EU-targeted measures against President Robert Mugabe and his wife, Grace, by building a state-of-the-art diary processing plan to process milk from their Gushungo diary estates.

The dairy, costing US$13.5 million, has been built by Guth South Africa, a leading supplier of equipment to the local diary, food and beverage market. It is a subsidiary of the German-owned, Guth Ventiltechnik.

The first family seized the Foyle dairy farm in the fertile Mazai Valley from its rightful owner, Ian Webster. It used to be one of the best dairy estates in the country.

Sources at Guth said the equipment would be installed at a big factory at Mugabe's rural home in Zuimba and not on the Gushungo estates. It is presumed the milk will be trucked away across the country from Mazai to Zuimba.

The dairy will produce anything you can think of in terms of dairy projects: milk, yoghurt, ice cream, cheese and juices, said the sources.

The Mugabes are unable to sell their milk to American or European Union (EU) companies, which are banned from doing business with the octogenarian leader and his circle, or businesses linked to them under a raft to target measures imposed on them for human rights abuses.

Zimbabwe's largest milk processor, the parastatal Dairiboard, which is riddled with mismanagement and corruption, was unable to pay the Mugabes for the milk. They therefore began selling to Nestlé, the Swiss-based multinational, but the public outrage around the world forced Nestlé to stop dealing with them.

Sources at the factory in Johannesburg told The Zimbabwean that the equipment was built over the past two years through funds channelled through the Reserve Bank of Zimbabwe (RBZ) where one of Mugabe's closest allies, Gideon Gono, is the governor. It is not clear whether the Mugabes have refunded the Reserve Bank from their own resources or whether taxpayers' dollars were used for the project.

Mugabe's official salary does not amount to US$13.5 million.

'We began to build the factory in 2005 and have now almost finished. Any time now it will be hitting the road to Zimbabwe. We are just waiting for Mugabe's people to come here and give their satisfaction before it leaves,' said an employee at Guth.

On how the alliance with the Mugabes began, the workers said that one of the company managers was a close business associate of Grace following many other jobs they have done for her.

'The boss is the only one that handles Mrs Mugabe's orders because he seems to have earned her trust. Her people always seem to come here and check on the equipment and they only deal with him,' said the source.

Other workers said the Mugabes had become popular and regular customers at the company, which is expected to send its regular experts to install the dairy in Zuimba. The company will also continue to send spare parts and after-sales service to the dairy, which will be up and running before the end of this year, according to the sources.

Despite several attempts, no official comment could be obtained from Guth SA as the company's manager, identified as Andrew by the receptionist, was said to be out of the office and he had not responded to telephone messages at the time of going to print. His deputy refused to comment, saying only that 'Andrew can talk about that'.

This is the only information I have to tell you on 'the dairy' at the moment, which started at the end of March 2010!

Now here is something around March: 'The MDC seeks justice' – and so they jolly well should!

More than a year after the formation of Zimbabwe's inclusive government amid post-election trauma, not one single person has been punished for the violence that killed 253 people, uprooted more than 200,000 and crippled the economy, parliament has been told.

MDC chief whip, Innocent Gonese, told parliament, after moving a landmark motion on the 2008 elections, that 2,401 homes, mainly belonging to MDC supporters, were destroyed countrywide between January and December 2008 by marauding militia.

He said that during the same period at least 253 people – 36 women and 217 men – were killed during the election-related violence in 2008 countrywide and there were many more unrecorded deaths.

Gonese has asked parliament to establish a select committee of the House to investigate the violence that took place after the 29th March 2008 elections and report its findings to parliament. But ZANU-PF legislators have rejected the MDC chief whip's first attempt because they fear a whitewash unless there are guarantees of immunity first.

ZANU-PF staged a walk-out after the motion was tabled.

Gonese said the post-election political violence that followed President Mugabe and ZANU-PF's devastating electoral loss provoked an operation of death and destruction, including the massacre of massive quantities of livestock: 4,211 recorded killings of fowl, 36 sheep seized and killed by militia, 128 pigs, 1,809 herds of cattle, 21 rabbits and 2,418 goats were reportedly seized and killed and feasted on by militia.

Amid remonstrations from ZANU-PF, Gonese told parliament that the operation was spearheaded by known perpetrators, including 65% ZANU-PF militia, 28% war veterans, 4% members of the Zimbabwe National Army, 1% Central

Intelligence Organisation operative and another 1% of Zimbabwe Republic Police operatives.

Gonese has asked parliament to approve the establishment of a Truth, Justice and Reconciliation Commission to probe human rights abuses that took place during the bloody and internationally condemned 2008 election. A similar body in South Africa shed light on apartheid crimes and to ease tensions.

'I have got suggestions and I think one of the most important things we should have done here is the setting up of a Truth and Justice Commission whereby those who are prepared to go and confess their acts can be forgiven,' Gonese said.

'It is easier for a person who is a victim to forgive a person who has shown remorse. But it is for people to come forward and confess what they did and that commission can then make a decision.'

Many want those found guilty of the slow-moving genocide and other human rights violations associated with the 2008 elections not to be eligible for amnesty.

The move comes amidst debate on how to deal with those implicated in the violence that broke out after the historic election in 2008. The issue is dominating Zimbabwean politics, weighing on local markets and being closely watched by the outside world.

President Robert Mugabe and Prime Minister Morgan Tsvangirai, who came together in the coalition to end the bloodshed in February last year, have been trying to push justice initiatives through the Troika of National Healing ministers, but the aged ministers have been accused of being lackadaisical in their approach and have also been hamstrung by a funding shortfall.

Special tribunal

Under pressure from home, especially its youth constitutency, which bore the brunt of the brutal election violence at the hands of the militia, the MDC proposes for a special tribunal. Some are calling for the court to be set-up by special degree by passing the legislature where the ZANU-PF has fiercely resisted any attempt at justice for perpetrators.

The Zimbabwean newspaper heard that the MDC had put together information on violence with a list of names of suspected chief perpetrators of the violence and that the dossier had been gathering dust at the attorney general's office. The dossier was seen by The Zimbabwean, sitting ministers and legislators.

Forgotten victims

Often forgotten in the political debate are the victims, the families of the bereaved, those still carrying wounds and the political refugees still sleeping rough in neighbouring countries.

There is deep resentment among Zimbabwe's 12 million people at a crisis perceived to have been caused by political leaders whipping up supporters along political lines and the lack of accountability afterwards.

Since the election crisis exposed Zimbabwe's instability, local markets have also become susceptible to the political mood.

Since the formation of the troubled coalition, Mugabe and Tsvangirai's respective factions have been endlessly squabbling over petty matters like protocol and also important matters of national policy, including outstanding issues from the Global Political Agreement that gave birth to the inclusive government.

So the 2008 violence motion in parliament has put a further strain on the bickering parties in the ruling coalition. Many fear more violence at the next election, scheduled for 2011, if those behind the 2008 election trouble get away free.

Gonese told the House, 'As Zimbabweans, I think we should be ashamed of what transpired. The country was in a state of war. We have a situation where people had to leave their homes and stay in the mountains. We had a situation where people had to leave their homes and comes to the urban areas. We had a situation where Harvest House (the MDC headquarters in central \Harare) resembled a refugee camp and where our office in Mutare also resembled a refugee camp. Madam speaker, I don't think we want such events to happen in our country ever again.'

Many are angry at Mugabe for failing to rein in his security forces during the crisis. Zimbabweans are sceptical of their own authorities' ability to bring the guilty to justice. A procession of past enquiries into million-dollar corruption scandals, land grab audits and other incidents of the '80's Gukurahundi violence, have all led to little other than huge bills for the taxpayer.

The headlines in the July papers just explain everything:

a) No accountability, no reconciliation (Sibanda).
b) Zimbabwe faces more food shortages – a 400,000-tonne cereal deficit.
c) False terrorism alarm.
d) Will Zimbabweans be chased out?
e) Chairman suspended.
f) Youths assaulted by MP.
g) Everyone is a foreigner somewhere.
h) Does the MDC have the audacity to ward of terror?
i) MDC-T activists abducted and arrested.
j) Councillors boycott allowances.
k) Opposition parties threaten constitution.
l) Women demand transitional ?
m) Protests over German-owned farm seizure.
n) South African rapper kicked out of Zimbabwe.

This is one newspaper in one day. Where in heaven's name is the progress of this once-beautiful, happy, wealthy country? The only thing we have not got is OIL!

I think it is high time to end the 'diary of politics' and say one thing: If you are a Zimbabwean, or lived there (as I did for 58 years) we might have lost everything, even our pensions, BUT we have got something that not many people in the world have got. Something no money in the world will, or could possibly buy, and that is the most wonderful and rare memories in the world.

We had it all: the Zimbabwean way of living; the people – nothing in the world was too much trouble to help and the reply was always 'It's but a pleasure'. There was no class distinction, everybody knew their place. The magic sunsets and the climate proved to be one of the best in the world. We loved our wonderful winter sunshine; no rain but cold at night with log fires, but warm in the day! The rainy season – we longed for the rain; our flying ants from the steamy ground having their natural flight and then their wings drop off and the Africans would eat them. The long, winding tarmac road for hundreds of miles, now full of potholes because of no maintenance for 28 years – we go by the potholes at night as all the street signs have been taken away.

And the water – some friends of ours have not had water for years, they collect it from friends that have a borehole or tap water for a few hours. But being Rhodesians we cope and all help each other.

'Sundowners' still exist – by 6.00 pm it is dark and we sit by our pools on our patios, not knowing who will pitch up. The ice is out and our bars are open, we never have light evenings, but who cares?

The most amazing thing in Zimbabwe is the avenues (we call them streets in the UK). Even without water before the rains they are all ablaze with colour: red, yellow and purple blossom. Some avenues have pink blossoms touching each other across the road – it is absolute magic with the royal blue cloudless skies and sunshine everywhere.

Then there were the magic holidays where our nearest seaside was Beira in Mozambique. The nation went there and we would meet at the Portuguese border and give each other a cold beer. Everyone knew everybody. We would go to Mana Pools Game Reserve in Kariba and one could have been on the Med with all the different islands with hotels on crocodile farms, watching the crocodiles on the riverbeds with their sly eyes looking at us; the hippos diving under the water and then after a few seconds coming up to the surface again; the jumbos crossing the Zambezi river in one lane, trunks hanging on to each others tales. At night we would listen to the Africans singing and having their homemade brew in the distance. What a happy country it was!

The servants in their white uniforms smiling at us with their beautiful white teeth showing up against their black skin. They have wonderful rhythm and when they dance and sing they harmonise so beautifully.

What a shame such a beautiful country has turned into utter violence, murder and corruption based on sheer greed. God along knows what is going to happen to Zimbabwe now. These days there does not seem to be much hope for Tsvangirai, or the country!

As for the whites – they just exist, filling up bottles, baths and buckets with water as they never know when their electricity or water will be cut off, or when the accounts come in one month and every account had the same amount in it! It is almost impossible to act like a normal citizen by paying the 'correct' amount for phone, water and electricity – you name it!

July 2011 – 'UK helps dictator buy 16 Paris homes as African leaders accused of stealing millions of US dollars in aid' – The Daily Mail

British taxpayers are funding the multi-million pound Paris property portfolio of an African dictator through aid payments to his nation, it has been claimed.

It emerged yesterday that Dennis Sassou Nguesso, President of the Democratic Republic of the Congo, owns 16 of the most luxurious houses and flats in the French capital.

This year, receiving £133 million, his country is amongst the biggest recipients of foreign aid from Britain. The figure of £133 million is due to almost double to £258 million by 2015, an increase that raises fresh questions over whether Britain's aid is actually alleviating poverty in the third world.

Sassou Nguesso is one of a number of African politicians said to have built up vast overseas property empires using public funds, including the proceeds of foreign aid from their countries' treasuries.

The details are contained in a report compiled by the anti-corruption groups, Transparency International and Sherpa and handed over to Paris prosecutors.

Ali Bongo, President of Gabon, owns at least 39 properties in Paris, while the portfolio of Teodoro Ubiang Nguema Mbasogo, President of Equatorial Guinea, includes an entire six-storey period building on the prestigious Avenue Foch, alone worth £15 million.

It is used by members of his family when they are on shopping trips in France. Mbasogo, who came to power in a bloody coup in 1979, prefers to stay in a £2,000 a night suite at the Hôtel Plaza Athénée off the Champs-Elysées.

French prosecutors are also investigating claims that deposed Arab Spring dictators, including Zine el Abidin Ben Ali of Tunisia and Hosni Mubarak of Egypt, have numerous homes in France. Libyan dictator, Colonel Gaddafi, who was honoured with a state visit to Paris by President Nicolas Sarkozy as recently as 2007, is also thought to own property in France as is Bashar Al-Assad of Syria.

The main accusation compiled in the legal dossier is that money flooding into highlighted African states was immediately used to fund the extravagant lifestyles of unelected leaders.

Paris prosecutors said all the families named in the files would definitely be investigated for acquiring real estate using misappropriated public funds. The enquiries are likely to take months, if not years, but judges will eventually have the power to freeze the assets before returning money to the countries from which it was stolen.

The £8.1 billion that England spends on foreign aid is set to increase to £11.4 billion in 2014, a 34% rise. Controversially, the Department of International Development is one of the few departments actually seeing its expenditure rise whilst most public spending is cut back to reduce Britain's huge deficit.

Britain's aid beneficiary, Sassou Nguesso, 67, has been president of the DRC since 1997 having ruled previously from 1979 to 1992. In his first period, he ruled a single-party regime under a Marxist agenda. Under very heavy pressure, he introduced multi-party politics in 1990 and he was booted out of power two years later. He returned in 1997 after leading rebel forces in a civil war and has still won two elections without meaningful opposition.

29th July 2011 – 'Robert Mugabe blows £12 million on jaunts abroad' – The Daily Mail

It is absolutely unbelievable to think that anyone could take so much public money for their own selfish benefits when people are starving. The money has been given to help them and Zimbabwe through these terrible times.

The Daily Mail tells us how Robert Mugabe has spent £12 million of public money on luxury foreign travel in the past six months!

The Zimbabwean dictator spent the cash on repeated first-class jaunts, often with an entourage of more than 70, according to the country's independently owned daily newspaper. Mugabe has overshot his £9 million annual travel budget by chartering jets from the state-owned Air Zimbabwe several times this year to travel to countries including Singapore and Italy.

The Daily Mail says that the £12 million that Mugabe has spent on travel could have funded life-saving medication for six months for nearly 600,000 HIV patients.

Joe Mabenge of the coalition on debt and development said, 'The meagre revenue by government should be directed towards critical needs like health, anti-retroviral drugs and education.'

Can't someone in this world stop all the hardship in this beautiful and once-wealthy country of Zimbabwe, instead of all the corruption?

About the only thing Zimbabwe has not got is oil. Maybe if we had, the world would come to our rescue!